If there's one book you need to read on fintech, this is it! *Financial Technology* is a must-read for anyone who wants a deep insight into this exciting industry.
Angela Yore, Co-Founder, SkyParlour

Financial Technology is a relevant, fresh and enlightening read for both seasoned finance veterans and those new to finance and fintech innovation. Niels Pedersen's case studies are largely drawn from the US and the UK, but his takeaways and insights are equally applicable to South East Asia or in a global setting.
Erik Jonsson, Head of Digital Partnerships, Techcombank

Niels Pedersen accurately captures the key elements that contribute to innovation in the financial technology ecosystem, making this publication relevant to anyone who has an interest in the sector.
James Nurse, Managing Director, FINTRAIL

Whether you are an established brand or a new innovator, fintech holds the key to driving digital and financial inclusivity. *Financial Technology* summarizes the great and the good in the world of fintech, with case study material to help new entrants learn about best practice, as well as, most critically, taking a hard look at fintech business models so the next generation of fintech leaders can avoid the common pitfalls.
Neil Harris, Chairperson, The Inclusion Foundation

Financial Technology

Case studies in fintech innovation

Niels Pedersen

KoganPage

First published in Great Britain and the United States in 2021 by Kogan Page Limited

2nd Floor, 45 Gee Street
London
EC1V 3RS
United Kingdom

122 W 27th St, 10th Floor
New York, NY 10001
USA

4737/23 Ansari Road
Daryaganj
New Delhi 110002
India

www.koganpage.com

Kogan Page books are printed on paper from sustainable forests.

ISBNs

Hardback   978 1 78966 545 1
Paperback   978 1 78966 543 7
Ebook   978 1 78966 544 4

British Library Cataloguing-in-Publication Data

A CIP record for this book is available from the British Library.

Library of Congress Cataloging-in-Publication Data

Names: Pedersen, Niels (Chartered accountant), author.
Title: Financial technology: case studies in fintech innovation / Niels Pedersen.
Description: London, United Kingdom ; New York, NY: Kogan Page, 2021. | Includes bibliographical references and index.
Identifiers: LCCN 2020042410 (print) | LCCN 2020042411 (ebook) | ISBN 9781789665451 (hardback) | ISBN 9781789665437 (paperback) | ISBN 9781789665444 (ebook)
Subjects: LCSH: Finance–Technological innovations–Case studies. | Financial services industry–Technological innovations–Case studies.
Classification: LCC HG173 .P43 2021 (print) | LCC HG173 (ebook) | DDC 332.10285–dc23
LC record available at https://lccn.loc.gov/2020042410
LC ebook record available at https://lccn.loc.gov/2020042411

Typeset by Integra Software Services, Pondicherry
Print production managed by Jellyfish
Printed and bound by CPI Group (UK) Ltd, Croydon CR0 4YY

To Sophie, for her unwavering
support, and love

CONTENTS

03   Behavioural economics and experience design: How to optimize user engagement 51

04   Artificial intelligence and automation in fintech: AI and machine learning in practice 76

05 Bitcoin, blockchain and cryptocurrencies: The applications of distributed ledger technology in finance 104

LIST OF FIGURES AND TABLES

ABOUT THE AUTHOR

Niels Pedersen is a senior lecturer on the MSc Financial Technology programme at Manchester Metropolitan University, UK, and a regular speaker on fintech. As a Chartered Accountant (ICAEW), he worked at PwC and the Financial Services Authority before coming to academia.

FOREWORD

The traditional global banking and finance system was once viewed as the backbone of trade and industry. Such governed and centralized financial systems are based upon government-issued (fiat) currencies, where key agents in the system are agreed on the value of cash via stock and local exchanges fuelling transactions and controlling economies. The physical nature of exchange between key agents and brokers excluded the masses from direct participation. Instead, the retail banking segment employed financial managers and experts to offer a portfolio of services to customers in return for interest payments on, for instance, loans and mortgages, etc – a distinct profit motive for the system. Over the centuries, this system monopolized the marketplace, presiding over consumer choic, underpinned by what could be described as a social contract of trust developed between the bank manager and consumer. This signifed a mutually productive relationship, packaged as safeguarding customers' financial interests and personal data (hardcopy ledger) while making a profit.

Before the global financial crisis of 2007–09 (GFC), discussions of the incumbent banks' dominant position and breaking of consumer trust would have been scorned for the lack of understanding surrounding the unique and socially embedded manager–consumer relationship. Since the GFC, we have seen a chain of events that gradually unpacked the macro-level centralized (and privileged) position of established financial institutions, revealing dubious trading practices with some reported reliance on underdeveloped algorithms making spurious transactions. In other words, failing to heed Ada Lovelace's warning: it [the algorithm] can only do whatever we know how to order it to perform. Enter the corporate rationalizers, introducing new technological innovations that challenge the extant system and its foundations, indeed, coining the term 'challenger' banks. Such innovation began to upset the equilibrium of the financial system, opening a pathway to a new decentralized form of exchange that shifts from physical to digital exchange, declaring the rise of the now-familiar financial technology (fintech) sector.

Today, we live in the 'digital economy', of which fintech plays a significant role in presenting substantial socio-technological and transformational challenges from new terminology and skills emerging from computer/data science. This is driving a mounting degree of technological development in enabling consumers greater choice in their financial decisions. The COVID-19 pandemic has reportedly driven acceleration toward a rethinking of our physical transactions with cash, finance and banking to full digitization or a cashless society. Thus, the once-revered discussion with the bank manager has been usurped by a digital 'bot' or assistant who can deftly answer those mundane questions about our bank balances or our likelihood of being granted a loan, for example. This socio-technical shift shows a reconceptualization of our social and physical relationship with finance to accessing online platforms. The power over our financial well-being and systems is moving away from larger financial institutions to that of the individual – decentralizing financial control and promoting agility in choice. We have neo-banks, challenger banks and fintech start-ups disrupting the plethora of services that was once the sole proviso of the financial agents monopolizing access to banking and finance.

How are organizations responding to this transformation of financial services? Simply put, technological innovation and collaboration has arrived and is cited as key for retaining a competitive advantage. Those who choose not to collaborate and engage with this next industrial revolution risk inertia – lacking agility in mindset and structure to adapt which could lead to exiting the marketplace. This is exemplified in the gradual closure of physical bank branches. The truth facing incumbents in banking and finance is: adapt, collaborate or die. Although they still retain customer mass over the new challengers, change is afoot.

Moreover, innovation invokes a myriad of digital regulations – albeit some rules and governance are also undergoing digital transformation to maintain pace with fintech innovation to ensure consumers do not fall foul of malpractice – back to Lovelace's warning around technology adoption. Yet, moving to a decentralized system is complex: finding a pathway through networks, APIs and new banking platforms (ie Open Banking platforms), and payments regulation. Thus, recognizing that buying off-the-shelf tech solutions without taking people into your network, organization or society with you may cause the profit motive to become unmoored. This is encapsulated in the first example of decentralized finance via distributed ledger technology underpinning blockchain and cryptocurrencies emerging since the GFC from the mysterious Satoshi Nakamoto. The limitations of a centralized system were writ large and the underpinning (almost 'hippy') central tenets focussed on changing the game of finance and decentralizing control over the system.

What has happened with decentralized finance since 2008 and what does this imply for organizations? As discussed, cultural and technical shifts of this magnitude necessitate time: as humans, we generally resist change that is forced rather than owned by us. Therefore, the current wave of innovation moves beyond disruption to signpost a new relationship with finance that will (eventually) benefit the masses. Admittedly, there's work to be done in this sphere, heralded by the Open Banking and finance movements.

Financial Technology provides an encyclopedic guide to the fintech arena. The use of topical examples helps garner an in-depth appreciation of fintech innovation while reducing fears of automation. The author embodies boundless thinking and agility tempered with caution over adoption, while celebrating technological innovation – which should not be stifled but balanced by safeguarding individuals' financial well-being. Thus, he addresses the need for financial inclusion across society, whereby ethical access and use of consumer data is central to creating trust in financial innovation, as consumers also adapt to the new digital financial landscape.

Pitched against this backdrop of an evolving digital economy witnessing unprecedented innovation, change and societal challenges, this book captures key aspects of the fluid fintech landscape while adding to the growing body of knowledge in this emergent field. Thus, the reader is offered methods to navigate through the minefield of decentralized financial innovation and seize aspects to embed within their organizations or facilitate further development across social and technological domains.

Dr Karen Elliott
Associate Professor of Enterprise and Innovation focussing
on FinTech at Newcastle University Business School, UK,
on the Standout 35 Women in FinTech Powerlist, and part of
the IEEE committee for Ethics, Trust and AI in Society

PREFACE

Every few years, a new buzzword makes its way into the headlines. From 'AI' to 'Big Data', and 'Cryptocurrency' to 'DLT', these terms are used to capture public imagination with grand promises and great expectations. To the cynic, the excitement around new technologies may seem like repetitions of past hype-cycles; however, as digitization accelerates, and reimagines the way we work, one can no longer remain a luddite. Instead, there is a need for learning and adaptation. This is not a one-off; rather it is a lifelong process. The opportunities of tomorrow belong to the curious.

When looking into new technologies, anyone without a background in computer science will almost immediately face stumbling blocks in the form of jargon. When looking up a new term, it is not uncommon to find oneself confronted with more jargon; in other words, end up with more questions than answers. This is a frustrating feeling, which leads many to give up, perhaps while thinking that 'technology is not for me'. Furthermore, even when one does overcome the jargon to gain some understanding, there is the feeling of being lost at sea. After all, how does it all fit together?

This book is an attempt to address these problems. It seeks to do so by giving the reader a basic yet thorough understanding of how the most important technologies work, and crucially, contextualizing these in terms of their impact on the financial industry. In doing so, the author hopes to instil a greater confidence in the reader, to dig deeper and learn more about those technologies that capture their imagination.

At first glance, the topics covered herein may seem disparate. The different technologies that are explored may seem unconnected. However, when seen from a bird's-eye view, the relationships become clearer. In this way, this book attempts to give the reader a 'lay of the land' in order to understand how different technologies are subject to the same underlying trends. For example, the ascent of artificial intelligence (AI) and cryptocurrencies would not have been possible without the processing power enabled by advancements in microchip technology; in other words, both innovations are part of the same story.

A core theme in this book is that the financial system and the internet are converging. Just as financial transactions contain information about people's preferences, so do clicks, reposts and instant messages. As both categories rely on the transmission of electrical signals, it is difficult to demarcate the two systems; indeed, with the increasing monetization of online user behaviour and the growing digitization of finance, perhaps they will soon be indistinguishable?

When exploring fintech through the lens of systemic convergence, between the financial and digital spheres, it becomes clearer how the various topic areas of this book fit together. While greater connectivity and better user interface design enable greater data collection, technologies such as blockchain and AI enable the emergence of new, and better, ways of doing finance. The net result of this is that financial services become increasingly decentralized, automated and user centric.

However, it is hoped that the reader will see fintech as more than making financial services faster, cheaper and more convenient by way of digitization. There is a paradox in using technology to reduce or remove humans from financial services, in that this actually increases the need for a human touch; in the absence of person-to-person interactions, the only thing distinguishing one financial institution from another will be corporate logotypes. In other words, a competitive advantage can be found in deploying a human touch in a fintech context.

Thus, it is hoped that the reader will use this book to benefit professionally from the wave of technological disruption sweeping through the financial sector. Whilst some professionals are dabbling in coding and others are honing their 'soft' skills, there is an opportunity in being a conduit between the two camps; in other words, being the link between decision makers (clients, senior management, etc) and the 'techies'. This book is written with those professionals in mind and aims to give them the requisite knowledge to pull this off.

ACKNOWLEDGEMENTS

In no particular order, thanks to David Gardner of TLT Solicitors, Dr Karen Elliott of Newcastle University and Mark Roberts of the Chartered Banker Institute for their feedback on earlier drafts of this work. In addition, the author would like to extend his gratitude to Michal Gromek and Pablo Neporozhnev for their productive conversations and encouragement in support of this work.

WALKTHROUGH OF FEATURES
AND ONLINE RESOURCES

Learning objectives

LEARNING OBJECTIVES

At the beginning of each chapter, a checklist of learning objectives outlines what you will learn from reading the chapter.

Case studies

 CASE STUDY

A range of case studies about different products, services and organizations bring the theory to life and illustrate how key ideas operate in practice.

Discussion points and suggested answers

 DISCUSSION POINT

An open question helps students probe further into the case study and stimulates discussion on topical issues.

 SUGGESTED ANSWERS TO DISCUSSION POINTS

Suggested answers, included at the end of the each chapter, explore points you may have missed and encourage further reflection.

Key takeaways

 KEY TAKEAWAYS

A clear summary of the most important lessons from each chapter, which allows you to reflect on what you have learned.

Glossary

A collection of technical terms and their definitions which helps cut through jargon and demystify key technologies in a clear and accessible manner.

Online resources

Supporting online resources for students and lecturers include supplementary case studies, which will provide more extensive examples, and PowerPoint lecture slides for each chapter of the book. The online resources can be found at koganpage.com/FinancialTechnology.

01

Networks, APIs and fintech banking platforms

How technology is decentralizing finance

LEARNING OBJECTIVES

This chapter will help you understand:

- How digitization is transforming finance.
- Why fintech start-ups are making inroads into banking.
- The possible business models that may emerge as a result.

Introduction

In many British cities, the word 'exchange' appears on old buildings and in place names: Royal Exchange, Exchange Square, Cotton Exchange, and so on. These remind us that, once upon a time, transacting face to face in financial markets was the norm: between 1870 and 1929, there were stock exchanges in a dozen cities across the UK.[1] However, over this period, the proportion of securities traded exclusively in London grew from *ca* 38 per cent to around 72 per cent.[2]

With the advances in technology and infrastructure seen during this time – in the form of the railway expansion, the telephone and radio communications – it is perhaps surprising that this centralization took place. Surely, the greater connectivity enabled by these innovations would have fostered greater de-centralization in financial markets?

This conundrum may be explained by a phenomenon known as *the network effect*: as a network grows, it becomes more attractive to its participants, due to the advantages that its greater size affords them.[3] These advantages are known as *network externalities*,[4] or, perhaps more commonly, *network effects*.

Liquidity and low transaction costs are network externalities of large financial markets (see Chapter 6). At the start of the 20th century, London was the world's largest capital market.[5] As a result, many companies, especially those seeking international expansion, were drawn to the capital.[6] In this way, London's size and international connections gave it an edge over its provincial rivals, which led to a concentration of financial services in the capital.

Just as regional stock exchanges have disappeared, bank branches are closing down across the UK. In 2017 alone, British banks closed 762 branches.[7] At the time, this represented a reduction of *ca* 8 per cent in the number of branches. What's more, this trend does not appear to be letting up: in 2018, it was reported that UK banks were closing *ca* 60 branches a month.[8] What is happening?

The answer appears to lie in the increasing digitization of finance. Though the internet and financial system are two distinct networks, both rely on the transmission of electrical signals: fundamentally, the physics of sending an email and making a digital payment are very similar. As a result, the increasing number of web-connected devices with financial applications is digitizing financial services, thereby reducing the need for bank branches.

This trend is evident in the decline of cash payments. In 2015, it was estimated that 57 per cent of all consumer payments were made without cash (ie with card, mobile or online – in effect, *digitally*).[9] Moreover, digital payments are growing fast: between 2012 and 2016, they grew at an annual rate of *ca* 10 per cent.[10]

Consumers appear to be embracing digital finance. For example, 84 per cent of Australian millennials say that they would bank with one of the large technology companies (ie Google, Apple, etc), if such services became available.[11] Given the global reach of anglophone millennial culture, there is little reason to believe that this figure would be much different in a survey of US or UK millennials.

Such willingness on the part of consumers to engage with web-based financial solutions was not always a given. For example, insurance providers struggled to gain traction online in the late 1990s:[12] consumers were initially reluctant to engage with financial solutions without a physical user interface. This was because potential problems were seen as easier to resolve in person than over the internet.[13] Moreover, there was the issue of brand recognition: on the internet, consumers were more disposed to trust established financial brands.[14] These factors made it more difficult for financial start-ups to break through. So, what changed?

For one, a larger portion of consumers are now *digital natives* – either they do not remember a time before the internet or were first exposed to it during their formative years. Digital natives make up a large portion of the millennial generation (usually defined as those born between 1980 and 2000). This generation was projected to become the largest living adult population in the United States by 2019,[15] and is therefore its largest consumer group. With a greater proportion of consumers being digital natives, it follows that more people are willing and able to engage with digitized financial solutions. That said, there may be a more profound reason for this: declining public faith in mainstream financial institutions.

Around the turn of the millennium, consumers were reluctant to trust purely web-based financial service providers because they did not have established brands.[16] However, as a result of the global financial crisis of 2007–09 (GFC), trust in mainstream financial institutions has been severely impaired.[17] Moreover, the behaviour of big banks since the GFC has done little to help: in the years 2012–16, the world's 20 leading banks incurred an estimated £264 billion in fines and other financial penalties in relation to various legal and regulatory transgressions.[18]

Thus, the tattered record of the mainstream financial institutions has lowered consumer expectations to such a degree that novel, and non-mainstream institutions, appear comparatively more reputable. At the very least, consumers are now more willing to give alternative financial providers the benefit of the doubt: by virtue of having been in business for comparatively less time, post-GFC financial start-ups have, on the whole, a comparatively limited history of disappointing consumers. Thus, strong, established brands are no longer significant barriers to entry in the financial industry. This, combined with a growing pool of consumers who are digital natives, is a boon for financial technology start-ups.

At this juncture, some nomenclature is called for. Generally speaking, the term *financial technology* (ie *fintech*) is used to describe the use of technology to enhance or deliver financial solutions;[19] in other words, leveraging technology to make finance cheaper, faster, more accessible and more convenient. Furthermore, some people take the term 'fintech' to mean financial technology start-up.

Fintech start-ups are shaking up the financial industry by harnessing the connectivity of the web. As the internet facilitates 'shopping around' for better products and services, this connectivity can be detrimental to customer loyalty:[20] in this way, fintechs are able to draw customers away from traditional financial institutions.

Moreover, many fintechs harness their customers' personal data to provide personalized financial services.[21] Unlike big banks – whose back-office processes tend to be paper-based and encumbered by legacy IT systems[22] – fintech start-ups have leaner behind-the-scenes operations, thanks to their smaller sizes and propensity to automate their activities as far as possible. As a result, their distribution costs tend to be lower than those of their branch-based competitors; after all, their user interfaces (ie their websites and smartphone apps) *are* their branches. In this way, the cost advantage of not having a physical branch network may allow fintechs to offer more competitive financial solutions.

However, such connectivity-spurred growth can also be a double-edged sword. On one hand, it allows fintech start-ups to poach customers from established players with the promise of more convenient and cheaper solutions; on the other, the digital nature of their propositions reduces switching costs for customers. As a result, businesses that engage customers with an exclusively digital proposition may struggle with customer retention: according to a study of digital user interfaces, solutions that contain a human element exhibit greater rates of customer retention than self-service solutions.[23]

In this way, humanizing customer interactions can be a way of building customer loyalty. This has not been lost on C. Hoare & Co., a family-run private bank dating back to 1672.[24] While Britain's largest banks scaled back their branch networks, C. Hoare & Co. announced the opening of an office in Cambridge in 2019, its first outside London.[25] Granted, it is a private bank that caters to an up-market clientele. Customers like these appreciate a high level of service and are therefore willing to pay for it. That said, when a bank that has been around for nearly 350 years bucks the industry trend to open a new branch, it says something about the importance of relationships in business.

Harnessing relationships

In some way, a business model can be viewed as a cluster of relationships, whereby the success of a company depends on how well it manages each relationship. To gain a competitive advantage, the company must leverage its distinctive capabilities (ie what it does well) in its relationships with customers, suppliers and other stakeholders.[26]

To stay ahead, companies must continuously seek to strengthen these relationships. To this end, reputation is paramount as it helps a company cultivate a sustainable competitive advantage.[27] The resources needed to compete (staff, technology, etc) can be readily acquired by competitors, but a sound reputation takes time to build;[28] by discouraging would-be competitors, a solid reputation can thus function as a barrier to entry.

To build and maintain a sound reputation, a business must, fundamentally, interact with its customers in a way that provides them with positive experiences. Given that millennial consumers are experience-orientated,[29] doing so consistently will help it establish a positive brand identity. In this regard, a company facing the end-user tends to be in the strongest position, as this allows its brand to occupy pole position in customers' minds. Retail banks have long held this advantage in that their branch networks allowed them to 'own' the customer relationship; however, this dominance is threatened by fintech innovation.[30]

Moreover, fintech is disrupting multiple sub-sectors: payments, consumer lending, wealth management, securities and insurance.[31] Of these, the payments sector is one of the more dynamic in terms of innovation and adoption of new technologies.[32] Given that payments form an integral part of the consumer experience,[33] this is perhaps no accident: this is an attractive sector because facilitating payments establishes a customer relationship, thereby laying the foundations for a brand identity. Down the line, this can be leveraged to generate additional revenue by providing additional financial solutions.[34] Investors in fintech understand this: between 2012 and 2017, start-ups in the payments sector attracted funding of more than US$21 billion.[35]

Thus, fintech start-ups are challenging established financial institutions by going after their most valuable assets: their customer relationships. This puts an onus on banks to upgrade their digital propositions. In the past, internet and telephone banking were seen as add-ons to branch networks; today, bank branches are becoming sub-components of greater digital networks.

Open Banking

Traditionally, large branch networks functioned as a barrier to entry in the banking industry. The name recognition afforded by these networks gave the advantage to incumbent banks.[36] Over time, the industry became increasingly oligopolistic, particularly in the UK, where five large banking groups came to dominate the sector: in 2018, it was reported that, between them, these banks controlled around 80 per cent of the UK's retail banking market.[37]

However, digital banking channels have removed the need to attend branches to withdraw funds.[38] As a result, customers can switch providers without the inconvenience of visiting a branch. In this way, digitization has allowed fintechs to pry customers away from long-established financial institutions.

However, incumbent banks still had a significant advantage in the form of large databases of customer transactions. Such data assets can be a source of competitive advantage as they can be used to inform product development, cross-selling decisions and credit risk management.[39]

This did not escape the attention of regulators in the European Union (including the UK). As a result, the EU's Second Payment Services Directive (PSD2) came into being, which became part of UK law in 2018.[40] PSD2 is also known as *Open Banking* because it seeks to increase consumer choice in the banking system and make it more competitive.[41] Open Banking makes customer data portable, that is to say, it allows bank customers to share their transaction history with other financial institutions; of course, there are a few conditions: the third-party institution must have regulatory approval; customers must consent to sharing their data; and customers can withdraw their consent at any time.[42]

Furthermore, bank customers can grant these third parties the ability to initiate payments from their accounts.[43] This allows customers to transact via third-party applications; in a way, this is similar to shoppers linking their bank accounts to online payment processors. However, Open Banking goes one step further in that the third-party applications do not hold customer funds; instead, they make payments on behalf of their users by accessing their users' bank accounts.[44]

The technology behind Open Banking is known as Application Programming Interfaces (APIs – see box below). This allows fintech start-ups to access customer data stored within bank systems, thereby enabling the development of third-party financial applications.[45] In Britain, the Open Banking API is managed by Open Banking Limited – an entity created by the Competition and Markets Authority to support the implementation of Open Banking in the UK.[46]

APPLICATION PROGRAMMING INTERFACES (APIs)

An API is a software tool that enables different computer systems to communicate with one another.[47] Much like diplomatic protocol dictates how different heads of state communicate, an API provides a framework for the transfer of information between different computer systems.

A restaurant waiter is a good metaphor for an API. This is because they serve as a communication interface between customers and kitchen staff. The diners and chef do not communicate directly; rather, a waiter takes orders from the table and passes these to the kitchen. In response, the chef prepares food and sends this to the diners via the waiter. In this way, a waiter enables the two parties to communicate indirectly, much like an API serves as an information conduit between different computer systems.[48]

The waiter metaphor is particularly fitting because it describes a situation wherein the two communicating parties do not know each other; restaurant diners do not usually enter the kitchen. Similarly, a computer system supplying data via an API is agnostic in regard to its recipients.[49] This allows organizations to make data available to whosoever queries their API,[50] thereby giving the process a self-service aspect.

Much like a restaurant menu, an API is a framework for relations between sender and receiver. Like a restaurateur, the organization supplying the data gets to set the terms. The difference is that there is no such thing as going off menu. In this way, an API is effectively a contract that governs the interactions between sender and receiver.[51]

Besides facilitating data sharing between organizations, APIs can be used within organizations to transfer data between different systems.[52] Thus, APIs can also be used to address tethering issues between banks' legacy systems. Moreover, APIs allow different organizations to integrate their services more readily, thereby allowing start-ups to develop complementary services, as is the intention with Open Banking.[53]

For example, TransferWise, a foreign currency exchange platform, allows fintechs to plug in their users via its API (see case study in Chapter 2).[54] In this way, TransferWise benefits from having greater volume on its platform, while the tributary fintechs gain from being able to offer their users more holistic customer propositions.

Of course, organizations do not have to share their data for free. As APIs can facilitate fee-based data sharing, these tools provide an automated way for organizations to monetize their data assets. This could lead to an economy where organizations and consumers maximize the value of their data via APIs.[55]

API-based business models in financial services

Over time, the greater transparency and competition brought on by legislative changes and technological change are likely to change the financial industry significantly by transforming its constituent business models. What's more, different institutions are likely to adapt to these changes in different ways: some banks may focus on originating financial products and distribute these via third-party intermediaries; meanwhile, others may opt to become these very intermediaries and focus on distributing third-party financial products via their user interfaces.[56]

The changes facing the banking sector have, to a greater degree, already occurred in the insurance sector. For instance, price comparison websites are used to distribute third-party insurance products.[57] In addition, some insurance providers routinely distribute products on behalf of third-party insurers while branding these as their own. This practice, called *white-labelling*,[58] is common in the insurance sector.

However, an origination strategy puts the originator's products at risk of commodification as it does not own the customer relationship:[59] as white-labelling does not expose the customer to the originator's brand, it forces the originator to compete on price. What's more, even when the product is originator-branded, the distributor can switch suppliers or use more than one supplier to begin with. In this way, product originators are often forced to compete on price. As a result, it is likely that banks pursuing a product origination strategy will want to brand their products as their own. In addition, these banks will likely supply a mix of own-brand and white-labelled products via a multitude of third-party channels, to avoid commodification and dependency on any one distributor.

A distribution-based strategy is the opposite of an origination-based one. This approach involves becoming a marketplace for financial services.[60] Taken to its extreme, this strategy would entail the bank having no products of its own, and instead serve as a data conduit between financial service providers and their customers.[61] Banks taking this road would need to engage customers with a compelling user experience – whether physical, digital or both – to avoid becoming just another price comparison website (for more on user interface/experience design see Chapter 3).

As the above-mentioned business models have inherent strengths and weaknesses, it is likely that some banks will pursue a mix of these, perhaps with an emphasis on one of the modalities; indeed, these strategies are not mutually exclusive.[62] In any case, it seems likely that larger banks will pursue a hybrid model as the scale and scope of their operations – and the glacial pace of change therein – make other paths difficult. Thus, large banks are on course to become platforms that provide customers with a holistic mix of in-house and third-party financial solutions; with the help of APIs, these banks may start to resemble financial application stores:[63] this model is sometimes referred to as Banking as a Platform (BaaP).[64] We explore BaaP further in the case study on Starling Bank below.

The economics of platform banking

Banking platforms are at the centre of what economists call *two-sided markets*: these are markets where an intermediary (ie a platform) has two distinct 'customer' groups, wherein the intermediary's actions in regard to either group affects the other.[65] As a result, the platform must consider the needs of both sides as part of its business strategy.

Conventional retail banking is also an example of a two-sided market as banks have both depositors and borrowers. As part of its business strategy, the bank has to consider the rate it charges its borrowers (who want it to be low) and the rate it pays its depositors (who want it to be high). In this way, the interests of each customer group are in direct conflict. As a result, the bank's actions regarding either are interdependent.

That said, a retail bank is not a perfect example of a two-sided market as its customers can be both borrowers and depositors, which is often the case concurrently. As a result, the distinction between these two customer groups can be unclear. However, under the BaaP paradigm, this distinction is not the case: on one side of the market, there are the consumers; on the other, financial solution providers.[66]

The bank itself sits in the middle of the market, and, as the proprietor of the platform, must figure out how to monetize its position as intermediary. This starts with an understanding of what both groups want. While the digitally savvy consumers desire a suite of personalized and convenient financial solutions, the financial solution providers want access to the platform's user base. Thus, the platform's revenue model depends on both sides' willingness to pay for access to the other.

In large part, the bank platform's approach to monetization will depend on its competitive strategy. According to conventional theory, businesses generally compete in one of two ways: by being the cheapest or by being unique, which are referred to as *cost-leadership* and *differentiation*, respectively.[67] To maximize profitability, businesses can either charge low prices to attract a high volume of low-margin customers; or they compete on quality, enabling them to charge a premium on a lower volume of high-margin customers.[68] In practice, many businesses have strategies that fall somewhere in between these two extremes.

In financial services, cost-based strategies can become a race to the bottom due to commodification. This is the case with online price comparison websites, where competition exerts downward pressure on prices.[69] As a result, many financial services firms instead pursue a differentiation-based strategy. What's more, some often seek to strengthen their proposition by homing in on specific segments. For instance, the Wesleyan Assurance Society, a Birmingham-based insurance provider, caters primarily to doctors, dentists, teachers and lawyers.[70] By focussing on these niche segments, Wesleyan is able to provide a specialized product offering, which allows it to charge a premium. This is referred to as a *differentiation focus* strategy.[71] Many banks already pursue some degree of specialization by focussing on certain product lines, customer segments or geographical regions. Therefore, it seems likely that these specializations will be transplanted onto banks' platforms to facilitate differentiation in their core markets; and, if nothing else, as a way of retaining customers.

To gain traction, platform businesses need to appeal to both sides of their markets.[72] On the one hand, a banking platform needs to curate a suite of financial solutions that is attractive to its customer base; on the other, it needs to offer financial solution providers a profitable user base. Thus, a higher quantity, and quality, of users should attract a greater number of financial solution providers, and vice versa. As a result, the more attractive a platform is to one side of its market, the more valuable it becomes to the other.[73]

Financial platforms often attempt to gain traction by offering generous terms to new users to attract solution providers. For example, Starling Bank does not charge its customers for making debit card payments or ATM withdrawals when abroad (see the case study below).[74] In this way, the bank incentivizes people to join its platform; once onboard, customers can be sold other, more profitable, solutions such as consumer loans or insurance. Thus, platforms can use loss-making solutions to draw in customers, thereby making themselves more attractive to third-party solution providers.[75]

Ultimately, the choice of revenue model depends on balancing the interests of users, solution providers and the platform itself. In this regard, the platform's competitive strategy becomes relevant, as cost-orientated users might be reluctant to pay for access; similarly, volume-driven solution providers will be unlikely to have significant margin to share with the platform. However, those pursuing a differentiation strategy may be able to charge a nominal fee for joining the platform, as a way of getting customers with looser purse strings to self-select. To succeed in this, a bank would need to build a holistic suite of financial solutions perceived to be worth paying a premium for. Thus, the success of a platform's revenue model depends, to some degree, on matching up its users with financial solutions that are commensurate with their needs and budgetary constraints.

Regardless of its revenue model, a platform-based business is threatened by disloyalty on each side of its market: on one side, there is the risk that solution providers service users directly, thereby dis-intermediating the platform; on the other, providers may service multiple platforms, thereby making its proposition less unique.[76]

To address these problems, the platform must incentivize loyalty in its user base and solution providers. For users, this can be achieved by offering a unique user experience (see Chapter 3) and loyalty incentives: in the UK, for instance, some banks offer higher rates on savings for long-standing (and no doubt profitable) customers. Meanwhile, as the success of a platform rests on connecting users with solution providers,[77] the bank must at all times put itself between these two groups. In practice, this can be achieved by imposing restrictive terms on solution providers, to prevent off-platform transactions with its users. In addition, trust-enhancing features such as user reviews or dispute-resolution mechanisms can encourage users to stay on the platform;[78] conceivably, such tools are effective because they decrease uncertainty relative to transacting off-platform. Of course, by branding third-party solutions as their own, platforms can achieve a similar effect, while further entrenching themselves in the customer relationship.

At this juncture, it should be evident that there is no one-size-fits-all model for platform banking. As a result, hybrids may emerge, incorporating aspects of both cost-focussed and differentiated models. Indeed, variations of the same platform could be deployed in different market segments: a low-spec, low-cost solution for mass-market consumption and a premium solution for up-market customers. As banks already do this within their business and personal banking offerings, a multi-layered approach to BaaP appears likely.

Bank–fintech collaboration

Regardless of how banks monetize their offerings, digitally enabled financial platforms are likely to transform banking, and financial services more generally. Indeed, it is not hard to imagine a large insurer or asset manager providing a BaaP-like solution: the key ingredients appear to be a large customer base and a willingness to engage with third-party solution providers, some of which are fintech start-ups. Perhaps then, large financial institutions will cease to focus on specific sub-sectors – such as banking, insurance or asset management – and leave the specialization to smaller players.

This progression can be described as the *un-bundling* of financial services: as part of this, fintech start-ups focus on providing specific solutions to compete against the most well-established players,[79] often in terms of convenience, customer engagement and/or cost; in turn, this draws customers away from incumbent financial institutions.[80] As a result, large financial institutions are forced to co-opt these fintech challengers, which, to some degree, re-bundles their innovative solutions via the incumbents' platforms.

Thus, the advent of BaaP-like solutions across the financial industry is likely to transform incumbent institutions into *one-stop shops* for financial services; where a solution cannot be offered in-house, it can be brought onboard via an external provider. As supplying the more innovative solutions that customers desire is, generally speaking, the domain of fintechs, established players find themselves drawn towards closer collaboration with the fintech sector.

Generally speaking, large financial institutions lack the agility and innovative culture of fintechs.[81] In addition, fintechs often start out by providing specialized solutions in niche markets,[82] which makes it hard to compete for generalist, mass-market financial institutions. Thus, to prevent fintechs from encroaching on their markets, banks must find ways of incorporating the most promising fintech solutions into their propositions.

Certainly, banks have much to offer fintech start-ups. For one, well-established financial institutions have large customer bases, and many fintech start-ups need access to these customers,[83] as even the most innovative financial solutions are worthless without users. In addition, large financial institutions have an abundance of capital, which many fintechs lack,[84] especially those that are not yet profitable, or indeed, without revenue.

Then there is the question of regulatory compliance. Large financial institutions have the requisite legal and regulatory expertise to navigate the complex environment of financial services regulation, something that many fintechs lack.[85] Although regulators have shown some forbearance (see Chapter 8) in regard to fintechs, these are not viable in the long term without access to regulatory expertise, especially as they scale up. Consequently, some start-ups may see partnering with an established financial institution as a way of gaining access to a well-resourced compliance department.

As incumbent institutions and fintechs have something to offer each other, it is unsurprising that banks are large investors in fintech start-ups. For example, by 2017, HSBC had invested US$200 million in fintech; its competitors, an array of global banks, are not far behind.[86] Investment can be seen as the most direct way of formalizing a relationship between a bank and a fintech provider. However, there are other, more informal, ways of building relationships with start-ups when their disruptive potential is not yet as clear.

Large financial institutions do this by sponsoring incubators: innovation centres wherein start-ups can experiment with, and build, novel technology solutions; these help established players identify and build relationships with promising start-ups.[87] By providing the necessary amenities and support, a sponsor may have first pick of novel fintech solutions relevant to its business model, thus effectively outsourcing innovation. Provided they can capitalize on the innovations nurtured within their incubators, this seems a much cheaper option than paying for management consultants or employing corporate innovation teams.

 CASE STUDY
Starling Bank: A marketplace of financial solutions

While many fintechs seek to partner with large banks to gain access to their customers, Starling is disrupting financial services by building its own platform. Founded in 2014, Starling is a mobile-based bank, which can be accessed by downloading its app on IOS and Android-based devices.[88]

Starling's core product is a current account with features such as: no fees on cash withdrawals and spending abroad; bill-splitting tools which help customers share the cost of group expenditures (eg restaurant meals); in-app customer-to-customer transfers; and personal budgeting tools. Furthermore, the app is serviced by a 24/7 customer support centre.[89]

The Starling platform is hosted on Amazon Web Services (AWS). In this way, Amazon provides the behind-the-scenes infrastructure that supports the app. By using AWS, Starling has achieved the back-end scale of a large bank, which gives it the capacity to handle millions of customer transactions.[90]

Though Starling appears to be a 'mobile-first' bank, it is not exclusively digital. In 2018, the bank announced an agreement with Royal Mail, the UK's postal service, which allows Starling customers to deposit cash at its *ca* 11,500 branches.[91] Given that there are between 7,000 and 8,000 bank branches in the UK,[92] this move effectively gives Starling a branch network that is larger than all other retail banks combined. Furthermore, the public service ethos of Royal Mail – a vestige from the time it was state-owned – means that these branches are located in convenient locations across the country. Thus, it is likely that Starling customers never have to travel too far in order to deposit cash.

The cash-depositing feature is unlikely to be as important to retail customers as it is for business customers, especially smaller businesses, who tend to receive a large portion of their revenue in cash. Thus, the partnership with Royal Mail makes Starling attractive to cash-based business owners such as trades people, market traders and freelancers. Perhaps then, it is no accident that Starling also launched a small business account in 2018.[93]

This solution was initially only available to small businesses with one director (ie where the owner and sole director are the same person, and, very often, also the only employee). However, in 2019 Starling became the first mobile bank in the UK to offer accounts to businesses with multiple directors.[94] As part of this solution, Starling provides real-time data integration with accountancy software packages.[95] Evidently, Starling has been paying close attention to the needs of industry: according to a 2017 survey of 100 large businesses around the world, integration of banking data with organizational management systems was a key challenge facing corporate treasury departments.[96]

That Starling, a small, start-up bank with only a few years on its back, should seek to disrupt the commercial banking market by offering customers something they have long desired, reflects the bank's customer-centric ethos. Indeed, Starling was founded 'out of a desire to create a new kind of bank and to make banking more inclusive by putting customer needs first'.[97]

Clearly, Starling aims to do things differently. This is evident in its expansive ethics policy which, amongst other things, commits the bank to partnering with institutions 'who themselves are committed to operating under ethical and environmental standards equivalent to our own – including in the fair treatment of customers, employees and other stakeholders'.[98]

Starling's commitment to fairness and its customer-centric approach appears to be paying off. In 2019, it was named 'Best British Bank' in the British Bank Awards.[99] As this award was decided by a poll of than more than 27,000 customers,[100] it appears that Starling's approach is striking a chord with the public.

Part of Starling's success could be attributed to its marketplace model, which provides customers with a suite of carefully curated financial solutions from third-party providers. Indeed, the bank appears to be making the most of APIs to enhance the appeal of its platform: in 2018, founder and CEO Anne Boden noted that it was 'time to celebrate a new age of banking – the age of the API... a traditional paradigm has been recast and unbundled to reflect advances in technology, culture, demand and practice'.[101]

During 2019, Starling announced the introduction of an insurance provider, and a credit-rating improvement service to its platform.[102, 103] These have complemented the borrowing and wealth-management solutions already on its platform, thus expanding the suite of innovative financial services. What's more, consumers appear to be taking note: by December 2017, the bank had more than 40,000 customers; a year later, this figure exceeded 350,000.[104] As a result, Starling's holistic approach to banking appears to be paying off. But what will happen once bigger players start to mimic this model at greater scale – can Starling stay ahead?

What are the strengths and weaknesses in Starling's business model?
(Suggested answer at the end of this chapter.)

Networked financial services

While a business can be viewed as a collection of relationships, it can also be analysed as a network. In this context, each business can be seen as a network of customers, employees and suppliers congregating on a shared platform. Thus, a business succeeds by strengthening the network effects associated with its platform.[105]

As a business grows, it becomes known to more people. In turn, this familiarity helps the business acquire new customers: as more users join, word of mouth enhances its reputation, thereby exerting pressure on people associated with existing customers to jump on the bandwagon[106] – if nothing else, just to fit in with their social circle. Human beings are influenced by the choices of their friends, colleagues and family members (see Chapter 3). This dynamic may partially explain the top-heavy concentration seen in the smartphone market, which is dominated by a handful of brands even though several dozen exist.[107]

Once a platform is sufficiently large and well established, its size attracts suppliers of complementary goods and services.[108] For example, many more third-party applications have been developed for the Windows Operating Systems than for Linux. This is because more people use Windows, which makes it more attractive to third-party developers. In turn, the greater availability of complementary solutions further strengthens the platform's appeal to potential users.

In the context of a financial platform, the network effect helps build and maintain a competitive advantage: as a platform grows its user base, consumer herd behaviour combines with supplier interest to increase the platform's appeal to potential participants – on both sides of the market. On one hand, consumers are drawn to the platform by the large number of people already on it as well as the availability of innovative financial solutions; on the other, fintech entrepreneurs are attracted to the platform by its large user base. This, in turn, enhances the product offering, thereby drawing in more users.

Despite the clear benefits that come with operating at scale, it would be fallacious to assume that every business should attempt to grow ad infinitum.

Every network will eventually suffer from growth pains; though network effects are generally positive, *negative network externalities* do exist.[109] In this way, network economics are similar to the concept of *economies of scale* from micro-economics: as a business grows it may benefit from advantages such as bulk purchasing discounts, easier access to finance and brand recognition. Thus, greater scale decreases the company's average cost per product made, thereby increasing its profit margins.[110] However, when a company becomes too large, its cost base can start to rise. For example, a large branch network is harder to manage than a single branch as upper management will find it more difficult to enforce frontline quality standards. This results in additional costs such as auditing expenses (ie a monitoring cost), resource waste and mis-aligned incentives. Such costs, known as *dis-economies of scale*,[111] are, to a degree, comparable to negative network externalities.

Platform businesses can be subject to negative network externalities and dis-economies of scale, as is evident in the problems facing large social media platforms in the form of abusive behaviour, privacy breaches and spam. As platforms grow, they become more attractive to bad actors on account of their greater size (ie a negative network effect). Thus, as data security and user privacy are paramount, the heightened risk of attack imposes additional costs on network-based businesses.[112]

In addition, such businesses may find that interventions designed to protect or enhance their platforms' network externalities affect participating groups asymmetrically; this can be especially pronounced if different sides of a platform are themselves subject to different network effects.[113] As a result, each group may respond differently to quality assurance measures imposed by the platform.

This dynamic complicates intermediation between the different sides of a financial platform: on the user side, the platform must seek to exclude bad actors and discourage unprofitable customers; on the other, it first has to vet, and then monitor, providers to ensure that they deliver positive user outcomes. Therefore, the platform must balance openness and inclusivity with security and profitability. Conceivably, there is more than one way of resolving this predicament. As a result, a platform may be afforded some flexibility when trading off these exigencies. However, the degree to which it leans one way or another is likely to depend, in large part, on its user base and competitive strategy.

Hitherto, we have focussed on the network effect as it relates to financial platforms. But what about the fintech start-ups themselves? Just like their much larger rivals, fintechs are subject to both positive and negative network externalities. However, there is an additional dynamic which complicates their early stage expansion: when a company is small, it lacks the network effects of its larger competitors.[114] In the context of fintech, this means many scale-dependent start-ups will be pushed in the direction of partnering with a larger institution.

At the same time, a start-up that grows too quickly may suffer from growth pains.[115] In the context of fintech, this can mean undergoing greater regulatory scrutiny and/or difficulty managing an increase in customer-related issues. As a result, network dynamics leave independent fintech start-ups in a tough spot. Naturally, this pushes many toward collaboration with larger players. Of course, independent platforms can succeed (as seen in the case study above), though for many, it may prove too difficult given the exigencies of platform economics and the network effect.

 CASE STUDY
Harnessing mobile networks for financial inclusion

One of the tragedies of today's financial system is the number of people who are excluded from it. Though no one knows the exact figure, it is estimated that *ca* 2 billion people living in emerging economies have little or no access to formal financial services.[116] Limited access to finance perpetuates poverty: if entrepreneurs cannot access capital, they cannot build job-creating businesses. Meanwhile, individuals cannot protect their wealth without access to financial institutions; storing one's money under the proverbial mattress leaves it vulnerable to theft while inflation erodes its value over time.

A well-functioning economy needs an inclusive financial system that directs capital to its most productive use by connecting savers and borrowers. Any system that leaves out a great number of people fails to achieve this, and thereby perpetuates inequality and poverty. Indeed, the economist Muhammed Yunus won the Nobel Peace Prize for his work relating to micro-credit in Bangladesh: with the bank he helped found, Yunus demonstrated that extending micro-loans to small entrepreneurs – who did not otherwise have access to credit – could help lift them out of poverty.[117]

Though this approach has been emulated around the world, there is still much room for improvement. Financial exclusion persists in developing countries because the infrastructure does not address the needs of poor and rural communities. Instead, financial service providers in emerging economies tend to cater to higher-income urban dwellers.[118]

However, technology is helping to foster greater financial inclusion. M-PESA is perhaps the most compelling example of this; first introduced in Kenya in 2007, this is a mobile-based payments solution run by Vodafone.[119] For some time, Kenyans had been using mobile top-up cards (ie plastic cards that contain phone credit in the form of minutes) as a substitute for cash.[120] While banking infrastructure was lacking in many areas, these cards could be bought at small convenience stores across the country. Thus, they became a store of value for Kenyans because a plastic card is much easier to transport (and hide) than a bundle of cash. Vodaphone expanded on this dynamic by allowing users to send each other electronic money via its mobile network, which can then be redeemed for cash at convenience stores registered with M-PESA.[121]

In this way, Vodafone has effectively fused its mobile network with a nationwide network of small merchants to supplement an underdeveloped financial system. The benefits of this are far reaching as it allows urban dwellers to send funds to their friends and family in less-developed rural areas, much like immigrants in advanced economies who send money to friends and family back home.

Over time, this additional liquidity should give rise to entrepreneurship and job creation, as much as micro-loans are intended to do. Indeed, there is evidence to suggest that M-PESA is transforming Kenya's economy: according to one study, it has succeeded in lifting 2 per cent of the country's households out of poverty.[122] In this way, mobile money solutions could make a big difference across sub-Saharan Africa, where an estimated 67 per cent of adults are without formal financial services.[123] With a mobile penetration rate that is growing rapidly and projected to reach 50 per cent by 2025,[124] millions more could escape poverty thanks to solutions like M-PESA.

M-PESA's model is being emulated across Africa, either by Vodafone itself or by one of its rivals. Unfortunately, some sub-Saharan governments have imposed taxes on mobile payments, which threatens to undermine the progress made in terms of financial inclusion.[125] However, as sub-Saharan Africa already had more than 100 million mobile money users by 2016,[126] the sea change brought on by mobile payments may prove too great for any government to bungle.

In addition, the growth in trade between China and Africa is another reason to be optimistic about fintech in Africa: standing at around US$100 billion in 2008, Sino-African trade had doubled to ca US$200 billion by 2018.[127] Indeed, in 2019, Alipay – a Chinese mobile payments platform with more than 1 billion users[128] – announced a partnership with a Nigerian business-to-business fintech to help facilitate payments between Alipay users and African merchants.[129] Thus, emerging economies appear to be leading the way in some areas of fintech innovation: by 2018, three quarters of millennial consumers in China had used mobile payments; the corresponding figure for US and UK millennials was around 50 per cent.[130]

How can political, economic, social and technological factors affect financial inclusion?
(Suggested answer at the end of this chapter.)

Chapter summary

The internet is reshaping business–consumer relationships. Greater digitization has reduced the time and hassle of shopping around for financial products. This, combined with the public loss of faith in the financial industry as a result of the financial crisis, has been detrimental to customer loyalty.

Consumers want something new, and fintech start-ups are answering this call by harnessing technology to make finance cheaper, faster, more convenient and more accessible. By automating their operations as far as possible, these start-ups have much leaner business models than many established players.

Furthermore, fintech start-ups are able to access customer data via Application Programming Interfaces (APIs), allowing them to develop innovative and personalized solutions based on incumbent banks' most valuable asset: their customers' transactions. This development would spell disaster for large financial institutions were it not for their inherent advantages in terms of access to capital, scale and regulatory expertise. As a result, incumbents and challengers find themselves drawn together.

As a result, banks are likely to find themselves reimagined as financial platforms, becoming marketplaces for the very fintech solutions that threatened to displace them. That said, different modalities are likely to emerge, which largely depends on each bank's readiness to engage its customers with a compelling user interface. Indeed, despite the advantages of established financial institutions, there is nothing to stop a fintech start-up from setting up its own financial platform as seen in this chapter's case study on Starling Bank. Consumers want something new and will flock to the institution that offers the most convenient, holistic, and personalized financial solutions.

 KEY TAKEAWAYS

The three most important ideas from this chapter are:

- Financial technology start-ups (fintechs) are encroaching on banks' territory by using technology to make financial services easier, faster and cheaper.

- This is likely to force many financial institutions to become financial platforms.

- Banks and fintechs both have competitive advantages over each other; thus collaboration, rather than competition, is a more likely route for most.

SUGGESTED ANSWERS TO DISCUSSION POINTS

 What are the strengths and weaknesses in Starling's business model?

Strengths in Starling's business model

The bank has a near-complete financial services platform, boasting borrowing, business, insurance and wealth-management solutions. The convenience of having all these solutions in one place is likely to help in attracting new customers, as well as retaining existing customers. Furthermore, the bank appears to be far ahead of many of its larger rivals in terms of the Banking as a Platform model: this gives it a 'first-mover' advantage while strengthening its reputation as an innovative bank.

In addition, Starling appears to have a strong, 'feel-good' brand because of its customer-centric ethos and ethical approach to banking. This is likely to increase customer loyalty because it appeals to customers who are disillusioned with mainstream banks. The fact that Starling has a de facto branch network via its partnership with Royal Mail gives it an edge over its digital-only fintech rivals, particularly with regard to business customers.

Weaknesses in Starling's business model

The bank relies on external partners to complete its suite of financial solutions. In this way, if there is a problem with one of these providers, it could damage Starling's reputation. Furthermore, as some of these providers are also on other platforms, this could undermine customer loyalty: though Starling technically owns the relationship with each customer, some customers may be more amenable to switching to a competing platform if they see a familiar financial provider on it. This could become especially relevant if one of Starling's providers stops servicing the bank's customers.

Furthermore, the bank's stringent ethics policy could become a problem if one of its partners fails to live up to Starling's standards. If a partner solution is used by a large portion of the Starling's customers, this could present a serious ethical dilemma for a bank that styles itself as values driven. Finally, there is the problem of potential financial exclusion: though Starling claims to take this value seriously, its platform is only accessible to users of IOS and Android smartphones.

 How can political, economic, social and technological factors affect financial inclusion?

Political

Government interference – either by way of excessive regulation or taxation – could discourage innovation and impede the adoption of fintech solutions, thereby hampering financial inclusion. On the other hand, pro-competition regulation, such as Open Banking, could encourage financial innovation, which would favour financial inclusion.

Economy

In the short term, a downturn in the global economy could lead financial institutions to become more risk averse. This would be detrimental to financial inclusion as financial service providers tend to see low-income customers as riskier. In the longer term, however, global economic growth driven by emerging economies could draw more financial institutions to emerging markets, thereby pushing more capital to the fringes, and thus increasing financial inclusion.

Social

With the free flow of information online and growing public awareness regarding environmental sustainability and inequality, it is likely that more people will become interested in financial inclusion. This will put pressure on financial institutions to offer more inclusive services. At the same time, it will inspire entrepreneurs to develop solutions that benefit financial inclusion.

Technology

Technological innovation enables financial service providers to reach more consumers digitally. This connectivity facilitates greater financial inclusion. In addition, technology enables organizations to automate the provision of financial services, thereby reducing the per unit cost of distributing financial products. Over time, this should decrease the costs to consumers, thereby making low-spec financial solutions accessible to previously financially excluded groups.

References

1,2,5,6 Campbell, G, Rogers, M and Turner, J D (2016) *The rise and decline of the UK's provincial stock markets, 1869–1929*, Queen's University Centre for Economic History, Working Paper 16-03, www.quceh.org.uk/uploads/1/0/5/5/10558478/wp16-03.pdf (archived at https://perma.cc/8EE3-FVU2)

3,4 Katz, M L and Shapiro, C (1985) Network Externalities, Competition, and Compatibility, *American Economic Review*, 75 (3), 424–40 (June)

7,92 White, L and MacAskill, A (2017) British banks set to close record 762 branches this year, *Reuters*, 23 August, uk.reuters.com/article/uk-britain-banks-branches-idUKKCN-1B31AY (archived at https://perma.cc/LW9G-6LG5)

8 Chapman, B (2018) UK bank branch closures reach 'alarming' rate of 60 per month, Which? finds, *The Independent*, 15 June, www.independent.co.uk/news/business/news/uk-bank-branch-closures-which-research-natwest-hsbc-a8399041.html (archived at https://perma.cc/ZDC6-VGU8)

9 Euromonitor, Passport (2015) in Govil, S, Whitelaw, D and Spaeth, P (2016) Accelerating global payment worldwide, Visa Inc, usa.visa.com/visa-everywhere/global-impact/accelerating-electronic-payments-worldwide.html (archived at https://perma.cc/2PTH-3XRG)

10 Gapgemini and BNP Paribas (2018) World Payments Report 2018, worldpayments report.com/wp-content/uploads/sites/5/2018/10/World-Payments-Report-2018.pdf (archived at https://perma.cc/R9QC-YRUT)

11 KPMG (2017) Banking on the future: The roadmap to becoming the banking partner of Gen Y professionals, home.kpmg/content/dam/kpmg/au/pdf/2017/banking-on-the-future-edition-3.pdf (archived at https://perma.cc/LH5Q-83ZH)

12,13,14,16,36 Christiansen, H (2001) Electronic Finance: Economics and Institutional Factors, OECD Financial Affairs Division, www.oecd.org/finance/financial-markets/2676135.pdf (archived at https://perma.cc/4GV2-5PAQ)

15 Fry, R (2018) Millennials projected to overtake Baby Boomers as America's largest generation, Pew Research Center, 1 March, www.pewresearch.org/fact-tank/2018/03/01/millennials-overtake-baby-boomers/ (archived at https://perma.cc/VPW6-NYAA)

17,19,38 Arner, D W, Barberis, J N and Buckley, R P (2016) The Evolution of Fintech: A New Post-Crisis Paradigm?, University of Hong Kong Faculty of Law Research Paper No. 2015/047, UNSW Law Research Paper No. 2016-62, papers.ssrn.com/sol3/papers.cfm?abstract_id=2676553 (archived at https://perma.cc/2B8N-2Y85)

18 CCP Research Foundation (2017) Conduct Costs Project Report 2017, 16 August, conductcosts.ccpresearchfoundation.com/conduct-costs-results

20,69 Ronayne, D (2019) Price Comparison Websites, Warwick Economics Research Papers, 25 April, warwick.ac.uk/fac/soc/economics/research/workingpapers/2015/twerp_1056b_ronayne.pdf (archived at https://perma.cc/Z68W-8H3M)

21 Gozman, D, Liebenau, J and Mangan, J (2018) The Innovation Mechanisms of Fintech Start-ups: Insights from SWIFT's Innotribe Competition, *Journal of Management Information System*, 35, 145–79

22 Olsen, T, Di Marzo, A, Ganesh, S and Baxter, M (2018) Wolf in Sheep's Clothing: Disruption ahead for transaction banking, Bain & Co, www.bain.com/insights/disruption-ahead-for-transaction-banking/ (archived at https://perma.cc/WMX4-GZ2A)

23 Scherer, A, Wangenheim, F and Wünderlich, N (2015) The value of self-service: long-term effects of technology-based self-service usage on customer retention, *MIS Quarterly*, 39(1), 177–200 (March)

24 C. Hoare & Co. (2019) About us, www.hoaresbank.co.uk/about-us (archived at https://perma.cc/KU38-NF68)

25 C. Hoare & Co. (2019) Cambridge expansion, www.hoaresbank.co.uk/news/c-hoare-co-cambridge-expansion (archived at https://perma.cc/9SSH-NFDM)

26,27,28 Kay, J (1993) The Structure of Strategy, *Business Strategy Review*, 4 (2), 17–37 (June)

29,33,130 Worldpay (2018) Global payments report: The art and science of global payments [report]

30,56,59,60,62,80 Deloitte LLP (2017) Open banking: How to flourish in an uncertain future, www2.deloitte.com/uk/en/pages/financial-services/articles/future-banking-open-banking-psd2-flourish-in-uncertainty.html (archived at https://perma.cc/TU5W-PAGC)

31,32,82 Lee, I and Shin, Y J (2018) Fintech: Ecosystem, business models, investment decisions, and challenges, *Business Horizons*, 61, 35–46

34,39 Badi, M, Dab, S, Drummond, A, Malhotra, S, Muxi, F, Peeters, M, Roongta, P, Strauß, M and Sénant, Y (2018) Global Payments 2018: Reimagining the Customer Experience, The Boston Consulting Group, 18 October, www.bcg.com/publications/2018/global-payments-reimagining-customer-experience.aspx (archived at https://perma.cc/VA6T-8ZJH)

35 PricewaterhouseCoopers and Startupbootcamp (2017) The state of fintech, www.pwc.com/sg/en/publications/assets/fintech-startupbootcamp-state-of-fintech-2017.pdf (archived at https://perma.cc/R2YG-6CRA)

37 Swinton, S and Roma, E (2018) Why Big UK Banks Are Worried about Open Banking, Forbes.com, 15 March, www.bain.com/insights/why-big-uk-banks-are-worried-about-open-banking-forbes/ (archived at https://perma.cc/QEQ9-ZXXB)

40,41,42,45,47,53 Open Banking Limited (2018) Background to Open Banking, www.openbanking.org.uk/wp-content/uploads/What-Is-Open-Banking-Guide.pdf (archived at https://perma.cc/N5FP-LGPH)

43,44,61 KPMG International (2017) PSD2 Strategy: Comply, Compete or Innovate?, assets.kpmg/content/dam/kpmg/nl/pdf/2017/sector/financiele-dienstverlening/psd2-strategy-comply-compete-innovate3.pdf (archived at https://perma.cc/3X3R-XSVV)

46 Open Banking Limited (2019) About us, www.openbanking.org.uk/about-us/ (archived at https://perma.cc/8ZGR-N236)

48 Chopra, A (2017) What is an API?, 9 October, www.quora.com/What-is-an-API-4?share=1 (archived at https://perma.cc/7PXE-YBUG)

49,50,52,55,63 Zachariadis, M and Ozcan, P (2017) The API Economy and Digital Transformation in Financial Services: Open Banking, Swift Institute, 15 June, swiftinstitute.org/research/impact-of-open-apis-in-banking/ (archived at https://perma.cc/73S7-T5YG)

51 Jacobson, D, Brail, G and Woods, D (2011) *APIs: A Strategy Guide*, O'Reilly Media, Sebastopol, CA

54 TransferWise (2019) TransferWise API, api-docs.transferwise.com/#transferwise-api (archived at https://perma.cc/3G2L-QEW9)

57 Brown, J R and Goolsbee, A (2000) Does the Internet Make Markets More Competitive? NBER Working Paper No. 7996, www.nber.org/papers/w7996 (archived at https://perma.cc/9Q9U-MEFB)

58 Tardi, C (2019) White Label Product, Investopedia, 10 April, www.investopedia.com/terms/w/white-label-product.asp (archived at https://perma.cc/2J87-296S)

64,66 Bouvier, P (2016) Exploring Banking as a Platform (BaaP) Model, Finiculture, 19 March, finiculture.com/exploring-banking-as-a-platform-baap-model/ (archived at https://perma.cc/DR64-43YC)

65,75 Rysman, M (2009) The Economics of Two-Sided Markets, *Journal of Economic Perspectives*, 23 (3), 125–43

67,68,71 Porter, M E (1980), *Competitive Strategy: Techniques for Analyzing Industries and Competitors*, Free Press, New York

70 Wesleyan Assurance Society (2019) About us, www.wesleyan.co.uk/about-us/ (archived at https://perma.cc/8T5G-B8GU)

72,77 Bonchek, M and Choudary, S P (2013) Three elements of a successful platform strategy, *Harvard Business Review*, 31 January, hbr.org/2013/01/three-elements-of-a-successful-platform (archived at https://perma.cc/H332-9V4C)

73,76,78,105 Zhu, F and Iansiti, M (2019) Why Some Platforms Thrive and Others Don't, *Harvard Business Review*, 97 (1), 118–25 (January–February)

74,89 Starling Bank Limited (2020) Personal current account, www.starlingbank.com/current-account/ (archived at https://perma.cc/SC9A-98AP)

79 International Organization of Securities Commissions (2017) IOSCO Research Report on Financial Technologies (Fintech), www.iosco.org/library/pubdocs/pdf/IOSCOPD554.pdf (archived at https://perma.cc/N5XH-CB5R)

81,83,84,85,86 MagnaCarta Communications and ACI Worldwide (2017) Innovation, distributed: Mapping the fintech bridge in the open source era, www.aciworldwide.com/-/media/files/collateral/other/aci-magna-carta-fintech-disruptors-report.pdf (archived at https://perma.cc/3PW8-N3S2)

87 CapGemini and LinkedIn (2018) World fintech report 2018, www.capgemini.com/wp-content/uploads/2018/02/world-fintech-report-wftr-2018.pdf (archived at https://perma.cc/4UDU-FNQC)

88 Starling Bank Limited (2019) About us, www.starlingbank.com/media/ (archived at https://perma.cc/D8PM-MCYD)

90 Amazon Web Services (2019) Breaking the Banking Mould: How Starling Bank is disrupting the banking industry, aws.amazon.com/solutions/case-studies/starling/ (archived at https://perma.cc/D3AF-QBPE)

91 Starling Bank Limited (2018) Introducing: Cash deposits at the Post Office, 12 November, www.starlingbank.com/blog/post-office-deposits/ (archived at https://perma.cc/JW7W-EEMA)

93 Starling Bank Limited (2018) Starling for business open for sole traders, 4 June, www.starlingbank.com/blog/sole-trader-bank-account/ (archived at https://perma.cc/8K7R-VVL6)

94 Smith, O (2019) Starling beats Tide to offering multi-director business accounts, Altfi, 25 July, www.altfi.com/article/5576_starling-beats-tide-offering-multi-director-business-accounts (archived at https://perma.cc/RNK7-5XXV)

95 Starling Bank Limited (2019) Introducing: Multi-owner mobile business accounts for limited companies, 25 July, www.starlingbank.com/blog/business-account-multiple-people-significant-control/ (archived at https://perma.cc/9JQS-LMQM)

96 Bannister, D (2017) Transaction Banking Survey: Challenges & imperatives of real-time payments & liquidity, Ovum Consulting, ovum.informa.com/resources/product-content/2017-transaction-banking-survey (archived at https://perma.cc/C3X4-MMJS)

97,98 Starling Bank Limited (2019) Our ethics statement, www.starlingbank.com/about/ethics-statement/ (archived at https://perma.cc/5Q66-9ECW)

99,100 Fotis, M (2019) British Bank Awards 2019: Winners, Smart Money People, 8 March, smartmoneypeople.com/news/post/british-bank-awards-2019-winners (archived at https://perma.cc/3KNP-L2NP)

101 Boden, A (2018) Welcome to Banking-as-a-Service, Starling Bank Limited, 10 October, www.starlingbank.com/blog/platformification-of-banking-industry/ (archived at https://perma.cc/ZUM6-K3XK)

102 Starling Bank Limited (2019) Direct Line Group partners with leading digital bank Starling, 24 June, www.starlingbank.com/news/direct-line-group-partnership-churchill-insurance/ (archived at https://perma.cc/9JJB-M45P)

103 Starling Bank Limited (2019) Introducing: CreditLadder, our new Starling Marketplace partner, 12 July, www.starlingbank.com/blog/introducing-creditladder-starling-marketplace/ (archived at https://perma.cc/V43B-9347)

104 Starling Bank Limited (2019) Annual report and consolidated financial statements for the year ended 30 November 2018, www.starlingbank.com/docs/Starling-bank-annual-report-2017-18.pdf (archived at https://perma.cc/JF3K-CV2L)

106 Leibenstein, H (1950) Bandwagon, snob, and Veblen effects in the theory of consumers' demand, *The Quarterly Journal of Economics*, 64 (2), 183–207 (May)

107 Kimovil (2020) All smartphone brands, www.kimovil.com/en/all-smartphone-brands (archived at https://perma.cc/CQ93-7XSU)

108,109 Liebowitz, S J and Margolis, S E (1994) Network Externality: An Uncommon Tragedy, *Journal of Economic Perspectives*, 8 (2), 133–50

110 Smith, A (1776) An Inquiry into the Nature and Causes of the Wealth of Nations, www.gutenberg.org/files/3300/3300-h/3300-h.htm#chap17 (archived at https://perma.cc/P3V7-CVLQ)

111 Cheung, S L (2016) Diseconomies of Scale, *The Palgrave Encyclopedia of Strategic Management*, 25 June, link.springer.com/referenceworkentry/10.1057/978-1-349-94848-2_66-1 (archived at https://perma.cc/4BEM-3NRQ)

112 Acemoglu, D, Malekian, A and Ozdaglar, A (2016) Network Security and Contagion, *Journal of Economic Theory*, 166, 536–85

113 Bakos, Y and Katsamakas, E (2008) Design and Ownership of Two-Sided Networks: Implications for Internet Platforms, *Journal of Management Information Systems*, 25 (2), 171–202

114,115 Weitzel, T, Wendt, O and Westarp, F V (2000) Reconsidering network effect theory, in: European Conference on Information Systems, Vienna: Association for Information Systems, https://aisel.aisnet.org/ecis2000/index.2.html (archived at https://perma.cc/LD4B-JJ7S)

116 Larios-Hernandez, G J (2017) Blockchain entrepreneurship opportunity in the practices of the unbanked, *Business Horizons*, 60 (6), 865–74 (November–December)

117 The Nobel Foundation (2006) Grameen Bank, Facts, www.nobelprize.org/prizes/peace/2006/grameen/facts/ (archived at https://perma.cc/P5Z6-FV2P)

118 Doi, Y (2010) Financial Inclusion, Poverty Reduction and Economic Growth, World Bank Group, 10 November, www.worldbank.org/en/news/opinion/2010/11/10/financial-inclusion-poverty-reduction-economic-growth (archived at https://perma.cc/98YR-Z7F8)

119,120,121 Vodafone (2019) M-PESA, www.vodafone.com/content/index/what/m-pesa.html# (archived at https://perma.cc/KCU6-LMF5)

122 Suri, T and Jack, W (2016) The long-run poverty and gender impacts of mobile money, *Science*, 354, 1288–92 (December)

123 World Bank (2018) The Little Data Book on Financial Inclusion 2018, openknowledge.worldbank.org/handle/10986/29654 (archived at https://perma.cc/9E7F-4RQK)

124 GSM Association (2019) The Mobile Economy: Sub-Saharan Africa, www.gsma.com/r/mobileeconomy/sub-saharan-africa/ (archived at https://perma.cc/AGD6-RCVG)

125 Ndung'u, N (2019) Taxing mobile phone transactions in Africa: Lessons from Kenya, The Brookings Institution, 5 August, www.brookings.edu/research/taxing-mobile-phone-transactions-in-africa-lessons-from-kenya/ (archived at https://perma.cc/GMY6-3A6Q)

126 McKinsey & Company (2017) Mobile financial services in Africa: Winning the battle for the customer, www.mckinsey.com/industries/financial-services/our-insights/mobile-financial-services-in-africa-winning-the-battle-for-the-customer (archived at https://perma.cc/KY5C-KBGM)

127 China–Africa Research Initiative (2019) Data: China–Africa trade, Johns Hopkins School of Advanced International Studies, www.sais-cari.org/data-china-africa-trade (archived at https://perma.cc/AVH2-4KQL)

128 Alipay (2019) About Alipay, intl.alipay.com/ihome/index.htm (archived at https://perma.cc/Z3U9-TFE2)

129 PYMTS (2019) Flutterwave Teams With Alipay To Enable China–Africa Transactions, 30 July, www.pymnts.com/news/mobile-payments/2019/flutterwave-teams-with-alipay-to-enable-china-africa-transactions/ (archived at https://perma.cc/4MUU-GG7Y)

02

Disruption and disintermediation

*How financial innovation and cloud computing
gave birth to the fintech revolution*

LEARNING OBJECTIVES

By the end of this chapter, you will have an understanding of:

- How technology is changing the role of financial intermediation.
- How the global financial crisis of 2007–09 has affected fintech.
- The role of cloud computing in enabling financial innovation.
- How and why novel fintech solutions are disrupting financial services.

Introduction

If you visit a home built according to traditional Chinese custom, you are likely to encounter a spring or fountain of some sort. This is because the flow of water is associated with wealth generation.[1] This metaphor is cogent: just as the flow of water sustains life, the flow of money brings prosperity. Perhaps then, it is not an accident that businesses with cash flow problems are said to have liquidity problems.

Financial intermediaries know that capturing money flows is key to building wealth. For centuries, they have sought to prosper by placing themselves between transacting parties; in this way, banks, insurers and asset managers have profited by acting as financial go-betweens.

However, the web is reshaping the role of financial intermediaries. Just as messaging apps and social media have transformed how people communicate, web-based financial services are changing the way people transact. Greater connectivity and information flow are narrowing the gap between transacting parties. Thus, technology reduces the need for financial intermediation, which puts pressure on traditional financial institutions.

Financial disintermediation

Financial intermediaries connect users of funds with providers of funds. Whether the intermediary is a bank, asset manager or insurer, the end result is the same in that money flows from those with an excess of capital to those with a deficit. In other words, from those who don't need money to those who do.

Generally speaking, capital providers come in the form of investors – debt, equity or otherwise – and savers (ie bank depositors). Meanwhile, the users of capital can be consumers, businesses or governments. Thus, many participants in the financial system are simultaneously providers and consumers of capital. For example, a bank customer can have a home loan and savings account at the same time.

Financial intermediaries facilitate transactions between parties whose financial needs complement one another. The presence of an intermediary helps overcome problems that would otherwise prevent or impede the transaction. For example, banks help their depositors and borrowers resolve a mismatch of liquidity preferences. On the whole, depositors want to access their funds within a shorter time frame than borrowers (ie for spending, etc); meanwhile, borrowers want to feel secure in their financing – they do not want their financiers to demand repayment at short notice.

Banks solve this problem by simultaneously diversifying their loan book and depositor base. Because customers do not require access to their funds at the same time, no one is left out of pocket. As a result, depositors can access their funds at short notice while borrowers are financed for a comparatively longer period of time. This is known as *maturity transformation*,[2] or colloquially as 'taking deposits short and lending long'.

Similarly, insurers help their customers spread the cost of providing for an unexpected cash outflow. By pooling customers' risks, the insurer *ensures* that no individual customer has to set aside a large amount of capital to make up for potential future shortfalls. In this way, insurance policyholders are both providers of capital and users of capital; by paying insurance premiums, they are all providers of capital, while those making claims are simultaneously also users of capital.

Of course, financial institutions are not charities. As a result, they seek to profit from their intermediary position. Often, this means charging fees and/ or a spread. For example, banks take deposits and lend at different rates of interest. This has been a profitable business model for centuries.

However, by facilitating information flows between users and providers of capital, technology is disintermediating traditional financial institutions, and, in some cases, making them obsolete. As seen in Chapter 1, this is exemplified by the fintech sector, wherein the smaller scale of fintech start-ups enables the specialization necessary to draw customers away from incumbents' packaged solutions.

For example, peer-to-peer lending platforms specialize in connecting savers and borrowers online.[3] Thus, they do not incur many of the costs associated with running a network of bank branches. As a result, they can afford to offer better rates of interest to both borrowers and savers,[4] and thereby pry customers away from conventional banks.

Such disintermediation is made worse by new players, such as Starling Bank, who aggregate fintech solutions via their digital platforms (see Chapter 1). In this way, people who would previously have consumed financial services via a few branch-based institutions now have access to holistic suites of innovative financial solutions from a single entry-point – their smartphones. As a result, fintech and financial disintermediation are a cause of concern in the financial industry: according to a global 2017 survey of financial services firms, 88 per cent of executives at incumbent financial institutions said they were concerned about losing revenue to fintech companies.[5]

Fintech and the financial crisis of 2007–09

To understand what fintech disruption means for the financial industry, it is necessary to examine the drivers behind it. In Chapter 1 we touched on the role of demography: the fact that the largest consumer group in the USA – the millennial generation[6] – is composed almost entirely of digital natives. This, along with the near ubiquity of web-connected mobile devices, appears to have made consumers more willing to embrace digital financial solutions.[7]

Although this is a major driver of the fintech revolution, two others stand out: the global financial crisis of 2007–09 (aka the 'GFC') and the rise of cloud computing.

Whereas technology and demography converged to lay the foundations for greater financial disintermediation, the GFC was a trigger event – the shot that set off the fintech revolution. Indeed, the GFC played, and continues to play, a multifaceted role in shaping fintech. Besides undermining public trust in mainstream financial institutions[8] – thereby giving fintech start-ups an in with consumers – the GFC has spurred financial innovation indirectly via a more competitive talent pool, lower interest rates and changes to financial regulation.

For starters, there is the question of available talent. As a direct result of the GFC, many people working in financial services lost their jobs. While some went on to work in other sectors, others joined or founded fintech start-ups. In this way, the GFC appears to have given fintech companies greater access to employees with the requisite financial services skills and experience.[9] Many of these people had seen the failings of the financial system from the inside. As a result, their combined experiences may have imbued the fintech industry with a desire for change and a willingness to do things differently, which may have helped foster a more innovative culture in many fintech startups.

Furthermore, the financial crisis had profound and long-lasting effects on capital markets. In 2007, the banking system was shocked by increasing home loan default rates in the United States, which many institutions were exposed to via *mortgage backed securities* (MBS) – bundles of mortgages sold as investments.[10] This *securitization* added a layer of opacity; as it was still the job of originating lenders to service the underlying mortgages, many MBS investors did not know who, or what, they were exposed to.

Consequently, banks feared the worst: with so many defaulting mortgages out there, someone would end up suffering catastrophic losses, though no one was sure who that would be. This uncertainty led banks to become reluctant to lend to one other.[11] As a result, the credit markets effectively froze.[12] This led some institutions to collapse, which further reduced banks' willingness to lend, thereby worsening the crisis.[13]

To prevent the financial system from collapsing, central banks around the world flooded the financial system with liquidity, by buying up government bonds and slashing benchmark interest rates. This caused global interest rates and bond yields to fall to historic lows. For example, the US Government's

10-year bond yield stood at *ca* 5 per cent at the end of June 2007.[14] This means that investors could have secured an annual return of *ca* 5 per cent by lending money to the US Government for 10 years starting in June 2007; by January 2009, this rate had halved.[15]

In financial parlance, the term 'interest rate' is often used synonymously with *yield*. This is because a bond yield is the annual rate of return that one receives for buying a bond and holding it to maturity (ie when the bond repays its notional value); much like depositing cash in a fixed-term savings account, this guarantees interest payments for a defined period of time, at the end of which the initial capital outlay is returned. For a bond, this means the investor receives the bond's notional value, which can, and often is, different from the bond's market price.

As a result, bond yields vary inversely with bond prices. This is because a bond is effectively an IOU whose future payments are fixed, while bond market prices fluctuate according to supply and demand. Thus, the rate of return that is attainable varies according to how much one pays for the bond: if bond prices are high, then bond yields will be low and vice versa. In this way, a bond's yield is a measure of its expected annual return given prevailing market prices.

By driving up bond prices, central banks caused global bond yields to decline to record lows. According to conventional financial thinking, United States *Treasuries* are seen as a risk-free asset because the US Government is 'too big to fail'. If the world's most powerful country were to default on its debt obligations, the whole financial system would collapse. As a result, all financial assets (stocks, bonds, etc) are priced in relation to United States Treasuries; whatever Uncle Sam pays, a riskier asset, such as a corporate bond, must yield more.

In this way, falling government bond yields have pushed investors into riskier assets. If a central bank buys your 'safe-haven' government bond, you are unlikely to use that money to buy another bond from the same government. Instead, you would either spend the money – on a new Tesla, for instance – or invest it in something with a greater expected return, and therefore more risk. Moreover, as bank interest rates barely keep up with inflation, investors looking to protect their wealth have been forced into riskier asset classes. As a result, their money has made its way into corporate debt, stocks and venture capital funds in order to secure a higher return.

As low interest rates have persisted since the GFC, large amounts of capital are cascading into fintech start-ups, often via venture capital funds: in 2013, total global fintech investments amounted to *ca* $19 billion; in 2018, this figure was *ca* $112 billion.[16] Thus, the financial crisis has indirectly spurred funding of fintech start-ups by causing global bond yields to collapse. Rather than putting their money in banks, many investors seem content to invest in innovative start-ups with a 'fail fast' attitude. In theory, astute selection and diversification should reward such risk taking with superior long-term returns, though there are no guarantees. Regardless, this has made it easier for fintech start-ups to secure funding; indeed, there is evidence to suggest a correlation between the availability of venture capital (VC) funding and the size of individual countries' fintech sectors.[17]

Regulation as a driver of fintech?

In the aftermath of the GFC, regulators and policymakers were roundly criticized for being too soft on banks in the years before the crisis. As a result, large financial institutions have since had to endure greater regulatory scrutiny and more stringent capital requirements. However, no regulator has infinite resources as they have to employ staff to supervise the institutions they regulate.

This means that regulators have had to prioritize their supervisory efforts and focus on firms that pose a comparatively greater risk to their regulatory objectives.[18] Though such objectives vary by jurisdiction, they, broadly speaking, involve protecting consumers while ensuring the financial system's stability. Consequently, regulators devote more staff time to supervising larger institutions; as these have more customers, they tend to pose a greater potential threat to regulatory objectives than, say, a fintech start-up.

In some jurisdictions, this has meant that fintech start-ups, by virtue of their small size, incur less regulatory scrutiny than their larger rivals.[19] Thus, the absence of a significant regulatory burden can be a competitive advantage for a small company, both from a cost perspective and, more crucially, from a business agility perspective (ie 'getting things done'). Less regulatory scrutiny means that fintech start-ups tend to worry less about what regulators might think before rolling out innovations – unlike their larger rivals.

Indeed, empirical evidence suggests that countries with comparatively liberal regulatory systems exhibit greater rates of fintech start-up formation than those with less flexible systems.[20] This presents regulators and policymakers with a dilemma. On one hand, they must fulfil their regulatory responsibilities; on the other, they do not want to discourage financial innovation. As a result, some regulators choose to engage with the fintech sector proactively. Perhaps most notably, the UK's Financial Conduct Authority (FCA) has a specialist unit dedicated to engaging with fintech start-ups: as part of this, the FCA aims to reduce regulatory barriers to innovation whilst maintaining robust consumer protection standards.[21] Seemingly, the FCA is attempting to embed a basic level of regulatory best practice into fintech start-ups. By making regulation easier to engage with, this will perhaps help foster a more robust compliance culture in the fintech sector, which was so badly missing at many banks in the run-up to the GFC.

Furthermore, some policymakers have attempted to make the legislative backdrop more accommodating for smaller firms. These changes are, at least in part, designed to address the 'too big to fail' problem in banking, which many see as the GFC's root cause: large banks were allowed by their shareholders to take on excessive risk because their failure would endanger the entire financial system, thereby securing an implicit government bail-out (which they got!). This moral hazard allowed large banks to access cheaper financing than their smaller competitors, causing them to grow even larger, thereby exacerbating the problem.

To address the too-big-to-fail problem, some policymakers have sought to make the financial system more competitive, in an effort to reduce concentration in the banking sector. In the UK, for example, Open Banking seeks to encourage innovation:[22] in this way, new and better-run institutions can emerge to chip away at the market share of larger banks. In an ideal world, no institution will be too big to fail; in practice, this is a long, long way off.

In this way, the GFC, its resulting regulatory forbearance and accommodative legislation have helped ease the compliance burden on smaller firms. As a result, regulation is no longer as significant a barrier to entry in the financial sector as it once was; particularly for fintech start-ups, which attract comparatively little regulatory attention.[23] Thus, large incumbent institutions can no longer rely on their scale to keep fintech challengers out.

Virtualizing IT infrastructure

Like regulation, access to large-scale IT infrastructure was once considered a significant barrier to entry into the financial sector. Unlike regulation, however, technology advances have made this barrier almost non-existent.

This behind-the-scenes story is often overshadowed by developments in consumer-facing technologies, such as smartphone apps, which have captured public imagination. It is not hard to see why: the story of digital natives coming of age to experiment with innovative new ways of doing finance is, on the surface, a far more compelling story.

However, the hardware story is no less important. In the past, organizations hosted their digital solutions internally. In practice, this would mean running data centres in out-of-town warehouses. For digitally based organizations, this represents a heavy cost due to the large amount of online traffic that has to be accommodated: the more digitally intensive the solution, the larger the data centre. However, an increasing number of solutions are being hosted externally, on *the cloud*. With its entire platform running on Amazon's cloud solution,[24] Starling Bank is a good example of this.

CLOUD COMPUTING EXPLAINED

Organizations operating their own behind-the-scenes data centres are faced with a resource allocation problem: as user activity varies throughout the day, it is difficult to optimize infrastructure spend. On one hand, enough computing power has to be available at peak times; on the other, running the same computer hardware 24/7 is both wasteful and costly.[25]

In fact, most organizations do not use their behind-the-scenes data centres all of the time. Therefore, it makes sense to pool these resources via a cloud solution. Rather than hosting their platforms internally, organizations can run them from the servers of a cloud provider. Meanwhile, the end-user, who engages with the customer-facing application, is none the wiser as the software interface remains the same. In this way, cloud computing is comparable to a time-sharing solution for data centres.[26]

This is where tech giants like Microsoft, Amazon and IBM come in. With their immense economies of scale, these companies can greatly reduce the cost of running a data centre.[27] To achieve these savings, cloud providers build their data centres in remote locations, often in colder climates, in order to save money on rent and electricity.

Cloud providers rely on automation to manage their service provision. This means using sophisticated algorithms to allocate computing resources.[28] In addition, cloud solutions tend to be self-service.[29] This enables cloud computing to be consumed on demand, like electricity or water, which can significantly reduce electricity costs for the client organization; by some estimates, the energy saving can be as much as 80–90 per cent.[30]

Cloud computing allows computing infrastructure to be consumed like utilities.[31] This gives organizations greater flexibility in regard to their IT spend.[32] Whereas building a super-computer in-house might be prohibitively expensive, renting the equivalent computing power for a few hours is not. In this way, cloud computing enables smaller organizations – such as fintech start-ups – to access powerful computing resources. As a result, the large upfront cost of setting up a data centre is no longer a barrier to entry into data-intensive sectors, like finance.

By virtualizing a physical resource, cloud computing has turned computer hardware into something that can be consumed on demand;[33] in this way, it has turned IT infrastructure into a service. This paradigm is not unique to computer hardware: whilst cloud computing is an example of infrastructure-as-a-service, Adobe Photoshop is an example of software-as-a-service.[34] This popular image manipulation package has gone from being sold on a licence basis to a subscription basis; whereas once you would buy the software package off the shelf, you now pay a monthly fee for accessing it.[35]

Thus, Photoshop's subscription model can be described as software-as-a-service (SaaS): rather than purchasing the package outright, users effectively lease it from Adobe. As part of this, users can rent storage space on Adobe's cloud solution.[36] Photoshop's transition from product to service was possible because software is intangible, which allowed it to be consumed digitally. As financial services are similarly intangible, it should, in theory, be possible to re-orient the financial industry towards a service-based delivery model.

Banking as infrastructure

Cheaper and more accessible IT infrastructure is hastening financial disinter-mediation. This, along with Open Banking, will force banks to reimagine their operating models. While some will pursue a platform model (see Chapter 1), others may become more like utility companies, by managing the financial system's background infrastructure: this could involve providing behind-the-scenes services such as payment processing and anti-money laun-dering checks.[37]

Becoming a banking utility would require institutions to reconfigure their revenue models, as they would no longer earn a spread from 'borrowing short and lending long'. This could involve levying periodic account management fees, charging per transaction, or a combination of the two. Indeed, different banks may come up with different models, much as home internet providers have done. Of course, the end customer may not have to bear such costs directly as these may be covered by the customer-facing firms relying on the banks' infrastructure.

To some, the prospect of becoming a utility may sound unattractive. That said, there are some advantages to this model. Large banks have the economies of scale to minimize operating costs per transaction, especially if they cede customer-facing areas to other players. Indeed, doing so may enable banks to focus on re-engineering their back offices, as opposed to competing against more innovative start-ups.

As scale helps keep costs down, the utility-banking sub-sector may see a push towards consolidation. Though further concentration in the banking sector may appear undesirable from a regulatory perspective, it need not be a deal-breaker. Large institutions are more closely scrutinized than their smaller fintech rivals. Thus, leaving the mundane parts of the financial sector to a few large – and well-regulated – institutions could lead to a greater level of security for customers and the financial system as a whole. Instead of breaking up large institutions, solving the 'too big to fail' problem may lie in allowing consolidation into lower-risk areas.

Banking as a Service (BaaS)

Just as cloud computing has enabled IT infrastructure to be consumed as a service, technology is making banking services accessible on demand. This paradigm is known as Banking as a Service (BaaS). It can be viewed as a cross between utility-based banking, as described above, and the Banking as a Platform (BaaP) approach.

In this way, the BaaS paradigm is analogous to cloud computing. A cloud solution contains three basic layers: infrastructure, platform and software.[38] Under the BaaS paradigm, large banks would provide a foundational layer of infrastructure in support of their own – or indeed, third-party – financial platforms.[39] Individual fintech providers would sit atop this *stack*, and be analogous to the customer-facing applications in a cloud solution.[40]

Application Programming Interfaces (APIs) would play a key role in a BaaS solution.[41] As in cloud computing, self-service and automation are at the core of the BaaS model. To this end, APIs would enable innovators to tether their solutions to the underlying financial infrastructure.[42] In this way, the scale and regulatory sophistication of large banks would be accessible to fintech start-ups,[43] almost as seamlessly as when using a cloud provider. In theory, this should enable fintech companies to create new solutions by using the services of larger – and more well-established – institutions as building blocks.[44]

In practice, the distinction between infrastructure, platform and solution provider is not always clear. Though a three-layer BaaS model seems appealing – chiefly because of its nod to cloud computing – it should be noted that, at the time of writing, no institution has successfully made the transformation from retail bank to being a banking utility or BaaS. The same can be said for financial platforms: very few, if any, mainstream financial institutions – save of course a few price comparison websites – play the role of platform-only businesses without any products of their own. Rather, large financial institutions remain, to varying degrees, hybrids of infrastructure, platform and financial solution providers.

Indeed, BaaS may be more viable as a two-layer model. With fintech start-ups becoming banks in their own right, there may be no need for long-established financial institutions to provide the underlying banking infrastructure. As the fintech-based banks incorporate third-party solution providers via their platforms, the infrastructure and platform layers may merge into one.[45]

This leaves banks between a rock and a hard place: for one, banks find themselves assailed from all sides by specialist solution providers who, product by product, unbundle banks' more holistic product suites; meanwhile, fintech-banks like Starling reassemble these specialist solutions on their platforms. Without an obvious role as infrastructure providers, this may force banks to face their competition head-on.

Disruptive innovation in financial services

Until now, much of the discussion has been focussed on the global drivers of change and how these are reshaping financial services. However, to be able to respond to fintech disruption, banks must seek to understand what their challengers are up to. In this regard, it is critical to consider the customer's perspective as it is their experience that determines success or failure. While regulations and technology shape the development of new financial solutions, there still needs to be a consumer demand for these, after all.

As touched on in Chapter 1, companies seek to compete by being the cheapest or by offering something that is sufficiently unique to command a premium. Both approaches can be strengthened by focussing one's proposition on a particular market segment.[46]

As established players focus on exploiting the most profitable segments, gaps emerge in the marketplace. Thus, some consumer groups are either overlooked or ignored because they are not viewed as being sufficiently profitable. As a result, a number of consumers find themselves either overcharged or underserved.[47]

This phenomenon can be readily observed in the retail banking industry: as banks close down branches in less profitable areas, some consumers find themselves alienated from the financial system as there is no longer a bank branch in their town, village or neighbourhood. This marginalization leaves a gap in the market for new competitors to enter the banking sector.

As a result, many consumers are drawn to digital solutions either by necessity or out of want for something new and different. This gives fintech start-ups, such as mobile-only banks, an initial customer segment to focus on. As these consumers are unlikely to be fully satisfied with incumbent financial institutions, they are easy to win over. By providing an alternative to overcharged and/or underserved consumers, fintech start-ups gain a foothold in the sector. Once a base has been established, the new entrants go on to compete in more profitable segments, encroaching on the turf of larger and more well-established players.[48] This process is known as *disruptive innovation.*[49]

This phenomenon tends to happen in industries where large groups of consumers find themselves either priced out or underserved. For example, low-cost airlines emerged because short-haul flights were too dear.[50] These airlines stripped out the non-essential add-ons such as 'free' food and generous baggage allowances, which many consumers were happy to forego in exchange for cheaper flights. Once these airlines had captured (and saturated) the short-haul market, some attempted to apply the low-cost model to longer-haul routes. Thus, these airlines have moved from what was once considered the fringes of the marketplace into the mainstream, competing with large and well-established long-haul operators.

Furthermore, industries with top-heavy structural concentrations tend to be more vulnerable to disruption. When only a few large players dominate an industry, it becomes oligopolistic. This reduces the incentive for firms to compete directly: large, well-established players are reluctant to compete too fiercely for fear of sparking a price war. After all, why rock the boat if everyone is making money?

This lack of competitive rivalry does little to improve customer outcomes, if at all. As a result, top-heavy sectors make attractive targets for disruptors. Perhaps then, it is no surprise that a swell of disruption is underway in the UK, where 80 per cent of the retail banking market is in the hands of just five institutions.[51] This potential for disruption is not limited to the UK, as similar concentrations exist elsewhere: in Australia, for example, four institutions account for approximately three quarters of the domestic banking industry.[52] Thus, disruptive innovation in financial services is a global phenomenon.

 CASE STUDY
TransferWise: Disintermediating currency markets

This company's genesis lends credence to the saying that 'necessity is the mother of invention'. The story starts with a nasty surprise: in 2008, Kristo Kaarmann, an Estonian living in London, sent £10,000 to his savings account in Estonia. When the money arrived, he was shocked to discover that the transaction had cost him *ca* £500.[53] Reflecting on the experience in an interview, Kristo said: 'I had foolishly expected that my UK bank would have given me the exchange rate I saw when I looked on Reuters and Bloomberg. Instead the bank had used an exchange rate 5 per cent less favourable.'[54]

To save money on future transfers, Kristo teamed up with his friend, and fellow Estonian, Taavet Hinrikus, who also lived in London, but happened to be paid in euros. As a result, the two friends had complementary currency needs. While Kristo wanted euros to service his mortgage in Estonia, Taavet needed sterling to pay the bills in London. To minimize transaction costs, the two friends agreed to swap currency at the mid-market rate and thereby avoid the spread. Once a month, Kristo would transfer British pounds to Taavet's UK bank account while Taavet would transfer an equivalent value in euros to Kristo's Estonian account.[55]

In 2010, the two friends founded TransferWise to help others do the same.[56] The company is founded on three core principles: transparency, low fees and a premium service for everyone.[57] By 2019, TransferWise reached 5 million customers,[58] who transfer US$4 billion every month.[59] According to its website, the company helps its customers save an estimated US$4 million a day in bank fees and transaction costs.[60]

TransferWise replicates the two friends' currency swapping scheme at scale. This enables users to send money abroad, to friends or family who use a different currency. By connecting groups of users with complementary currency needs, TransferWise solves the counter-party matching problem: rather than transacting peer to peer, users transact with pools of other users. In this way, an individual's transaction can be matched against several other users from the other side of the market.

Thus, users do not transact directly. Instead, the matching process takes place behind the scenes with reference to the mid-market rate. With greater scale comes greater liquidity, and, as TransferWise has grown, it has taken on more currency pairs (eg USD–EUR, GBP–AUD, etc). As a result, its users can now transact in dozens of currencies.

TransferWise levies a conversion fee on each transfer. Depending on the currency pair, these fees typically range from around 0.3 per cent, for the most liquid currency pairs, up to ca 2.8 per cent, for less liquid pairs.[61] According to a study commissioned by the company, this represents a significant cost reduction for sending money across borders. The study examined the cost of using mainstream European banks to send €250 to local-currency accounts in the UK, United States, Australia, as well as within the Eurozone: for example, when compared to banks in Germany, using TransferWise cuts transaction costs by as much as 75 per cent; against Irish banks, TransferWise saves ca 90 per cent.[62]

In 2018, the company launched its Borderless Account,[63] a multi-currency bank account that is registered as local in the UK, United States, Australia, New Zealand and the Eurozone. This means that users can receive payments in GBP, USD, AUD, NZD and EUR without incurring conversion charges. Furthermore, the account allows users to hold dozens of currencies, which they can spend using the solution's debit card. This enables users to transact on local terms when travelling abroad, thereby minimizing transaction costs on foreign spending.[64]

The solution is not entirely free as users suffer conversion fees when acquiring foreign currencies via the TransferWise platform, though these are low when compared to mainstream banks (see above). Furthermore, there is a nominal fee for sending money from the account of ca 65p, though this varies by currency. That said, there are no account management fees and users can make ATM withdrawals of up to £200 every 30 days without incurring additional charges.[65]

TransferWise has offered a proposition for business customers since 2016.[66] In essence, it is a more sophisticated version of the company's Borderless Account. Built with business needs in mind, the account facilitates payroll processing and batch payments.[67] In addition, the solution can be integrated with Xero,[68] a popular accountancy package. This allows businesses to send money to large groups of payees from a spreadsheet,[69] while transactions feed directly into their accounting systems.

Furthermore, TransferWise allows businesses to tether their systems to its platform via its API.[70] This has enabled financial institutions to integrate their platforms with TransferWise. This group includes banks in the UK (Monzo), Germany (N26), France (BPCE) and Estonia (LHV).[71] This allows their customers to access TransferWise from their own platforms. In this way, these institutions have effectively outsourced their foreign currency services to TransferWise.

How is TransferWise disrupting international payments?
(Suggested answer at the end of this chapter.)

Convenience as a business model

Once disruptors gain a beachhead, they move on to more profitable market segments.[72] As seen in the TransferWise case study above, this requires a more sophisticated service proposition. As a result, fintech banks assemble suites of innovative financial solutions via their platforms; rather than doing everything themselves, they select specialist partners that will enhance their overall proposition. At the same time, these platforms focus on building strong customer relationships and optimizing their user experience (for more on this, see Chapter 3).

If conventional financial institutions are to survive as anything other than, perhaps, infrastructure providers, they must seek to emulate their fintech rivals. If banks cannot compete on price – which seems doubtful, given that they are routinely undercut by more innovative players – they have to find other ways of differentiating their propositions. This can be achieved by making their services more convenient. But what does this mean in practice?

To understand 'convenience', one must start with the idea of inconvenience. Every interruption, delay or effort – whether physical or mental – takes an emotional toll on the customer. Thus, financial transactions are subject to what can be called mental transaction costs.[73] Humanity has never had more information at its fingertips, and thus there is a heightened risk of suffering from *decision fatigue*. As a result, consumers need things to be as simple and straightforward as possible.[74]

Fintech banks recognize the importance of mental transaction costs. By assembling a holistic range of financial solutions on their platforms, they lower search and comparison costs for consumers. This increases transparency, thereby reducing uncertainty: by providing access to an open smorgasbord of financial solutions, fintech banks allay user concerns of not getting the best deal, or otherwise missing out. Such uncertainty is, in itself, a transaction cost.[75] Thus, the reduction of the mental transaction costs is a core part of many fintech business models; to this end, they strive to make their service propositions as convenient as possible.

To make their services more convenient, banks must look at things from their consumers' perspective. This can be achieved by recasting their propositions as potential solutions to consumer problems: rather than buying products, people increasingly hire businesses to help them solve problems.[76] These problems can be multifaceted, subtle and difficult to quantify. Thus, it is useful to understand each customer's problem as a job that needs to be completed.[77]

To this end, it is useful to analyse the customer's problem as a process and distil this into its sub-components. In this way, each 'job' can be defined as a series of steps to be completed by the customer; companies can innovate by finding ways of helping customers through each step. This can be achieved by removing hassle, lowering costs, increasing access, or allowing greater flexibility, etc.[78]

Moreover, it is conceivable that a similar approach to innovation can be adopted internally; after all, like customers, employees are, quite literally, trying to complete a job. Regardless, this is an ongoing and iterative process.[79] As the world is dynamic, banks must continue to improve their processes, whether externally or internally; if they do not, they risk being displaced by the innovators who do.

Thus, the ongoing cycle of convenience-led process optimization resembles the Japanese manufacturing philosophy of continuous improvement (aka Kaizen), one that focusses on making improvements on an iterative basis.[80] As these compound over time, even the smallest innovations can make a difference in the long run. Perhaps then, it is time for a Kaizen approach to financial services?

CASE STUDY
Wealth Wizards: Robo-advice with a human touch

A robo-adviser is a financial planning application that surveys its users in order to gauge their risk appetite. On the back of this, the application recommends a portfolio of investments in line with each user's risk appetite.[81] Consequently, users that exhibit greater risk appetite will be steered towards higher-risk investments, and vice-versa.

Generally speaking, this means recommending a portfolio of exchange traded funds (ETFs)[82] – investment vehicles that track well-known market indices, which can be readily traded like company shares – to gain exposure to various asset classes, such as stocks, bonds or gold. The idea is to recommend a target asset allocation which can be rebalanced periodically (usually one to four times per annum). In this way, the investor achieves diversification and avoids the guesswork of when, where and how to invest.

Many robo-advisers rely on end-to-end automation: all the customer ever has to do is take a risk quiz, set up an account and deposit money in it; the robo-adviser takes care of the investing, plus any periodic rebalancing of the portfolio. This enables consumers to 'set it and forget it', assured that their investment decisions were made in a sober manner and in keeping with their long-term financial goals.

Robo-advice appears to be gaining ground with consumers: according to one survey, 58 per cent of Americans expect to be using a robo-adviser by 2025.[83] Elsewhere, regulatory intervention has helped create a demand for robo-advisers: in the UK, post-crisis regulation mandates that financial advisers charge for their time, rather than taking commission on the investments they recommend to their clients.[84] These rules were implemented in response to widespread mis-selling of financial products, which was seen as the result of commission-based remuneration structures.[85] As a result, many financial advisers either left the industry or moved up market, to serve clients who could afford to pay by the hour. This has left many low- and middle-income earners without adequate access to financial advice. Robo-advisers have stepped in to fill this gap, by using automation to provide low-cost financial advice at scale.

Granted, robo-advisers are not perfect: unlike human advisers, computers cannot ascertain whether clients truly understand the risks of investing by taking cues from their facial expressions and tone of voice. Indeed, a human adviser can ask their client to affirm, orally, that they understand the advice given. These pieces of information are not available to robo-advisers. Instead, customers tick boxes, confirming that they have read, and understand, the terms and conditions, which may cause some consumers to make financial decisions they don't really understand;[86] after all, who actually reads the small print?

Wealth Wizards appears to be aware of this flaw in the robo-advice model. Thus, its retail solution, branded as MyEva, takes a hybrid approach: though the user interface is a mobile application, it does not provide financial advice, as such; rather, the MyEva chat bot engages users by asking them questions about their finances, enabling them to 'feel more in control' of their money.[87] In doing so, it helps identify areas where financial advice may be needed, giving users the option of being referred to a professional human adviser.[88]

Wealth Wizards was founded in 2009.[89] According to the company's marketing director, Wealth Wizards represents a 'marriage of financial advisers and digital solutions... to make financial advice affordable and accessible to all in a way that speaks human, not finance and engages the right people, at the right time'.[90] The company's MyEva solution can assist users with a range of financial services, including pension planning, mortgages and insurance.[91] Thus, MyEva offers a more holistic solution than many other robo-advisers, which mainly focus on investments.

Wealth Wizards estimates that financial advisers spend up to 43 working days a year doing admin tasks that could be automated.[92] Thus, it is unsurprising that the company also has a solution for professionals which seeks to minimize the administrative burden on financial advisers. By digitizing routine tasks, the company claims that this application, branded as Turo, can make the advice process up to 50 per cent faster.[93] According to Wealth Wizards, Turo therefore enables financial advisers to spend more time with their clients,[94] whether in person or digitally via the Turo app.[95]

As these professionals are competing against digital-only robo-advisers, this may help improve customer retention outcomes. Indeed, digital services that involve a human touch have been demonstrated to exhibit greater levels of customer loyalty than pure self-service solutions.[96] Thus, it can be said that Wealth Wizards is using digitization to enable, rather than replace, financial advice.

How is Wealth Wizards making financial advice more accessible and convenient?

(Suggested answer at the end of this chapter.)

Chapter summary

Though novel technologies like blockchain and AI hold much promise, one of the biggest enablers of financial services innovation can be found behind the scenes, in the infrastructure. Cloud computing is a significant part of this story: just as the democratization of consumer technology and faster connectivity has enabled greater access to digitally based financial services, cloud computing has, and is, enabling the development and distribution of innovative fintech solutions.

Cloud computing gives small fintech start-ups flexible access to computing infrastructure that would previously have required the financial resources of a large bank. By enabling the use of hardware on demand this allows fintechs to scale quickly and be more responsive to consumer needs. In this way, large data centres – along with branch networks – are no longer barriers to entry in financial services.

Furthermore, the global financial crisis of 2007–09 (GFC) has, and continues to have, profound effects on financial services. The crisis spurred greater regulatory scrutiny of large financial institutions and a political desire to de-risk the financial system. This has allowed smaller start-ups to enjoy comparatively greater regulatory forbearance – for now – as regulators focus their resources on institutions that are 'too big to fail'. As a result, scale (which has traditionally been an advantage when dealing with the regulatory burden) is no longer as much an edge as it once was.

Lower barriers to entry, combined with lower capital costs, have allowed new players to enter the industry. As a result, fintech start-ups are encroaching on the turf of traditional financial institutions. What's more, these newcomers leverage each other's innovative solutions by integrating their services via APIs. This is accelerating financial disintermediation.

Thus, the financial industry is facing a wave of technology-led disruption. As digitalization reduces the distance between providers and users of capital, this puts pressure on traditional financial intermediaries. As a result, conventional financial institutions will have to anticipate, and constantly respond to, change. Otherwise, they risk being swept away.

In every sub-sector, innovators are entering the market by focussing on a neglected segment whose needs are not being met. Most often, this means providing them with a better service or lower price, if not both. To respond, incumbents must rethink their value propositions and consider things from the customer's perspective.

For large financial institutions this involves reframing their services, away from product-based solutions, to focus on solving customer problems. In short, it means removing friction from the financial intermediation process and making their service provision as convenient as possible. This will be an ongoing and iterative process: if banks are not challenging themselves, someone else will.

 KEY TAKEAWAYS

The three most important lessons from this chapter are:

- The global financial crisis of 2007–09 lowered barriers to entry in the financial industry by making the regulatory environment more accommodative to financial innovation, lowering interest rates and widening the talent pool available to fintech companies.

- Much of the fintech revolution has been driven by cheaper and more flexible access to computing infrastructure, chiefly via cloud computing.

- Incumbent financial institutions must make their propositions more convenient by helping their customers solve problems, rather than try to sell them products.

SUGGESTED ANSWERS TO DISCUSSION POINTS

 How is TransferWise disrupting international payments?

TransferWise is a good example of disruptive innovation in action: it started life by pursuing a financial sub-sector (international retail payments) where customers found themselves overcharged. By pursuing a cost-based strategy, it gained a foothold. Since then, it has moved on to compete in more complex, and profitable, market segments, such as international business payments.

It is hard to see how TransferWise could have done this in any other way. The platform needs a large user base to a make it sufficiently liquid. Without millions of retail users, TransferWise would find it difficult to facilitate larger business payments.

Interestingly, TransferWise's ethos of low cost combined with a premium service turns conventional competitive strategy on its head: in theory, this should be a difficult balancing act because any service-based differentiation increases the company's cost base to a point where it can no longer offer the lowest prices.

Indeed, it would be interesting to see what would happen to TransferWise if a rival platform were to achieve the same scale. Would customers jump ship or stick with the company which has treated them so well? Of course, TransferWise has a very strong position via the network effect: the size of its user base begets more liquidity on its platform, which makes its solution more cost effective, which attracts more users. In this way, it has a significant advantage over would-be competitors.

Finally, via its partnerships with other financial institutions, TransferWise may slowly be transforming the market for international payments. As partnering with TransferWise enables banks to offer cheaper foreign exchange services, this will exert pressure on all banks. In this way, the growth of TransferWise will put downward pressure on fees across the industry.

 How is Wealth Wizards making financial advice more convenient and accessible?

Convenience

For many people deciding when, where and how to invest feels like a chore. Wealth Wizards makes this more convenient by enabling consumers to access financial advice digitally, from the comfort of one's home. In addition, the company's retail solution provides additional convenience in that it encompasses a multitude of financial services – not just investment advice. In this way, it takes away the hassle of having to deal with multiple organizations via different customer interfaces.

From a job-based view, the company helps consumers complete the task of finding financial advice that is commensurate to their needs. In this way, it lowers search costs for consumers. Moreover, some consumers are afraid of making financial planning mistakes as these could have a significant impact on their long-term financial well-being. Thus, Wealth Wizards allows its customers to feel more secure in their financial decisions, thereby lessening the mental transaction cost of money-related anxiety.

Furthermore, Wealth Wizards reduces the administrative burden on financial advisers by automating many of their routine admin tasks. This frees up the advisers' time to see more clients, enabling them to generate more fee revenue. In addition, less admin means less stress, a lower cognitive load and a smaller chance of suffering from decision fatigue. This should hopefully translate into better service and improved customer outcomes.

Accessibility

Wealth Wizards is improving accessibility to financial advice by making it quicker and easier to obtain. In addition, the company makes it easier to provide financial advice via its professional solution by allowing financial advisers to engage with their customers digitally. In theory, this should lower the cost of providing financial advice as financial advisers are able to reach more clients this way, thereby achieving greater per customer economies of scale.

Furthermore, by automating behind-the-scenes paperwork, Wealth Wizards is helping to free up adviser time. In this way, its solution facilitates the customer-engagement process by removing admin tasks that are unlikely to be enjoyable and add comparatively little value to the business. By making the financial advice process less onerous, administratively speaking, Wealth Wizards is increasing the supply of financial adviser time in the market. This, in theory, should help lower the cost of financial advice to consumers, and thereby improve accessibility.

References

1 Xu, P (1998) Feng-Shui models structured traditional Beijing courtyard houses, *Journal of Architectural and Planning Research*, 15 (4), 271–82

2 Tkac, P and Dybvig, P (2012) Maturity Transformation: An Interview with Phil Dybvig [interview transcript], Federal Reserve Bank of Atlanta, www.frbatlanta.org/news/conferences-and-events/conferences/2012/120409-fmc/media/dybvig-interview/12fmc_dybvig_transcript.aspx (archived at https://perma.cc/BV5E-MCYJ)

3,4,7 Lee, I and Shin, Y J (2018) Fintech: Ecosystem, business models, investment decisions, and challenges, *Business Horizons*, 61, 35–46

5 PricewaterhouseCoopers LLP (2017) Redrawing the lines: Fintech's growing influence on financial services

6 Fry, R (2018) Millennials projected to overtake Baby Boomers as America's largest generation, Pew Research Center, 1 March, www.pewresearch.org/fact-tank/2018/03/01/millennials-overtake-baby-boomers/ (archived at https://perma.cc/Z5L4-KLKD)

8,9,18,19,23 Arner, D W, Barberis, J N and Buckley, R P (2016) The Evolution of Fintech: A New Post-Crisis Paradigm?, University of Hong Kong Faculty of Law Research Paper No. 2015/047, UNSW Law Research Paper No. 2016-62, papers.ssrn.com/sol3/papers.cfm?abstract_id=2676553 (archived at https://perma.cc/AUX9-B5F5)

10,11 Brunnermeier, M K (2009) Deciphering the Liquidity and Credit Crunch 2007–2008, *Journal of Economic Perspectives*, 23, 77–100

12,13 Mishkin, F S (2011) Over the Cliff: From Subprime to the Global Financial Crisis, *Journal of Economic Perspectives*, 25, 49–70

14,15 Federal Reserve Bank of St. Louis (2020) 10-year Treasury Constant Maturity Rate, 1 May, fred.stlouisfed.org/series/GS10 (archived at https://perma.cc/8CU8-CZD5)

16 KPMG (2019) The Pulse of Fintech – H2' 2018: Bi-annual analysis of global investment trends in the fintech sector, 13 February, home.kpmg/xx/en/home/insights/2019/01/pulse-of-fintech-h2-2018 (archived at https://perma.cc/E97B-6GN5)

17,20 Haddad, C and Hornuf, L (2019) The emergence of the global fintech market: economic and technological determinants, *Small Business Economics*, 53, 81–105

21 Financial Conduct Authority (2018) FCA response to the European Commission's consultation on 'FinTech: A More Competitive and Innovative European Financial Sector', 2 August, www.fca.org.uk/publication/corporate/fca-response-eu-commission-fintech-consultation.pdf (archived at https://perma.cc/VN7S-DMK6)

22 Open Banking Limited (2018) Background to Open Banking, www.openbanking.org.uk/wp-content/uploads/What-Is-Open-Banking-Guide.pdf (archived at https://perma.cc/S5HM-A2B2)

24 Amazon Web Services (2019) Breaking the Banking Mould: How Starling Bank is disrupting the banking industry, aws.amazon.com/solutions/case-studies/starling/ (archived at https://perma.cc/M2HN-TP4S)

25,27,28,30,31,32 Armbrust, M, Fox, A, Griffith, R, Joseph, A D, Katz, R, Konwinski, A, Lee, G, Patterson, D, Rabkin, A, Stoica, I and Zaharia, M (2010) A View of Cloud Computing, *Communications of The ACM*, 2010, 53 (4), 50–58 (April)

26,34 Hayes, B (2008) Cloud Computing, *Communications of The ACM*, 51 (7), 9–11 (July)

29 Mell, P and Grance, T (2011) The National Institute of Standards and Technology Definition of Cloud Computing, United States Department of Commerce, Special Publication 800–145

33,38 Lenk, A, Klems, M, Nimis, J, Tai, S and Sandholm, T (2009) What's inside the cloud? An architectural map of the cloud landscape, in Proceedings of the 2009 ICSE Workshop on Software Engineering Challenges of Cloud Computing, Vancouver: Institute of Electrical and Electronics Engineers, 23–31 (May)

35,36 Adobe (2020) Adobe Creative Cloud, www.adobe.com/uk/creativecloud.html (archived at https://perma.cc/2GH4-JWK8)

37 Deloitte LLP (2017) Open Banking: How to flourish in an uncertain future, www2.deloitte.com/uk/en/pages/financial-services/articles/future-banking-open-banking-psd2-flourish-in-uncertainty.html (archived at https://perma.cc/HZ6D-K9ZU)

39,40,43 Life.SREDA Venture Capital and Fintech Ranking (2016) Overview of APIs and Bank-as-a-Service in FINTECH, www.bank-as-a-service.com/BaaS.pdf (archived at https://perma.cc/9XZX-JER8)

41,42,44 Dintrans, P, Anand, A, Ponnuveetil, M, Acharya, A and Chardukian, A (2016) How Banking as a Service Will Keep Banks Digitally Relevant and Growing, Cognizant, www.cognizant.com/whitepapers/how-banking-as-a-service-will-keep-banks-digitally-relevant-and-growing-codex2047.pdf (archived at https://perma.cc/6EAU-8MAB)

45 Scholten, U (2016) Banking-as-a-service: What you need to know, VentureSkies, 20 December, www.ventureskies.com/blog/banking-as-a-service-categorizing-the-services (archived at https://perma.cc/4FMC-FYZD)

46 Porter, M E (1980), *Competitive Strategy: Techniques for Analyzing Industries and Competitors*, Free Press, New York

47,48,49,72 Christensen, C M, Raynor, M and McDonald, R (2015) What is Disruptive Innovation?, *Harvard Business Review*, 44–53 (December)

50 Raynor, M E (2011) Disruptive innovation: The Southwest Airlines case revisited, *Strategy & Leadership*, 39 (4), 31–34

51 Swinton, S and Roma, E (2018) Why Big UK Banks are Worried About Open Banking, Forbes.com, 15 March, www.bain.com/insights/why-big-uk-banks-are-worried-about-open-banking-forbes/ (archived at https://perma.cc/GWT4-SWV8)

52 Commonwealth of Australia (2018) Background paper 1: Some Features of the Australian Banking Industry, Royal Commission into Misconduct in the Banking, Superannuation and Financial Services Industry, 9 February, financialservices.royalcommission.gov.au/publications/Documents/some-features-of-the-australian-banking-industry-background-paper-1.pdf (archived at https://perma.cc/VMD5-67A5)

53,54 Smale, W (2019) The mistake that led to a £1.2bn business, BBC News, 28 January, www.bbc.co.uk/news/business-46985443 (archived at https://perma.cc/P9GE-AKWG)

55,56,59,60 TransferWise (2019) The TransferWise story, transferwise.com/gb/about/our-story (archived at https://perma.cc/J42Q-N8SU)

57 TransferWise (2019) We're building money without borders, for people without borders, transferwise.com/community/mission-and-philosophy (archived at https://perma.cc/T8ZV-UHZP)

58 TransferWise (2019) Annual report and consolidated financial statements for the year ended 31 March 2019, transferwise.com/gb/blog/annualreport2019/ (archived at https://perma.cc/2QKJ-UQNJ)

61,64,65 TransferWise (2019) Borderless account and card pricing, transferwise.com/gb/borderless/pricing#conversion_fees (archived at https://perma.cc/523B-78XS)

62 TransferWise (2019) How does TransferWise compare to leading banks, transferwise.com/gb/blog/how-does-transferwise-compare-to-leading-banks (archived at https://perma.cc/W6GJ-JCDD)

63 TransferWise (2018) TransferWise's next chapter starts today, and it's bright green, 9 January, transferwise.com/gb/blog/transferwise-debit-card-launch (archived at https://perma.cc/CE42-WV9J)

66 TransferWise (2016) We're launching TransferWise for business, 26 May, transferwise.com/gb/blog/a-wiser-way-to-make-international-business-payments (archived at https://perma.cc/3RZG-KFKT)

67,69 TransferWise (2018) Building multi-user access at TransferWise, 23 August, transferwise.com/gb/blog/multi-user-access-transferwise (archived at https://perma.cc/Y823-BQWK)

68 TransferWise (2019) The new and improved TransferWise for business, transferwise.com/gb/business/#/howitworks (archived at https://perma.cc/6KYE-K2GN)

70,71 TransferWise (2019) TransferWise API, api-docs.transferwise.com/#transferwise-api (archived at https://perma.cc/F466-BW8M)

73,75 Nick Szabo (1999) Micropayments and Mental Transaction Costs, nakamotoinstitute.org/static/docs/micropayments-and-mental-transaction-costs.pdf (archived at https://perma.cc/S66M-GFH6)

74 The Behavioral Insights Team (2010) Mindspace: Influencing behaviour through public policy, UK Cabinet Office, www.bi.team/publications/mindspace/ (archived at https://perma.cc/USU5-77DS)

76,77,78,79 Bettencourt, L and Ulwick, A (2008) The Customer-Centred Innovation Map, *Harvard Business Review*, 86 (5), 109–14 (May)

80 Brunet, A P and New, S (2003) Kaizen in Japan: An empirical study, *International Journal of Operations & Production Management*, 23 (12), 1426–46

81,82 Jung, D, Dorner, V, Glaser, F and Morana, S (2018) Robo-advisory: Digitalization and Automation of Financial Advisory, *Business and Information Systems Engineering*, 60, 81–86 (January)

83 Business Wire (2018) Nearly 60 Percent of Americans Expect to Use Robo Advice by 2025 According to New Schwab Report, 1 November, www.businesswire.com/news/home/20181101005790/en/ (archived at https://perma.cc/2ULP-C56W)

84,85 Financial Conduct Authority (2019) Evaluation of the Retail Distribution Review and the Financial Advice Market Review: Call for input, www.fca.org.uk/publication/call-for-input/call-for-input-evaluation-rdr-famr.pdf (archived at https://perma.cc/MXZ6-YDCY)

86 Fein, M (2015) Robo-Advisors: A Closer Look, Social Science Research Network, papers.ssrn.com/sol3/papers.cfm?abstract_id=2658701 (archived at https://perma.cc/M8ZL-LD4S)

87,88 Wealth Wizards (2019) About MyEva, myeva.com/about-myeva/ (archived at https://perma.cc/D3XE-6KHJ)

89,92 Wealth Wizards (2019) Is 43 working days a year the cost of slow digital adoption for the advice industry?, 17 June, www.turoadviser.com/blog/is-43-working-days-a-year-the-cost-of-slow-digital-adoption-for-the-advice-industry (archived at https://perma.cc/J9XD-LLBV)

90 Basten, L (2019) We're here to help you take control of your finances, Wealth Wizards

91 Wealth Wizards (2019) Our terms of business, 1 June, myeva.com/app/uploads/2019/06/2019-06-06-MyEva-Terms-of-Business.pdf (archived at https://perma.cc/D52H-54CP)

93,94 Wealth Wizards (2019) Spend more time servicing your customers, www.turoadviser.com/services-for-advisers (archived at https://perma.cc/UWD7-P46F)

95 Wealth Wizards (2019) Reach more customers with a great digital experience, www.turoadviser.com/services-digital (archived at https://perma.cc/43C7-JMA2)

96 Scherer, A, Wangenheim, F and Wünderlich, N (2015) The Value of Self-service: Long-term Effects of Technology-Based Self-Service Usage on Customer Retention, *MIS Quarterly*, 39 (1), 177–200 (March)

03

Behavioural economics and experience design

How to optimize user engagement

LEARNING OBJECTIVES

This chapter will give you an overview of:

- Why users adopt certain technologies and innovations over others.
- How users make choices, and how these can be influenced.
- The psychological principles underlying user interface design.
- How these shape the user experience in digital and branch settings.

Introduction

In this chapter, we seek to integrate basic interface design principles with behavioral economics. Our overarching objective is to examine how the user experience can be improved, both digitally and in the branch. That said, this chapter should not be construed as a be-all and end-all guide, as the body of relevant literature is both broad and deep. Instead, the aim is to help the reader identify some of the common – though not necessarily obvious – pitfalls of physical and digital user experience design. Thus, it should be read as a starting guide; as a first step in building a knowledge base of behavioral and design interventions that may be relevant to customer engagement in financial services.

This chapter is structured to contextualize behavioural economics within some facets of the Technology Acceptance Model[1] – a well-known analytical framework for technology adoption – as well as user interface design, community-based innovation and retail reinvention. Consequently, it combines different fields, strung together by various ideas from behavioral economics. However, as these ideas were chosen for their relevance, this chapter is not an exhaustive review of the literature pertaining to behavioral economics.

The tools presented in this chapter are laden with ethical dilemmas. As is the case of many technologies, there is a risk that bad actors will use behavioral economics for nefarious purposes; namely, to deceive and mislead. Unfortunately, these tools are only as good – or indeed as ethical – as the people using them. In addition, there is also the risk that these will be misused unwittingly. As a result, some discussion is devoted to the ethics of applying behavioral economics.

User experience as a competitive advantage

In a world of shortened attention spans, where services are rendered on demand via digital interfaces, there is an onus on businesses to capture their customers' emotions, not just their imaginations. This is particularly pressing in financial services where whole business models risk becoming commoditized by digitization; after all, a mortgage is no more than numbers on a screen, which, in essence, is not much different from, say, a life insurance contract.

In addition, convenience-led experiences like Amazon's 1-Click Ordering service have trained consumers to expect greater convenience in all manner of transactions. Of course, Amazon is not solely responsible for raising the bar: on-demand solutions like Uber and Netflix have also increased consumer expectations regarding the ease and speed of which services are rendered. In other words, these technology companies have collectively reduced the mental transaction costs[2] that consumers are willing to bear. Thus, financial institutions must reduce friction in their customers' experiences in order to keep up with market expectations.[3]

In the so-called 'Now Economy', consumers expect their needs to be met instantly. As a result, there is an onus on retailers to make their customers' transactions seamless, in order to remove as much friction from the customer journey as possible. In this way, the minutiae of effecting transactions do not distract customers from the experiences they are paying for.[4]

However, convenience alone is not enough. Customers expect automated and integrated journeys tailored to their individual needs.[5] That said, it would be a mistake to treat automation as a panacea; in fact, there is evidence to suggest that over-reliance on automated, self-service solutions can be detrimental to customer loyalty.[6] When viewed through the customer experience lens, the reason for this becomes clear: according to what is called channel expansion theory, the perceived richness of an interface depends, in part, on the user's unique experiences with it;[7] in this way, it is conceivable that human interaction adds to the uniqueness of a user's experience, thereby increasing its perceived quality.

Thus, financial institutions are facing the predicament of digitizing their services for the sake of efficiency and, at the same time, having to retain a personal touch to improve customer retention. To surmount this, financial institutions can look to consumer technology, where product design has moved from being technology led to design led,[8] as technology companies have recognized that the user experience is paramount to success.

Apple's iPod is perhaps the most famous example of this; the company didn't invent the MP3 player, it simply made it cool. A few years later, Apple did the same thing for internet-connected mobile phones with the launch of the iPhone. These experience-led products propelled Apple to become one of the world's most valuable companies by market capitalization after years of stagnation; likewise, the financial institutions that succeed in the future are likely to be those that provide the best user experiences.

The drivers of technology adoption

Optimizing user engagement goes beyond minimizing friction in the user journey and adding an attractive veneer. In the context of software applications and new technologies, user engagement depends, in large part, on how users perceive the solution on offer: if users view the technology as easy to use and useful, then they are more likely to use it.[9]

In this way, the success of a technology-led solution hinges on user perceptions regarding its usefulness and ease of use. Under the technology acceptance model (TAM),[10] a solution's perceived usefulness is influenced by certain factors: empirically speaking, output quality, relevance to the task at hand and results demonstrability correlate positively with perceived usefulness.[11] In addition, perceived ease of use appears to have a positive effect on perceived usefulness.[12]

On the surface, it may not be obvious how the TAM ties into fintech innovation. However, on examination of its component drivers, the links become clearer: if one takes a jobs-based view of innovation – the idea that service providers help their customers complete jobs[13] – then output quality and task relevance become critical. Moreover, the notion of result demonstrability suggests saving users' time, effort and money, and making them notice it; in other words, disruptive innovation.[14]

The emphasis on usefulness, demonstrable results and ease of use in the TAM suggests that users' desire for a human touch may be grounded in pragmatism. Indeed, interfaces with human interaction enable greater personalization in that the they allow customers to explain their problem/s in detail;[15] even if this does not to lead a quicker resolution, it does allow users to feel that someone is addressing their issue/s. Thus, interface designers should consider when and how to deploy staff in the user journey; in other words, ask themselves: where are customers likely to face the greatest uncertainty?

USER INTERFACE (UI) AND USER EXPERIENCE (UX) DESIGN

These terms are sometimes used in the same context because there is some amount of overlap between the two. That said, it is worth examining how they differ. Whereas UI design addresses the usability and aesthetics of user interfaces, UX design goes deeper: it focuses on the value and meaning that users derive from the interaction.[16]

Though UI is an integral part of UX design, it is not everything; user interfaces can look good and be usable, yet still provide a poor user experience. For example, a movie review website may have an excellent user interface but let its users down if it lacks breadth of content; if the website only focusses on mainstream releases, it may disappoint users interested in independent films.[17]

By some estimates, the look and feel of a user interface contribute comparatively less to the user experience than the relevance of the content to the user's goals; *ca* 40 per cent and 60 per cent, respectively.[18] As a result, it makes sense to design user experiences from the bottom up, with users' needs and expectations as the primary focus.

UX design is relevant to the entire customer journey. It goes beyond simply meeting customer needs and aims to satisfy these in a way that is both simple and elegant, as well as pleasant for the customer. Thus, designing a top-notch user experience requires a combination of skills, including those of interface designers, marketers and engineers.[19]

As suggested above, it may be useful to stage staff interventions at points in the customer journey where users suffer the greatest uncertainty, which tends to arise at decision-making junctures. As an additional remedy, UX designers can employ behavioral *nudges*. These design interventions are based on behavioural economics and intended to prod users towards certain decisions whilst affording them some degree of agency.[20]

Behavioural economics is a departure from classical economics in that its proponents do not take for granted that individuals make rational decisions. Instead, decision making is seen as context dependent;[21] rather than making self-interested decisions based on all available information, individuals can be swayed into irrationality by their circumstances.

As user interfaces can influence users' decisions, it is useful to consider basic design principles in light of behavioural economic theory. This will be examined from two perspectives: that of the interface and that of the user. This distinction is somewhat arbitrary and is merely an implement to provide structure to a disparate set of ideas. In addition, some of the interventions listed below may feel intuitive; this is likely because the reader will have been on the receiving end of these as a consumer.

The principles of user interface design

The ideas presented in this section have been chosen because they are relevant to financial services and backed by empirical evidence. In other words because they can be applied and tested in a fintech context. That said, much has been written about both user interface design and behavioral economics. Thus, this section is not intended to be an exhaustive list. In addition, some of these interventions, when applied in practice, may not produce the expected results; after all, what works in one cultural context may not work in another. Therefore, it is incumbent upon the designer to measure and test the effectiveness of different user interfaces. Moreover, as the world is dynamic, this must be done on a periodic and iterative basis.

Let's start with the cliché that **less is more**, which is actually a basic design principle. Just as writers strive to be parsimonious with their words, good user interfaces require only a minimum amount of effort from their users;[22] in other words, the shortest user journey is usually the best, as this minimizes the cognitive load on the users. In turn, this reduces the likelihood of *decision fatigue*.

As an idea, decision fatigue is closely related to **choice overload**:[23] that too many options lead to sub-par decision making. For example, a study of employment-based retirement schemes found that when people were offered a wide range of funds to invest in, they tended to select riskier, less diversified and more expensive investment funds[24] – exactly the opposite of what a 'rational' investor might be expected to do. Thus, a user interface must be careful not to offer its users too many alternatives: by reducing these, one can minimize the feeling of uncertainty that comes from choice overload.

Another way of reducing uncertainty is by **signposting the user journey**, and having a clear beginning and end. This journey must flow logically and conform to user expectations with easily recognizable patterns of input and output. These prescriptions make users more apt to engage with the interface because they create an experience that is distinct from the user's surrounding reality.[25]

Signposting can be applied in a more subtle manner, by offering users default settings; if the user does not make an active choice, the default setting becomes their choice.[26] This is an effective nudging strategy because people tend to passively accept default settings.[27] For example, auto-enrolment pension schemes that offer their employees the option of leaving – rather than joining – have been shown to exhibit greater rates of participation.[28] In the context of digital interfaces, default settings can manifest as pre-checked boxes.[29] These provide users with subtle guidance, thereby reducing uncertainty.

In addition, user interfaces must feel **relatable and culturally relevant** to the user.[30] In this regard, simplicity is important as users are more likely to engage with things they can easily understand.[31] In practice, this means attaching meaningful labels to information on user interfaces: it has been shown empirically that people are able to integrate more quantitative information into their decision-making processes when this information contains qualitative labels.[32] For example, food labels in the UK are colour-coded: high-sugar foods are labelled red while low-sugar foods are labelled green; thus, labels can be visual as well as verbal.

To facilitate information processing, quantitative information should be presented on a scale that is relatable to users' qualitative reality. For example, restating motor vehicles' energy consumption as gallons per 10,000 miles – as opposed to miles per gallon – has been shown to help consumers estimate their energy efficiency with greater accuracy.[33] As people pay for gallons, not miles, the restated measure was closer to their lived experience, and therefore easier to process.

The example above alludes to the importance of **reference points**. Users attach expectations to the information they are given, which, in turn, influences their behaviour.[34] This effect is known as *anchoring*,[35] and has been observed in credit card users: when one provider amended its statements to remove a message stating that the minimum repayment was 2 per cent, the average monthly repayment increased from £99 to £175.[36] Thus, the information displayed in a user interface can unintentionally affect user behaviour by way of anchoring their expectations.

Closely related to anchoring is priming: the idea that people's decisions can be influenced subconsciously if they are exposed to certain cues beforehand.[37] These can take the form of sounds, images or words. Priming effects can be remarkably powerful: for example, one experiment found that placing an image of two eyes above an honesty box in a self-service coffee bar increased donations almost three-fold.[38] Consequently, designers should **employ visual and auditory elements judiciously**; the interface must be designed with the user experience in mind, not the other way around.[39]

Just as cues in the environment can influence users' decisions, so can emotional stimuli:[40] often, experiencing positive emotions puts people in a more receptive emotional state. This is why billboards often contain attractive people; they pique our interest by arousing our emotions. In this way, decision making can be emotionalized, and thereby be made less rational.[41] In one experiment, an advertisement for a loan that carried an image of an attractive woman increased uptake amongst male customers to the same degree as a 25 per cent reduction in the loan's interest rate.[42]

Eliciting emotions is particularly important because consumers make decisions based on a small number of facts: according to one study, people think of only half the things they consider relevant when making decisions.[43] Thus, it makes sense to **focus user attention** on the most important aspects of the interface. This can be achieved by employing the principle of salience, the idea that users pay attention to that which appears simple, novel, and relevant.[44]

Salience can be engineered via bright colours, contrast, movement and visual metaphors. It's why important text is often in bold: waving a flag signals offside; a red light means 'stop'; and the image of a skull signifies toxicity. However, these interventions are only tactical; strategically, simplicity and relevance are paramount.[45]

The design principles highlighted above implicitly treat the user as a passive actor. However, successful user interfaces **invite input from users** and provide them with feedback, to make them feel they are affecting the interface;[46] this reassures users that they are some way towards having their needs met. This can take subtle forms, such as highlighting a hyperlink as the user hovers over it with their cursor.

However, this feedback can also be more overt. Indeed, some interfaces employ mechanisms from games in order to increase user engagement.[47] This is known as gamification, of which examples include progress bars, the accumulation of points or badges and even a degree of competition between users.[48] These tools are powerful because they engage people both cognitively and emotionally.[49]

As a result, gamification is a powerful way of inviting user input, which in itself, is an effective engagement tool as it builds commitment; by investing time and effort in the interface, users implicitly commit to it. This builds engagement because it taps into a basic psychological exigency: the need that people have for their current actions to be consistent with prior behaviour.[50] There is a good reason for this, as failing to live up to one's commitments can entail reputational damage and social exclusion.[51] Indeed, this effect is so powerful that merely writing down a commitment has been shown to increase a person's likelihood of following through with it.[52]

How users make decisions

The section above explores certain design principles in the context of behavioral economics. However, it does so from the perspective of the interface not the user. As user choices are also shaped by their internal economics, it is necessary to examine engagement from the opposite angle – that of the user.

Let's start by examining how users view themselves; in other words, what their egos say. In general, **people tend to overestimate their own capabilities**. Few people are happy to admit that their skills are below average in, well, most domains. For example, in one study of American college students, 93 per cent of respondents rated their own driving skills as better than those the median driver.[53] This points to a significant degree of overconfidence in the general population given that, by the laws of mathematics, 50 per cent of people are below average. This overconfidence is also present in retail investors: one study found that affluent retail investors are prone to overestimate their own stock picking skills and underestimate the impact of broader market movements on their investment returns.[54]

In addition to overestimating themselves, **people pay a disproportionate amount of attention to small probabilities**.[55] Thus, a change in a probability estimate from 5 per cent to 10 per cent looms larger in the mind than an equivalent change from 50 per cent to 55 per cent.[56] This effect goes some way in explaining the attraction of lottery-based savings products, such as premium bonds[57] and, perhaps, insurance-based savings products (ie life insurance).

Closely related to this is the notion of loss aversion: the idea that **losses have a greater emotional impact than gains**.[58] Thus, incentives matter more when they are negative. This idea has been applied to great effect in the UK: in 2015, the government introduced a 5 pence surcharge on plastic bags in English supermarkets;[59] in the first six months, like-for-like plastic bag usage fell by *ca* 80 per cent.[60]

What's more, negative incentives have been shown to be effective in helping people lose weight: in one experiment, participants were asked to put an amount of money into escrow, which would then be returned to them, plus an add-on reward, if they met their weight-loss targets.[61] At the end of the study, these participants showed significant improvement when compared to the control group.[62] Some of this outperformance may be explained by what is called the endowment effect;[63] the idea that individuals value more highly what they see as theirs. Thus, individuals with money in escrow may feel a greater motivation to act in order to meet their goals than those who simply stand to be rewarded – even though the net financial reward is the same.

There is a common theme running through the above-mentioned effects: that people are, in general, not particularly good at interpreting quantitative information dispassionately. The internalization of quantitative measures of success, progress or achievement – in other words, accounting measures – can affect people's behaviour to such a degree that it becomes irrational;[64] in other words, the subjective meaning that one assigns to financial incentives can lead to behaviour that fails to maximize financial gains and/or minimize risk.

For example, a study of New York City cab drivers found that setting a daily earnings target led people to finish early on good days and work longer on bad days.[65] This is the opposite of what a rational actor would do: rationally speaking, it makes sense to work a standard shift on a good day to build up an earnings buffer against bad days, thereby reducing the need to work longer hours on an unplanned basis, while minimizing uncertainty. The explanation for this phenomenon lies mental accounting, in that **people tend to interpret financial gains and losses in isolation**,[66] thereby losing sight of the bigger picture.

This explains why people can exhibit traits of both conservative investors and gamblers concurrently, often within the same portfolio.[67] For example, investors may hold low-risk investments, while, at the same time, speculating on the 'next big thing' via a selection of high-risk penny stocks.[68] In this way, they mentally put their assets into separate buckets: those that provide protection from poverty and those that promise riches.[69] Of course, this strategy is unlikely to be optimal as it may lead investors to allocate too much capital to low- and high-risk asset classes, thereby neglecting medium-risk investments and thus failing to achieve optimal diversification.

Other behavioral effects impede rational portfolio decisions: in the absence of information, **people tend to allocate attention, resources and money evenly across different categories.**[70] This is called naive allocation and can be used to nudge investors to take less risk: by separating low-risk investment funds into separate sub-funds while combining higher risk funds.[71] For example, a low-risk bond fund could be separated into corporate and sovereign sub-funds; at the same time, a highly volatile technology fund could be combined with an emerging markets fund and labelled as a 'frontier' fund. Given naive allocation in this simple investment universe, the allocation towards high risk vs low risk would change from 2:1 (ie technology and EM vs bonds) to 1:2 (ie corporate bonds and government bonds vs 'frontier').

Regardless of interface design or user disposition, **people suffer, to a lesser or greater degree, from myopia and prefer to receive positive outcomes sooner;**[72] after all, a bird in the hand is better than two in the bush. As a result, people tend to procrastinate and are biased towards seeking instant gratification. For this reason, savers have to be compensated with returns for delaying gratification and not spending their money in the present. This is one of the reasons why returns on long-term investments tend to be higher than short-term investments.

To overcome consumer myopia, interface designers can provide users with immediate and/or salient incentives; people need rich and compelling reasons, and a feeling of progress, to make choices that benefit them in the long term. This is why people are willing to put time and effort into learning a new language: the promised richness of the future experiences (ie improved communication skills, experiencing a different culture, etc) is enough to make some people forego leisure time.[73]

Communities, social norms and culture

A user interface must conform to the cultural norms of its users.[74] This is especially important in the use of metaphors, particularly when these are visual. This is because metaphors activate memories and construct associations;[75] in other words, metaphors prime users. Thus, financial institutions must exercise cultural sensitivity when deploying metaphors.

To gauge the cultural relevance of a metaphor, one must consider its social context: according to a sociological theory known as *symbolic interactionism*, human beings do not independently derive meaning from objects; rather, they rely on social interactions to imbue these with significance.[76] Therefore, it is critical to understand the social context of symbols and metaphors, as well as their connotations, before deploying these as part of a user interface.

As an example, consider the use of grain as a metaphor for growth and prosperity. For some European financial institutions, particularly those with agrarian roots, wheat has long been a favoured symbol; in Asia, however, it is rice. This difference can be explained by wheat and rice being the chief staples in Europe and Asia, respectively. Thus, each crop has been cemented in the public imagination via the dinner table.

Because culture shapes social norms and intra-group expectations, its role goes beyond rebranding user interfaces to suit local sensibilities: according to the TAM, users consider how they might be perceived by people they respect, and the potential impact on their reputation, before adopting new technologies.[77] Thus, innovators would do well to view their customers as communities of users, and not atomized consumers.

Furthermore, UX designers must consider how users engage with their innovations in social settings. Where a social setting is not obvious or does not exist, it can be accentuated or manufactured by making reference to other users: in one study, a hotel updated its bathroom signs from asking guests to reuse their towels to stating that 'most' guests reuse their towels. Even though this was lie, the proportion of guests who reused their towels at least once during their stay increased from 35 per cent to 44 per cent.[78]

Social pressure and image concerns are relevant in the context of the network effect: the greater the size of a network, the more valuable it is to its members.[79] In this regard, social effects can add to individual benefits of network membership.[80] For example, being part of a country club is valued because it provides individuals with positive experiences, and because it can build and maintain social relationships.[81] Indeed, social ties shape network participants' behaviours more so than would be predicted by economic logic.[82] Thus, the social benefits of being part of a network, incentivizes individuals to 'fit in' in order to minimize any risk of exclusion.

This dynamic can be observed in the design and marketing of certain consumer technologies. For example, messages sent between Apple devices via the iMessage app appear in a different colour (blue) from those that are not (green).[83] This can be interpreted as a signal to Apple users that they are different from non-Apple users, and therefore part of an in-group; in theory, this should make them more reluctant to use non-Apple products for fear of alienation.

User motivations go beyond network effects: research into equity crowd-funding campaigns suggests that people fund these for reasons that are not strictly financial, but also social and emotional.[84] This implies that users desire the feeling of being part of a community, which is also a driving force behind open-source communities.[85] Of course, this has not been lost on some innovators: in 2019, PayPal launched a localized advertising campaign for its point-of-sale payment solution, iZettle,[86] which featured images, names and addresses of local shopkeepers in the UK. In this way, PayPal targeted two user groups, shopkeepers and their customers, by playing on people's desire to participate in their local communities.

Community-centred innovation is not a new phenomenon; indeed, open-source user communities have brought us an alternative operating system (Linux) as well as a peer-to-peer currency (Bitcoin). These communities spring up because users grow impatient with existing solutions.[87] This leads them to collaborate in order to develop solutions that better meet their needs; as users, they have a first-hand understanding of these needs, and are thus better equipped to develop solutions for them than the market.[88]

For this reason, a company may engage its users to co-create innovative solutions, and thereby turn its customer base into an open-source community.[89] For example, in 2019, Tandem, a UK-based fintech, announced that it would seek customer input as part of developing a mortgage proposition.[90] Thus, by turning to their users for innovation, companies like Tandem are effectively crowd-sourcing market research and product development.

When engaging a community of users, it is best to start with its leaders, as other users are likely to emulate their behaviour.[91] People tend to mimic the behaviour of those they hold in in high esteem and/or identify with: for example, one study found a 1,000 per cent increase in teenagers who smoke when two of their friends smoke; by comparison, the increase is only 26 per cent when one parent smokes.[92]

In addition to taking cues from their role models and peer group, people are also influenced by markers of authority. These signify credibility, thereby enabling people to take a mental short-cuts.[93] This is why toothpaste adverts make references to dentists: such appeals to authority allow users to outsource their decisions to 'experts', thereby minimizing their own mental transaction costs.

Markers of authority can be subtle, and still be effective: for instance, 'research assistants' have been shown to be more effective in changing people's behaviour than 'trained facilitators' and 'teachers' when delivering the same health advice.[94] Thus, it appears that even subtle markers of authority can be enough to shape people's behaviour.

Engaging customers in the branch

Although the ideas above can be implemented digitally, a digital-only interface may not be optimal. Humans are social creatures, and if financial institutions digitize their user interfaces uniformly – all in accordance with behavioral principles – individual user experiences would, perhaps somewhat paradoxically, not feel unique. Taken to its logical extreme, this would mean that the only difference between various propositions would be institutional logotypes and on-brand colour schemes.

Thus, digital-only interfaces may not be an option for many institutions, despite ever-increasing automation. In the gap between some degree of digitization and full automation, there is space for a human touch. As automation frees up staff time, excess resources could be redeployed towards tasks that require empathy and creativity;[95] in other words, towards providing users with more personal experiences. However, as no solution is applicable to all, each institution must reimagine its user interfaces to support increasingly unique customer experiences in the context of its own business model. As no 'quick fix' exists, these interventions must be deployed incrementally; moreover, this process is likely to be iterative.[96]

So, what do people seek in their dealings with financial institutions? According to a survey of North American consumers, many expect a personalized service that helps them save money, time and effort.[97] Customers want financial institutions to be on their side: for example, wealth management clients desire timely and holistic advice that is specific to their financial circumstances;[98] rather than being 'sold' a product, they want their advisers to help them understand why certain financial solutions may be relevant to them. In this way, the bank branch of the future may resemble a doctor's office, whereby bank staff help customers diagnose problems and offer solutions.

Just as customers seek a return on their money, they also want a return on their time. As with other in-store retail experiences, going to a bank branch is an investment of customer time. In this way, banks, like other retailers, can offer the customers tangible experiences, something that cannot be attained digitally;[99] in other words, create a strong incentive to attend the branch.

On a basic level, this can mean redesigning the branch, to make it a more pleasant space to spend time in, thereby minimizing the pain of having to wait around; it can also mean giving the branch a local touch, to make customers see it as an integral part of their community. In addition, as no retail concept is permanent,[100] banks must refresh their branches on a periodic basis; in doing so, they speak to their customers' desire for novelty. Finally, retail propositions succeed by integrating in-store and online channels;[101] thus, a bank's branches must complement its online and mobile interfaces.

 CASE STUDY
A new branch at Lloyds Bank

With more than 30 million customers,[102] Lloyds Banking Group (LBG) is of the UK's largest banks. Its main brands include Lloyds Bank, Bank of Scotland and Halifax; together, these account for *ca* 20 per cent of bank branches in Britain.[103] Perhaps, then, it is unsurprising that LBG's stated purpose is 'to help Britain prosper'.[104] As part of this, LBG's aims to provide a 'leading customer experience', by offering personalized and digitized customer solutions.[105]

In 2017, LBG opened a new type of branch in central Manchester, intended to combine 'face-to-face expertise with new technology'. Speaking about the launch, Lloyds Bank Managing Director, Robin Bulloch said: 'While digital services are becoming increasingly important to our customers, we continue to recognize the significant value of human interaction – people want to deal with people when it matters.'[106]

With floor-to-ceiling transparent windows, the exterior of the branch resembles those of neighbouring retail outlets. Outside, on the pedestrianized street, stands a chalkboard advertising baked goods. As you enter, the first thing you see is the cafe, complete with a barista and artisan coffee from a local roaster.

The branch is open seven days a week, albeit with shorter hours during the weekend.[107] The cashiers' windows are at the back of the branch, while self-service kiosks stand closer to the entrance. The branch is staffed by people who, in addition to being impeccably dressed, have a pleasant demeanour about them.

Upstairs, there is a business hub. Upbeat music fills the air. Here, the armchairs are furnished in the colours of Lloyd's Bank. They are spotless and comfortable. Adorning the walls, are artworks with images of horses – motifs inspired by LBG's logo, which features a rearing horse.

The business hub appears to be something of a mix between a co-working space for entrepreneurs and a small business bank. There is free Wi-Fi and desk space for business people to meet and work. Moreover, specialist support is on hand, and, if needed, the bank can facilitate contact between start-ups and local advisory firms.[108] In this way, the branch functions like a start-up incubator of sorts.

The branch regularly hosts networking events and talks by expert speakers.[109] In addition, the branch works with local charities to help homeless people access basic financial services; this is an important step towards being reintegrated into society, as people without a bank account cannot get a job or claim state benefits.[110]

LBG has followed on up its success in Manchester by launching similar branch formats in London and Glasgow, under its Halifax and Bank of Scotland brands, respectively.[111] However, this new format isn't LBG's only branch-centred innovation: in 2018 it launched 41 'micro-branches'.[112] Herein, customers serve themselves via tablet computers while help is at hand from one of the two staff members on duty.[113] In addition, specialist mortgage advice can be accessed via video link.[114] Speaking about this concept, Jakob Pfaudler, Lloyds' Retail Chief Operating Officer said: 'Think Apple store, as opposed to bank branches.'[115]

**With its new approach to branch banking,
how is LBG engaging customers?**
(Suggested answer at the end of this chapter.)

The ethics of nudging

Nudging was brought into the mainstream by two academics, Richard Thaler and Cass Sunstein, with the publication of their 2008 book, *Nudge*.[116] The idea that behavioural economics could be used to guide – rather than force – people towards better choices struck a chord with the neo-liberal establishment: Thaler was subsequently appointed as a special adviser to the Obama administration.[117]

Though the intentions of Thaler and Sunstein may have been good, the ideas they present in their book – and indeed, behavioural economics more generally – could be applied malevolently: in other words, to sway users into making decisions that are fundamentally not in their own interests. In addition, behavioral economics can be deployed unethically even where this is not the intention of the interface designer; indeed, it is much harder to judge whether an intervention is unethical than malevolent; the latter requires bad intent, the former can be accidental.

Whilst nudges must not be deployed against users' interests, they must also not interfere with users' ability to exercise free will; interventions that deceive users violate this principle.[118] Thus, the line between easing the user along the customer journey and manipulation lies at the point at which the user is unable to provide informed consent.

Of course, this line is blurred, and regulators know this. For this reason, many jurisdictions have laws mandating a right of return for products purchased both in-store and online, thus implicitly recognizing that a certain amount of manipulation takes place in these settings; these cooling off periods allow the customer to reassess their purchases when they are in a different, and perhaps more rational, frame of mind.[119]

Users do not want to feel like they are being manipulated. When this becomes overt, it stops working and user engagement falls. The 'click to read more' button found on many blog-based websites is a good example of this: it is there to increase the amount of ad space that users see as they click sideways through a single article. Over time, this tool has become less effective at fostering engagement; once fooled, users learn from their disappointing experiences and see these obvious attempts at manipulation as markers of low quality.

Thus, organizations need to tread carefully when deploying nudges. As an initial remedy, clear and unambiguous disclosure could be used to make users aware of the potential consequences of their choices. Such disclosure can be seen in some domains like investment management (eg 'Your capital is at risk'), albeit for compliance reasons. As a result, it would be refreshing to see financial institutions voluntarily disclose to their customers the most important implications of their choices as a matter of best practice, rather than out of regulatory necessity. For starters, this would help manage customers' expectations and may, perhaps surprisingly, foster greater engagement: indeed, appearing to present information that is seemingly against one's own interest is an effective way of building trust with customers.[120]

However, not all users are equally sophisticated, and therefore some groups are more vulnerable than others. Indeed, there is evidence to suggest that people from lower socio-economic groups are more susceptible to certain behavioural nudges.[121] As a result, taking a disclosure-based 'buyer beware' approach may not suffice as this will likely to lead to consumer detriment. To see how this can impact the bottom line, one need only look at the more than £37 billion paid out by UK financial institutions in compensation for mis-sold insurance products.[122]

In addition, it is pertinent to consider things from the user's perspective: if a behavioral intervention cannot be demonstrated to be in the user's interest, should it be there? This begs the question: how does one know what these interests are? Thus, applying nudges starts ethically with knowing one's users and understanding their needs. In this way, one can establish the suitability of one's proposition, something which no amount of nudging can change. That said, users are not a monolithic group; indeed, what may be appropriate for one type of user may not be appropriate for all users.[123]

CASE STUDY
Applied nudging

Let's consider a hypothetical mobile app, one that seeks to maximize user engagement by employing some of the nudges described in this chapter. This application is a budgeting tool, designed to help users save and invest money. However, its developers have overlooked its potential ethical and practical ramifications: this is your job.

When the user first opens the application, they are asked a series of questions about their income, spending habits, age and attitude to risk. The final question is as follows: *Do you see yourself as a financially responsible person?* Whatever the answer, the next screen displays the proportion of their monthly income that the average user of the application saves each month; this is combined with a pre-ticked box for the option of saving a somewhat higher proportion of monthly income. This option is labelled with a smiley face. The only other option is a free entry 'other' box.

At the end of the sign-up process, there is a last-minute 'special offer' for mobile-phone insurance. This is accompanied by an image of a woman appearing distraught as an unsavoury-looking man snatches her handbag. This up-sell is accompanied by a countdown timer. This was done because studies have demonstrated that imposing limited time windows on opportunities motivates users towards positive action;[124] in other words, instilling in them a 'fear of missing out'.

Each user is given a sign-up bonus of 50 euros. However, this is conditional on the user hitting their savings target for the first year. At the end of this period, the user can double their bonus by meeting their savings target for another six months. As the user saves, they earn 'savings points' according to how far they have progressed towards their annual target. These points become redeemable for the sign-up bonus at the end of the first year.

Users have the option of nominating another user to be their 'savings buddy'. As part of this, each user records an audio or video message addressed to the other stating their own savings goal while wishing the other good luck in reaching theirs. The name of each user's buddy is visible on the home screen along with their total savings points.

After a week of using the app, the user is asked to upload an image that represents their savings goal. For example, this can be an image representing the home, car or holiday that the user is saving for. Users are offered a small amount of savings points for complying with this request. This then becomes the header image on the user's home screen. If the user neglects to do this, they are reminded to do this via text or email on a weekly basis for three weeks in a row, and on a monthly basis thereafter.

The app invests users' savings according to either a short, medium or long-term time horizon. Each setting contains different combinations of the same basket of investment funds, covering equities, real estate, government bonds and cash deposits. In this way, short-term savers have comparatively more exposure to government bonds and cash deposits than long-term savers. Users cannot change their investment settings unless they elect to change the stated time horizon of their savings plan.

The home screen displays each user's account balance next to their points total. Underneath, there is a graph showing the evolution of the user's account value. As a fixed amount is invested automatically each month, this graph is generally upward-sloping. In order to see the actual investment gains (or losses) in percentage terms, the user must click on the graph. Investment gains are stated in green, whereas losses are stated in blue, a much cooler colour than red, thereby avoiding unnecessary stress.

What potential issues do you see with the nudges employed by this application?
(Suggested answer at the end of this chapter.)

Chapter summary

At this point, it should be clear that applying behavioral economics as part of the user experience is no panacea. Indeed, interventions that make sense at a tactical level, may not be appropriate at a strategic level; consumers, after all, are people and expect to be treated as such. Thus, the competitive edge will belong to those financial institutions that succeed in bridging the gap between self-service and authenticity; that is to say, leveraging automation whilst retaining a personal touch in the experience. As no two business models are the same, this is likely to manifest in different ways across different sub-sectors and business models.

 KEY TAKEAWAYS

The most important ideas from this chapter are:

- The user experience depends on more than just branding and superficial aspects of user interface design.

- Though users make choices that are not always rational, erring on the side of simplicity is generally a good design strategy.

- The nudging tools presented in this chapter are more powerful than most people think and so they must always be applied with the user's best interests in mind.

SUGGESTED ANSWERS TO DISCUSSION POINTS

 With its new approach to branch banking, how is LBG engaging customers?

Everything about the branch signals 'come in': the floor-to-ceiling windows, the chalkboard advertising baked goods and the visibility of the cafe at the entrance. This is likely to put customers in a positive frame of mind; thus, it is perhaps no accident that the cashiers' windows – which may bring back memories of waiting in queues and feelings of frustration for some customers – are placed at the back of the branch.

The pleasant music, spotless furniture and well-presented staff help separate the experience of being inside the branch from the hustle and bustle of the busy high street outside. In addition, the excellent sartorial presentation of the staff is an implicit symbol of authority, which helps build trust with the customer. Moreover, the imagery of horses in nature are likely to prime customers towards feelings of freedom, aspiration and positive action.

Hosting a co-working space and networking events builds a community around the branch. However, this goes beyond business, as can be seen in the branch's charity work. In this way, the branch embodies LBG's slogan of 'Helping Britain Prosper'. This makes customers feel part of a community and good about being customers of the bank.

Furthermore, the introduction of micro-branches shows that LBG is attentive to the needs of different types of customers. By making the experience in its micro-branches similar to that of an Apple store, it offers something that is familiar to many of its customers. This, along with remote access to mortgage advisers (which, presumably, reduces the need for multiple appointments) minimizes customers' mental transaction costs.

 What potential issues do you see with the nudges employed by this application?

Though nudging users towards saving a greater proportion of their income may be well intentioned, it could be sub-optimal to nudge all users towards saving an above-average proportion of their income, as different users have outgoings of varying flexibility. For example, some users spend a higher proportion of their income on rent (a fixed cost) than others, and so may be able to save less. Moreover, by forcing users to input an amount freely, there is the possibility of user mistakes. This could result in costly errors, in terms of rectification costs, reputational damage and inconvenience to users.

Moreover, using time pressure to up-sell mobile phone insurance may not be entirely ethical. In addition, this final hurdle in the sign-up process may cause some customers to drop out. Finally, the emotive image of the woman being robbed may prime customers in a negative way and therefore detract from their user experience.

Though the points scheme seems like a good way of keeping customers on track, there is some question about what to do with the points after customers have earned their maximum bonus. To keep customers engaged, they could be given badges for accumulating points, or better yet, some sort of voucher. In addition, the proportion of income saved per month would need to be some minimum amount; otherwise, customers would be able to game the system by saving a peppercorn amount (say 1 per cent) to pick up the sign-up bonus.

Asking users to upload images may involve privacy and, when taken from the internet, copyright issues. In addition, the app has to be careful with regards to the information that is shared between users on grounds of potential privacy/data protection issues. Perhaps sharing only point totals and not incomes (or percentages thereof) would be useful as a safeguard. Furthermore, nudging users who have not uploaded an image more than just a few times may annoy them. The UX designers need to tread carefully here.

There is a question regarding the appropriateness of each of the savings options as the distinctions between the three time horizons (low, medium, and long term) seem somewhat rudimentary. Different types of savers have different risk preferences, and, indeed, different time horizons. As a result, some medium-term savers may end up with investment settings that are too risky while some long-term savers may find themselves not taking enough risk. As a result, more needs to be done in order to make the investment settings more specific to each user's risk appetite.

References

1,9,10 Davis, F D. Perceived usefulness, perceived ease of use, and user acceptance of information technology, *MIS Quarterly*, 1989, 13 (3), 319–40 (September)

2 Szabo, N (1999) Micropayments and Mental Transaction Costs, www.fon.hum.uva.nl/rob/Courses/InformationInSpeech/CDROM/Literature/LOTwinterschool2006/szabo.best.vwh.net/berlinmentalmicro.pdf (archived at https://perma.cc/ARY5-EF88)

3,5, Badi, M, Dab, S, Drummond, A, Malhotra, S, Muxi, F, Peeters, M, Roongta, P, Strauß, M and Sénant, Y (2018) Global payments 2018: Reimagining the Customer Experience, The Boston Consulting Group, 18 October, www.bcg.com/publications/2018/global-payments-reimagining-customer-experience.aspx (archived at https://perma.cc/K3RD-GP8Z)

4 Worldpay (2018) Global payments report: The art and science of global payments

6,15 Scherer, A, Wangenheim, F and Wünderlich, N. The Value of Self-Service: Long-Term Effects of Technology-Based Self-Service Usage on Customer Retention, *MIS Quarterly*, 2015, 39 (1), 177–200 (March)

7 Carlson, J R and Zmud, R W. Channel Expansion Theory and the experiential nature of media richness perceptions, *Academy of Management Journal*, 1999, 42 (2), 153–70

8 Maeda, J (2017) Design in Tech Report 2017, designintech.report/2017/03/11/design-in-tech-report-2017/ (archived at https://perma.cc/77LM-BY98)

11,12,77 Davis, F D and Venkatesh, V. A Theoretical Extension of the Technology Acceptance Model: Four Longitudinal Field Studies, *Management Science*, 2000, 46 (2), 186–204 (February)

13 Bettencourt, L and Ulwick, A. The Customer-Centred Innovation Map, *Harvard Business Review*, 2008, 86 (5), 109–14 (May)

14 Christensen, C M, Raynor, M E and McDonald, R. What is Disruptive Innovation?, *Harvard Business Review*, 2015, 93 (12), 44–53 (December)

16 Law, E L C, Roto, V, Hassenzahl, M, Vermeeren, A and Kort, J (2009) Understanding, scoping, and defining User eXperience: A survey approach [conference proceedings], in: CHI 2009 – User Experience, Boston, MA, 7 April

17,19 Nielsen, J and Norman, D (n.d.) The Definition of User Experience (UX), www.nngroup.com/articles/definition-user-experience/ (archived at https://perma.cc/2C8W-YBTG)

18 Berry, D (2000) The user experience: The iceberg analogy of user experience, IBM, 1 October, www.ibm.com/developerworks/library/w-berry/index.html (archived at https://perma.cc/T3CU-ANHG)

20 Sunstein, C R. Nudging: A very short guide, *Journal of Consumer Policy*, 2014, 37, 583–88

21,34 Kahneman, D. Maps of Bounded Rationality: Psychology for Behavioral Economics, *The American Economic Review*, 2003, 93 (5), 1449–75

22 Dünser, A, Grasset, R, Seichter, H and Billinghurst, M (2007) Applying HCI principles to AR systems design, HIT Lab NZ, www.researchgate.net/publication/216867606_Applying_HCI_principles_to_AR_systems_design (archived at https://perma.cc/6B9E-Z4EV)

23 Iyengar, S S and Lepper, M R. When Choice is Demotivating: Can One Desire Too Much of a Good Thing?, *Journal of Personality and Social Psychology*, 2000, 79 (6), 995–1006

24 Cronqvist, H and Thaler, R H. Design Choices in Privatized Social-Security Systems: Learning from the Swedish Experience, *American Economic Review*, 2004, 94 (2), 424–28

25,30,39,46,74,75 Blair-Early, A and Zender, M. User interface Design Principles for Interaction Design, *MIT Design Issues*, 2008, 24 (1), 85–107

26,27,31,56 Dolan, P, Hallsworth, M, Halpern, D, King, D, Metcalfe, R and Vlaev, I. Influencing behaviour: The mindspace way, *Journal of Economic Psychology*, 2012, 33, 264–77

28 Madrian, B and Shea, D F. The Power of Suggestion: Inertia in 401(k) Participation and Savings Behaviour, *Quarterly Journal of Economics*, 2001, 116, 1149–87

29,119,123 Johnson, E J, Bellman, S and Lohse, G L. Defaults, Framing and Privacy: Why Opting In-Opting Out, *Marketing Letters*, 2002, 13, 5–15

32 Peters, E, Dieckmann, N F, Västfjäll, D, Mertz, C K, Slovic, P and Hibbard, J H. Bringing meaning to numbers: The impact of evaluative categories on decisions, *Journal of Experimental Psychology*: Applied, 2009, 15 (3), 213–27

33 Larrick, R P and Soll, J B. The MPG Illusion, *Science*, 2008, 320, 1593–94

35 Tversky, A and Kahneman, D. Judgment under Uncertainty: Heuristics and biases, *Science*, 1974, 185 (4157), 1124–31 (September)

36 Stewart, N. The cost of anchoring on credit card minimum payments, *Psychological Science*, 2009, 20, 39–41

37,40,41,44,45 The Behavioral Insights Team (2010) Mindspace: Influencing behaviour through public policy, UK Cabinet Office, www.bi.team/publications/mindspace/ (archived at https://perma.cc/5S49-5YLP)

38 Bateson, M, Nettle, D and Roberts, G. Cues of Being Watched Enhance Cooperation in a Real-World Setting, *Biology Letters,* 2006, 2 (3), 412–16

42 Karlan D, Bertrand M, Mullainathan, S, Shafir, E and Zinman, J. What's Advertising Content Worth? Evidence from a Consumer Credit Marketing Field Experiment, *Quarterly Journal of Economics*, 2010, 125, 263–306

43 Bond, S D, Carlson, K A and Keeney, R L. Generating Objectives: Can Decision Makers Articulate What They Want?, *Management Science*, 2008, 54, 56–70 (January)

47 Terrill, B (2008) My Coverage of Lobby of the Social Gaming Summit [blog], 16 June, www.bretterrill.com/2008/06/my-coverage-of-lobby-of-social-gaming.html (archived at https://perma.cc/G4L8-3EP6)

48 Huotari, K and Hamari, J (2012) Defining gamification – A service marketing perspective, in Proceedings of the 16th International Academic MindTrek Conference, 3–5 October, Tampere, Finland, ACM, 17–22

49 Mullins, J K and Sabherwal, R. Gamification: A cognitiv–emotional view, *Journal of Business Research*, 2020, 106, 304–14 (January)

50,52,93,120 Cialdini, R B (2007) *Influence: The Psychology of Persuasion*, HarperBusiness, New York, revised edition

51 Bicchieri, C (2006) *The Grammar of Society: The Nature and Dynamics of Social Norms*, Cambridge University Press, New York

53 Svenson, O. Are we all less risky and more skillful than our fellow drivers?, *Acta Psychologica*, 1981, 47, 143–48

54 De Bondt, W F M. A portrait of the individual investor, *European Economic Review*, 1998, 42, 831–44 (May)

55,58 Kahneman, D and Tversky, A. Prospect Theory: An Analysis of Decision Under Risk, *Econometrica*, 1979, 47, 263–91

57 Tufano, P. Saving whilst Gambling: An Empirical Analysis of UK Premium Bonds, *American Economic Review*, 2008, 98, 321–26

59,60 HM Government, Department for Environment, Food & Rural Affairs (2019) Single-use plastic carrier bags charge: data in England for 2015 to 2016, 31 July, https://www.gov.uk/government/publications/carrier-bag-charge-summary-of-data-in-england/single-use-plastic-carrier-bags-charge-data-in-england-for-2015-to-2016 (archived at https://perma.cc/WQH9-RLVP)

61,62 Volpp, K G, John, L K, Troxel, A B, Norton, L, Fassbender, J and Loewenstein, G. Financial Incentive-Based Approaches for Weight Loss: A Randomized Trial, *JAMA*, 2008, 300 (22), 2631–37

63 Kahneman, D, Knetsch, J L and Thaler, R H. Experimental Tests of the Endowment Effect and the Coase Theorem, *Journal of Political Economy*, 1990, 98 (6), 1325–48.

64,66 Thaler, R. Mental accounting matters, *Journal of Behavioral Decision Making*, 1999, 12, 183–206

65 Camerer, C, Babcock, L, Loewenstein, G and Thaler, R H. Labor Supply of New York City Cabdrivers: One day at a Time, *Quarterly Journal of Economics*, 1997, 112, 407–41 (May)

67,68 Utkus, S P and Byrne, A (2013) *Understanding how the mind can help or hinder investment success,* Vanguard Asset Management

69 Shefrin, H and Statman, M. Behavioral Portfolio Theory, *The Journal of Financial and Quantitative Analysis*, 2000, 35 (2), 127–51 (June)

70 Johnson, E J, Shu, S B, Dellaert, B G C, Fox, C, Goldstein, D G, Häubl, G, Larrick, R P, Payne, J W, Peters, E, Schkade, D, Wansink, B and Weber, E U. Beyond nudges: Tools of a choice architecture, *Marketing Letters*, 2012, 23, 487–504 (June)

71 Benartzi, R and Thaler, R H. Naive Diversification Strategies in Retirement Savings Plans, *American Economic Review*, 2001, 91, 79–98 (March)

72 Loewenstein, G F and Elster, J (1992) *Choice Over Time*, Sage, New York

73 Soman, D, Ainslie, G, Frederick, S, Li, X, Lynch, J, Moreau, P, Mitchell, A, Read, D, Sawyer, A, Trope, Y, Wertenbroch, K and Zauberman, G. The Psychology of Intertemporal Discounting: Why are Distant Events Valued Differently from Proximal Ones? *Marketing Letters*, 2005, 16, 347–60

76 Aksan, N, Kisac, B, Aydin, M and Demirbuken, S (2009) Symbolic interaction theory, in: World Conference on Educational Sciences 2009, Procedia – Social and Behavioral Sciences, 1, 902–04

78 Goldstein, N J, Cialdini, R B and Griskevicius, V. A Room with a Viewpoint: Using social norms to motivate environmental conservation in hotels, *Journal of Consumer Research*, 2008, 35 (3), 472–82

79 Katz, M L and Shapiro, C. Network Externalities, Competition, and Compatibility, *American Economic Review*, 1985, 75 (3), 424–40 (June)

80,81 Liebowitz, S J and Margolis, S E. Network Externality: An Uncommon Tragedy, *Journal of Economic Perspectives*, 1994, 8 (2), 133–50

82 Uzzi, B. The Sources and Consequences of Embeddedness for the Economic Performance of Organizations: The Network Effect, *American Sociological Review*, 1996, 61 (4), 674–98 (August)

83 Apple Inc (2019) About iMessage and SMS/MMS, 19 September, support.apple.com/ en-us/HT207006 (archived at https://perma.cc/U6RR-SDHY)

84 Lukkarinen, A, Teich, J E, Wallenius, H and Wallenius, J. Success drivers of online equity crowdfunding campaigns, *Decision Support Systems*, 2016, 87, 26–38

85,89 Lakhani, K R and Panetta, J A. The Principles of Distributed Innovation, *Innovations*, 2007, 97–112

86 iZettle AB (2019) About us, www.izettle.com/gb/about-us (archived at https://perma.cc/ EUC6-5S6C)

87,88 Von Hippel, E (2005) *Democratizing Innovation*, The MIT Press, Cambridge, MA

90 Tandem Money Limited (2019) Tandem customers to design mortgage, 7 August, www. tandem.co.uk/blog/tandem-customers-to-design-mortgage (archived at https://perma.cc/ LQM3-SEVC)

91 Von Hippel, E. Democratizing Innovation: The evolving phenomenon of user innovation, *Journal für Betriebswirtschaft*, 2005, 55 (1), 63–78

92 Duncan, O D, Haller, A O and Portes, A. Peer influences on aspirations: A reinterpretation, *American Journal of Sociology*, 1968, 74 (2), 119–37

94 Webb, T L and Sheeran, P. Does changing behavioural intentions engender behaviour change? A meta-analysis of the experimental evidence, *Psychological Bulletin*, 2006, 132 (2), 249–68

95 Martinho-Truswell, E. How AI Could Help the Public Sector, *Harvard Business Review*, 2018, 53–5 (January–February)

96,97 Accenture Consulting (2016) Banking on Value: Rewards, Robo-Advice and Relevance, North America Consumer Digital Banking Survey, www.accenture.com/t20160609t222453__w__/us-en/_acnmedia/pdf-22/accenture-2016-north-america-consumer-digital-banking-survey.pdf (archived at https://perma.cc/CF2E-76Q4)

98 Nanayakkara, N C and Hennessey, P (2019) Global Wealth Management Research Report: How do you build value when clients want more than wealth? EYGM Limited, www.ey.com/en_gl/wealth-asset-management/how-do-you-build-value-when-clients-want-more-than-wealth (archived at https://perma.cc/5JY5-XWG5)

99,101 Burggraaff, P, Schuuring, M and Urda, B (2015) Four Digital Enablers: Bringing Technology into the Retail Store, The Boston Consulting Group, www.bcg.com/publications/2015/technology-strategy-four-digital-enablers-bringing-technology-into-retail-store.aspx (archived at https://perma.cc/WJC3-YG5Z)

100 Aubry, F and Souza, R (2011) The Art and Science of Retail Reinvention, The Boston Consulting Group, www.bcg.com/publications/2011/retail-consumer-products-art-science-retail-reinvention.aspx (archived at https://perma.cc/G6VL-SWNZ)

102 Lloyds Banking Group (2019) Fast facts about Lloyds Banking Group, www.lloydsbankinggroup.com/Media/media-kit/faqs/lloyds-banking-group-fast-facts/ (archived at https://perma.cc/HJS2-SXWB)

103,105,112 Lloyds Banking Group (2019) Annual Report and Accounts 2018, www.lloydsbankinggroup.com/globalassets/documents/investors/2018/2018_lbg_annual_report_v2.pdf (archived at https://perma.cc/B4G7-T3W8)

104 Lloyds Banking Group (2020) Helping Britain prosper, www.lloydsbankinggroup.com/our-purpose/ (archived at https://perma.cc/54QB-ZJ3B)

106,108,109 Lloyds Banking Group (2017) Lloyd's Bank opens state-of-the-art branch offering new banking experience, 25 September, www.lloydsbankinggroup.com/Media/Press-Releases/press-releases-2017/lloyds-bank/lloyds-bank-opens-state-of-the-art-branch-offering-new-banking-experience/ (archived at https://perma.cc/8W9Q-462Q)

107 Lloyds Banking Group (2020) Welcome to our Market Street, Manchester branch, www.lloydsbank.com/branch-locator/market-street-manchester.html (archived at https://perma.cc/EVE6-VTCQ)

110 Lloyds Banking Group (2019) Banking for homeless people, www.lloydsbankinggroup.com/our-purpose/helping-people/making-banking-easier-for-homeless-people/ (archived at https://perma.cc/54QB-ZJ3B)

111 Lloyds Banking Group (2019) Bank of Scotland opens state-of-the-art Argyle Street branch following multi-million pound refit, 16 December, www.lloydsbankinggroup.com/Media/Press-Releases/2019-press-releases/bank-of-scotland/bank-of-scotland-opens-state-of-the-art-argyle-street-branch-following-multi-million-pound-refit/ (archived at https://perma.cc/P6ME-5AL7)

113,114,115 Milligan, B (2017) Lloyds Bank to shrink hundreds of branches in size, BBC News, 3 April, www.bbc.co.uk/news/business-39457961 (archived at https://perma.cc/K8KM-U2HZ)

116 Thaler, R H and Sunstein, C R (2008) *Nudge: Improving Decisions about Health, Wealth and Happiness*, New Haven, CT: Yale University Press

117,118 Hausman, D M and Welch, B. Debate: To Nudge or Not to Nudge, *The Journal of Political Philosophy*, 2010, 18, 123–36

121 Durantini, M R, Albarracín, D, Mitchell, A L, Earl, A N and Gillette, J C. Conceptualizing the Influence of Social Agents of Behavior Change: A meta-analysis of the effectiveness of HIV-prevention interventionists for different groups, *Psychological Bulletin*, 2006, 132 (2), 212–48

122 Financial Conduct Authority (2020) Monthly PPI refunds and compensation, 3 March, www.fca.org.uk/data/monthly-ppi-refunds-and-compensation (archived at https://perma.cc/CYJ6-6ZQ2)

124 Shu, S B and Gneezy, A. Procrastination of enjoyable experiences, Journal of Marketing Research, 2010, 47 (5), 933–44

04

Artificial intelligence and automation in fintech

AI and machine learning in practice

LEARNING OBJECTIVES

This chapter will help you gain an understanding of:

- What is meant by the term AI and its history.
- The basic approaches to machine learning.
- Practical considerations of using AI in finance.
- Ethical pitfalls associated with the widespread application of AI.

Introduction

The term *artificial intelligence* (AI) is often used very liberally, especially amongst media commentators and people who have – at best – a superficial understanding of its meaning. This is unfortunate because it over-simplifies the critically important conversation that needs to be had about AI and its role in business, society, and finance.

Though written with very little assumed knowledge, this chapter seeks to elevate readers' understanding of AI. At the end of this chapter, the reader should have a solid grounding in artificial intelligence; what it is, how it works, and a keen appreciation of how its widespread application could impact the financial sector and society as a whole.

Whilst the developments in this fledging field are exciting to some, they are threatening to others. Therefore, it is hoped that readers will use this chapter as a springboard for gaining a deeper understanding of AI. This will help them prepare for the incoming disruption, and thereby position themselves to seize the opportunities brought on by the widespread use of AI in finance.

A definition of artificial intelligence

The genesis of AI as an academic field can be traced back to 1950 when Alan Turing published his seminal paper *Computing Machinery and Intelligence.*[1] Herein, Turing set out a framework for assessing whether or not machines demonstrate intelligent behaviour: if a machine produces behaviour indistinguishable from intelligent human behaviour, then the machine itself can be considered intelligent.[2] This has become known as the *Turing Test*, which can be considered a definition of artificial intelligence.

The Turing Test takes a narrow view on artificial intelligence: whereas a computer can be programmed to trade currencies autonomously – which might satisfy the Turing Test – it cannot at the same time drive a car or make a cup of coffee. To understand why, it is useful to consider the historical context. Computing was developed following a period of rapid industrialization across the world, a time that saw revolutions in science, medicine and mathematics. At the peak of this period in the early 20th century, the concept of *scientific management* became part of the zeitgeist: this is the idea that manufacturing can be reduced into individual sub-tasks, and therefore be optimized like a machine;[3] the invention of the conveyor belt was perhaps the clearest manifestation of this kind of thinking.

As societies in the 1950s were still heavily industrialized, it is unsurprising that early thinkers on AI viewed intelligence as reducible to the performance of individual tasks. After all, the great industrialists had succeeded by taking a similarly mechanistic view of human labour: by breaking labour into its component tasks, they had enabled workers to specialize in different parts of the chain of production in order to optimize manufacturing.

Thus, the Turing Test finds itself at home in a world where everything can be measured, deconstructed, and optimized. In this way, machines performing the same hyper-specialized tasks as humans can be considered intelligent as long as these tasks, simple as they may be, require some modicum of intelligence to be performed by humans. As a result, the Turing Test implies that agency is a prerequisite for intelligence: in other words, some sort of decision must be made, whether by a human being or a machine.

The Turing Test can be used to differentiate between automata and machine intelligence. Whereas an automaton facilitates human labour, it does not replace human decision making. For example, a cartridge-based coffee maker is an automaton: it greatly speeds up the act of making a coffee when compared to more traditional methods, yet it cannot operate without human input (ie loading cartridges, refilling the water supply and pressing a button). In contrast, a vending machine can be said to exhibit a higher degree of intelligence under the Turing Test as it can take payments and serve customers.

Granted, a vending machine is probably not the best example of an artificial intelligence. That said, it has a higher degree of autonomy than the coffee maker in that it does not require supervision or input by its master. Furthermore, it is easy to imagine a vending machine that performs a greater number of tasks independently. For example, facial recognition technology could be installed to identify regular customers and address them by their first name. This raises two important points: 1) artificial intelligence can be graded on a spectrum; and 2) the degree of artificial intelligence increases with the degree of autonomy.

These points lead us to an important distinction, that of narrow AI vs broad(er) AI: an AI is narrow when it performs a single task.[4] For example, an algorithm that trades currencies is an example of narrow AI because it only does one thing. An artificial intelligence becomes broader the more tasks it performs autonomously, and, crucially, the more domains in which it acts. Thus, a vending machine that recognizes its customers based on their facial features is a broader AI than a vending machine that does not. Similarly, a driverless car, which must choose whether to accelerate, brake or slow down, in addition to a multitude of other tasks, is an even broader AI.

If this car's sound system were to offer its users musical selections based on the scenery, weather or time of day, then it would be broader still. Yet it would still not be broad AI per se. This term is reserved for an AI that acts in all domains, and in doing so, becomes an artificial general intelligence.[5] At the time of writing, no such AI exists.

A brief history of artificial intelligence

From the late 1950s to the early 1970s, the field of AI progressed steadily;[6] the world had great hopes for AI and what it could do for humanity.

However, these early years of great expectations were followed by years of disappointment and a loss of public interest. So went the first AI-infused boom–bust cycle: a period of technological advancement and great hopes, known as an 'AI spring', followed by a period of stagnation, known as an 'AI winter'.[7]

The world has seen several of these cycles. The development of AI hit a stumbling block due to a lack of computing power in the early 1970s. Then, for a few years in the 1980s, the invention of deep learning (see below) reignited interest in AI. However, technological progress soon slowed, causing another winter, which lasted until the mid–late 1990s.[8]

Since then, the world has been in a multi-decade AI spring.[9] In the late 1990s, AI rode on the wave of the dot-com boom. However, this current AI spring has outlived the dot-com boom: in 2016, Google's AI, AlphaGo, defeated the world champion of the ancient Chinese game Go, with a score of 4-1;[10] in 2017, its successor machine, AlphaGoZero, defeated AlphaGo 100-1.[11] However, unlike AlphaGo, AlphaGoZero was developed without human guidance or input, save for the rules of the game Go.[12] In this way, AlphaGoZero was closer to self-programming AI than its predecessor.

The current AI spring has been facilitated by improvements in chip technology, which has lowered the cost of processing power, and cloud computing, which has broadened accessibility to powerful computing resources.[13] In this way, the story of the current AI spring is more about improvements in computer hardware than revolutions in mathematics; cheaper, and more powerful, hardware facilitates the gathering and processing of data to facilitate innovations in AI. This has enabled more experimentation with AI and has thereby broadened the scope of its applications. It is this greater scope that has captured the public's imagination. As more businesses experiment with AI, this produces a steady stream of news headlines about the potential uses of AI. This, in turn, helps maintain public interest in the sector.

While sensor technology enables computers to gather data in physical spaces, data hungry websites and smartphone apps glean information about user behaviour online. Given the growing connectivity of the web around the world, the 2017 claim that humanity had created 90 per cent of its data in the preceding two years[14] is not entirely unbelievable. Whether most of this data is useful is, of course, a separate matter.

Big Data vs artificial intelligence

The term *Big Data* may sound familiar because it was once the buzzword du jour. Like AI, it was used as a catchall to describe anything that involves computer-based quantitative analysis. Though it seems to have given way to AI in popular parlance, it is useful to examine in order to understand what AI is, and what it is not.

While its origins are disputed, Big Data started to gain traction as a term in the 1990s.[15] The core idea is that computer-based analytical tools allow us to gather, process and analyse vast, and ever-increasing, amounts of data.[16] Whilst your laptop computer may hold a few hundred gigabytes of hard-disk space, the size of the data sets used for Big Data analysis are often counted in thousands (terabytes), if not millions, of gigabyte (petabytes). This is what puts the 'big' into Big Data.

This abundance of data enables businesses to make faster and better decisions.[17] Whereas classical statistical methods deal with much smaller data sets, sometimes with sample sizes of a few hundred cases, Big Data allows for the timely processing of data sets with cases many times that number. This increase in scale makes Big Data analytics a compelling idea; that, given enough data, we can make better decisions on the basis of quantitative information.

That said, Big Data does not preclude the use of conventional statistical methods.[18] However, the data sets under examination are often so large that they require complex data management systems.[19] As a result, the surrounding infrastructure and the size of data sets distinguish Big Data from other analytical approaches.

In addition, Big Data methodologies sometimes employ machine learning algorithms.[20] As these techniques are also used in artificial intelligence,[21] there is some overlap between Big Data and AI. Indeed, these terms are sometimes used interchangeably. So, what then, is the difference?

AI can be distinguished from Big Data analytics by invoking the Turing Test: in this way, AI is different from Big Data because it is more autonomous. A data-driven decision that is not automated still requires human input, and therefore cannot be considered to be AI. For example, an investment fund may use a machine learning algorithm to analyse stock market data to generate trading signals. These trades could be executed by a human, which would make this an example of Big Data analytics. However, if the computer instead makes these trades without human input, then this becomes an example of AI.

Machine learning vs artificial intelligence

Early AI researchers took a mechanistic view of intelligence; if the rules underpinning intelligent human decision making could be defined, then it should be possible to engineer human intelligence. As a result, AI was initially conceived as rules-based expert systems, which would be programmed to emulate expert decision making.[22]

The rules-based approach started to run aground in the 1980s when it became clear that writing a rule for every decision would be too onerous;[23] whereas some decisions are, in theory, easy to break into a series of steps in order to arrive at the 'right' answer, others are more nuanced and subject to informational uncertainty. In addition, rules tend to degrade over time as they become subject to new complexities.[24]

Following the decline in expert systems, machine learning (ML) algorithms became a core part of the AI story.[25] ML is a probabilistic approach to decision making wherein large quantities of data are used to inform the rules of decision-making algorithms.[26] The term 'machine learning' is sometimes used interchangeably with AI;[27] to a degree, this is less erroneous than conflating AI with Big Data. However, it is still not technically correct, as ML algorithms are enablers of AI systems,[28] and not the systems themselves. For the purposes of our discussion, however, AI shall be taken to mean ML algorithms that facilitate automated decision making, which thereby meet the Turing Test.

MACHINE LEARNING EXPLAINED

ML algorithms use data to construct their decision-making rules.[29] They do so by classifying known outcomes in data sets based on their characteristics; in other words, by detecting patterns.[30] This enables the algorithms to make predictions about unknown outcomes based on exhibited characteristics in new cases and the degree to which these are similar to those of known outcomes.[31] For example, if a review of patient data associates smoking and obesity with heart disease, then an algorithm may predict that people who exhibit these characteristics are at greater risk of suffering from this.

ML algorithms are 'trained' and tested separate data sets.[32] In this way, their predictive accuracy can be readily ascertained: with the benefit of hindsight from outcomes in the training sample, an ML algorithm should be able to predict outcomes in the testing sample where similar characteristics are present.[33] Once validated, ML algorithms are deployed to predict outcomes in data sets where outcomes are unknown, thereby enabling predictive decision making. As a result of this work-cycle, ML algorithms require vast quantities of data to inform their decision-making rules.

FIGURE 4.1 Machine learning overview

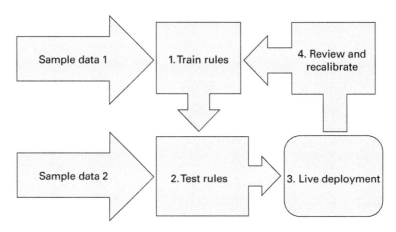

Though there are different approaches to machine learning, the calibration of each algorithm follows the same basic process: (1) The algorithm's decision-making rules are trained on a sample of data; 2) The algorithm's proficiency is then tested on an independent sample to ascertain its accuracy; 3) The algorithm is deployed predictively, by classifying cases with unknown outcomes; 4) Finally, the proficiency of the algorithm is reviewed periodically and its rules are recalibrated accordingly.

As technology advances, humanity generates ever-growing volumes of data.[34] The increase in web-connected devices, such as laptops, voice assistants and smartphones, facilitates data gathering via text messages, video and audio recordings. In this way, the writing of rules for ML algorithms has become crowdsourced: rather than relying on experts, this has been outsourced to millions of brains via the internet. The more user-generated data the better: this is why search engines and text-correction features have improved over time.

There are five basic types of ML algorithms: decision trees, genetic algorithms, nearest-neighbours, Bayesian classifiers and neural networks.[35] Though these approaches vary, they share basic facets: all are concerned with classifying new cases based on known cases, which necessarily involves two steps: using past data to inform the algorithms' decision-making rules and testing their predictive accuracy on a separate sample. To understand how they differ, we must examine each type of algorithm in turn.

Decision trees and random forests

These algorithms take on the basic structure of a tree, whereby decisions are made in sequence according to simple rules.[36] This allows an algorithm to direct users down 'branches' depending on their input; in this way, cases can be classified according to their exhibited variables.[37]

For example, some chat bots rely on decision trees: to invite user input, the bot poses a question such as, 'How may I help you today?' Then, depending on key words or phrases in the input – such as 'mortgage' or 'lost credit card' – the bot directs users towards an appropriate human adviser. If user input is not clear or sufficiently specific, the bot may invite further input by asking clarifying questions.

At every juncture, decision trees split cases into two groups based on probabilistic inference;[38] in other words, based on their similarity to known cases. Thus, the algorithm splits cases into progressively smaller groups.[39] As in the example of the chat bot above, this allows the algorithm to direct users towards increasingly case-specific solutions.

The classification of cases into progressively smaller groups results in case groupings at the base of the tree with constituent cases that have many variables in common. This enables predictive classification of new cases based on their exhibited variables, the accuracy of which can be tested on a separate sample of known cases.[40]

Decision trees do not have to be deployed in isolation; indeed, their predictive accuracy can be improved employing a multitude of trees, known as a

FIGURE 4.2 Decision tree simplified example

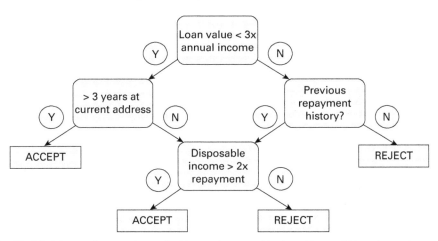

A simplified decision tree for assessing credit risk. Based on a combination of four variables – loan to income ratio, disposable income, repayment history and time at current address – the lender can classify the would-be borrower as likely or unlikely to default and thereby come to a lending decision (ie accept or reject). For more context on tree classifiers and credit risk see the Zopa case study at the end of this chapter.

forest.[41] The trees in such forests can number in the hundreds of thousands.[42] Though there are different types of forest models, the so-called random forest is widely used.[43] This forest is 'random' because each tree is given only a random selection of variables to consider.[44] In this way, different trees may reach different conclusions as individual trees process different aspects of the data set. As the final decision is decided collectively via a vote,[45] random forests are likely to benefit from a *wisdom of the crowds* effect (see Chapter 6).

Bayesian classifiers

Bayesian classifiers owe their name to Thomas Bayes, an 18th-century English priest,[46] who formalized a way of updating existing beliefs for new evidence.[47] After Bayes's death, the French mathematician Pierre-Simon Laplace built on his work to formulate what is known as Bayes' Theorem.[48] This can be expressed as follows:

$$p(x|y) = p(y|x)p(x)/p(y)$$

The expression above states that the probability of outcome x given outcome y is the probability of outcome y given outcome x, multiplied by the probability of outcome x, compared to the probability of all outcomes y. In plain English, this would read as: don't forget to consider the big picture.

Bayes' Theorem can be understood in the context of diagnosing a disease.[49] Let's suppose you are randomly screened for an infectious disease. You have no symptoms, but your test result is positive. Even if the test is 90 per cent accurate, this does not mean you have a 90 per cent chance of actually having the illness. The key to understanding why this is the case lies in considering the prevalence of the disease in the general population and the chance of your test result being a false positive.[50] In other words, not losing sight of the bigger picture.

Let's say 20 per cent of the general population suffer from this disease; given that the test is 90 per cent percent accurate, this means that for every 100 people tested, 18 (20 per cent × 90 per cent) true positives are found. However, this also means that, out of the healthy population, it will produce 8 false positives (80 per cent × 10 per cent). Thus, your true probability of having the disease after seeing a positive test result would be:

$$p(x|y) = 18/(18+8) = 69\%$$

Granted, you are still likely to have the disease, but significantly less so than was suggested by the high accuracy rate of the test. As no other symptoms were present, the diagnostic test was but one piece of evidence. By virtue of being a member of the general population you are, on average, exposed to many other factors that could cause you to have the disease, or not. Therefore, the possibility of false positives must also be considered.

Consider then, what your best-guess likelihood would have been without a test result, positive or negative. In other words, without any evidence for or against having the disease. If this were the case, your best estimate would be 20 per cent. Why? Because we know that 20 per cent of the people have the disease and, in the absence of any data (eg a diagnostic test result), the population average is the best starting point. In this way, the 69 per cent likelihood of having the disease given a positive test result was just the population average adjusted upwards for an additional variable (ie the positive test result).

Bayes' Theorem allows us to incorporate multiple variables into our predictions; in the example above, the positive test result was an aggravating factor as it made having the disease more likely than the population average. However, mitigating factors may also exist, such as exercise habits and diet.

Thus, Bayes' Theorem can be restated as: the posterior probability of an outcome is proportional to its prior adjusted for the likelihood of the data.[51] In plain English, this would be: start with the population average (ie the prior) and adjust according to each variable present to arrive at an estimated probability that accounts for all available data (ie the posterior). As more data becomes available, our probability estimate grows ever more specific to the case at hand. In this way, Bayes' Theorem allows us to calculate the probability of an outcome given case-specific variables: a multivariable estimate can then be used predictively, by classifying whether an unknown outcome is more or less likely than the population average. Thus, Bayesian classifiers are rooted in the application of Bayes' Theorem to cases with multiple variables. In practice, this relies on complicated mathematics, though a simplification can be illustrated with ratio multiplication as in the case study below.

CASE STUDY
Bayesian classifiers and car insurance

In 2016, Admiral, a UK-based insurance company, made headlines by announcing that it would use drivers' Facebook data to price car insurance premiums.[52] In theory, a customer's social media data can help an insurer estimate their probability of making a claim: for example, customers who travel often and visit more accident-prone parts of the country are conceivably at higher risk of having an accident than those who do not. Thus, social media data could allow an insurer to charge its customers premiums that are more in line with their individual risk profiles.

Although Admiral's data initiative was blocked by Facebook on privacy grounds,[53] this does not appear to have dented its appetite for collecting user-specific data to facilitate more granular pricing decisions. To this end, Admiral uses telematics,[54] which involves installing a small box in the customer's car that tracks various aspects of how the customer drives, such as their speed, rate of acceleration and how often they brake sharply:[55] in theory, this yields a more detailed, and personalized, picture of each customer's risk profile.

Car insurance premiums have traditionally been calculated based on group-based factors such the driver's age, type of vehicle, location and annual mileage.[56] This effectively allows drivers to pool their risks with those who exhibit similar risk factors;[57] thus, this pricing model ignores personal driving habits. This model disadvantages younger drivers,[58] who have not yet had the opportunity to demonstrate that they are safe and careful drivers by driving for several years without an accident.

Telematic car insurance addresses this problem by reducing the information asymmetry between driver and insurer.[59] If most people are honest, they can tell you whether or not they are careful drivers; unfortunately, the insurer cannot ascertain this from the group-based risk factors used in their pricing models. The more granular information provided by telematics addresses this problem by helping the insurer establish whether the customer is indeed a good driver based on how they actually drive.[60]

Thus, telematic car insurance may incentivize customers to drive more carefully, as doing so will help keep their premiums down. For instance, a driver who regularly exceeds the speed limit will, all else being equal, incur higher premiums than one who does not. In this way, drivers from 'at risk' groups, such as younger drivers, are, by driving carefully, able to demonstrate that they are a lower insurance risk than their peer group. In this way, both parties win: careful drivers pay lower insurance premiums, while the insurer avoids bad drivers, or at least charges them accordingly.

It is conceivable that a Bayesian classifier could be used to estimate a customer's risk of having an accident, and by extension, pricing said customer's insurance premiums. For the purposes of this discussion, let's assume that the insurance policy only covers car accidents, thereby leaving out things such as theft, vandalism or environmental damage, which might also give rise to insurance claims; of course, this is a simplification, but it will do. In addition, we will assume that the insurer's risk appetite is such that it will only insure drivers who exhibit a below-average risk of having an accident. Thus, the classifying decision becomes insure or do not insure; in other words, a 'yes' if the customer's risk is below average, and a 'no' if it is average or above average.

As a starting point, we estimate a prior probability; that is, a population average given no other information concerning the individual case. Given that the average car travels 7,134 miles per year in the UK[61] and the casualty rate is 484.5 for every billion miles,[62] we can estimate the average probability of having an accident per year as follows:

$$7,134 \text{ miles} \times (484.5 \text{ accidents}/1 \text{ billion miles}) = 0.35\%$$

This estimate is a simplification as it implicitly assumes that road accidents and casualties are equivalent – not all accidents result in injury or death; that said, it will suffice as a starting point. Our prior probability can now be adjusted for additional information to derive a posterior probability. Let's say the driver lives in London: according to Admiral, London drivers are the safest in the country based on their telematic tracking data.[63] Let's say that this makes London drivers half as likely as the national average to have an accident. Using ratio multiplication, the average London driver's adjusted probability can be estimated as follows:

$$p(\text{accident}) = (0.35\%) \times (1/2)$$

$$= 0.35\%/2$$

$$= 0.175\%$$

As seen above, the London driver's probability of having an accident was estimated by scaling down the national average. Though this calculation is a simplification of the mathematical operations behind the algorithm, it is a cogent illustration of how Bayesian classifiers work: by adjusting the population average (ie prior probability) according to the variables present.[64]

The above probability estimate was based on a single data point: the fact that the driver lives in London. To get a clearer picture of the driver's risk of having an accident, more variables must be accounted for. For instance, say a London driver regularly exceeds the speed limit, which increases their accident risk by 33 per cent. When combined with the other fact that this person lives in London, this modifies their posterior probability as follows:

$$p(\text{accident}) = (0.35\%) \times (1/2) \times (1.33/1)$$

$$= (0.35\% \times 1.33)/2$$

$$= 0.23\%$$

As can be seen, the risk of an accident has increased but is still below the national average; as a result, the insurer would agree to underwrite this driver, based on its policy of insuring drivers with a below-average accident risk. Of course, this example is fictional: in practice, an insurer would base its decision on more variables. In this way, the more drivers that use telematic insurance solutions, the more data an insurer like Admiral will have to use for its underwriting decisions.

Indeed, ML algorithms can employ a multitude of different variables. Thus, adding a new variable is like adding weight to different sides of a scale; in most cases, the presence of a variable either increases the risk of a claim, or causes it to decline. In this way, the addition of each new variable helps the algorithm decide whether the individual case is more or less likely to result in a claim than the population average.

 Given the scaling factors in the table below, if the policy of an insurance company is to accept only those drivers with a risk below the national average, will the algorithm accept or reject a case that exhibits all of the factors in the table?
(Suggested answer at the end of this chapter.)

TABLE 4.1 Accident risk factors

Risk factors	Effect on accident risk
Always observes speed limit	40% reduction
Young driver	50% increase
Lives in an accident-prone area	20% increase
Drives outside rush hour but not at night	15% reduction

Nearest neighbours

These algorithms are analogous to a doctor making a diagnosis based on the symptoms present in that they seek to classify new cases by comparing them to known cases. Nearest neighbour algorithms do this by assessing each new case's degree of similarity with known example cases; the new case will be classified according to the example case that it resembles most. This approach is employed in e-commerce, for example, where online shoppers are recommended products because these have been purchased by similar customers.[65]

Nearest neighbour algorithms rely on vector algebra to classify new cases.[66] As individual variables can be represented by axes on a plane, distinctions can be made between example cases based on their 'score' along each axis; some examples are more x, while others are more y. Thus, a line can be drawn to demarcate the boundary between two different classes on a plane;[67] new cases are then classified according to the side of the boundary they are on – in other words, on their similarity to existing cases.

Though the paragraph above is a simplification of the mathematical processes that take place, it may still read like a foreign language to some. As a result, it is useful to look at an example: imagine an algorithm that is built to distinguish between boys and girls aged 16 based on their reported height and weight. Say, for example, that girls in this age group are known to exhibit slightly higher body-mass-indices (BMIs) than boys, then a person's height relative to their weight can be used to distinguish between boys and girls. As the BMI is derived by dividing an individual's weight (in kilograms) by their height squared (in metres),[68] the difference between girls and boys can be shown on a plane: if height is the y-axis and weight is the x-axis, then boys will exhibit higher readings for y relative to x and vice versa. By plotting each case on a graph, one could draw a dividing line above and below which there would be more boys and girls, respectively.

Of course, this algorithm is overly simplistic and is likely to make classification errors; after all, some 16-year-old girls are underweight while some 16-year-old boys are obese. Thus, our algorithm's accuracy could be improved by adding an additional dimension: GCSE exam results. GCSEs are standardized tests that 16-year-olds take in the UK, somewhat comparable to SATs in the United States. Historically speaking, girls outperform boys on these tests.[69] Scoring cases for this variable along an additional axis could help reduce the error rate as we'd now have more information to help us distinguish between boys and girls.

Of course, our dividing line would no longer lie on a plane, but in a three-dimensional space. But why stop there? We could invoke more variables by adding more dimensions. With each new dimension, the classification decisions should become more accurate. However, an increasing number of variables quickly increases the algorithm's complexity,[70] which makes it harder and more time consuming to process; given thousands of variables, this could be a serious problem, even in the age of cloud computing. Fortunately, computer scientists have found ways around this problem by breaking it into multiple parts.[71] How this works, however, is beyond the scope of this book (for more information see Domingos (2015)).

Genetic algorithms and genetic programming

This class of algorithms takes an evolutionary approach. The core idea is that the process of evolution is a problem-solving mechanism. Whereas our DNA determines our survivability, computer code determines an algorithm's capacity for problem solving or making predictions.[72]

At a basic level, an algorithm can be represented by strings of bits (ie 1s and 0s), also known as binary. Thus, a population of algorithms can be generated by randomly scrambling strings of 1s and 0s. These algorithms can then be set to work at solving a problem, after which they can be ranked according to the quality of their output. In this way, the relative fitness of each algorithm can be determined.[73]

Following this, the weaker algorithms are discarded, leaving the more successful algorithms to reproduce. This is done by splitting each parent algorithm's bit string at the same randomly chosen point; the resulting strings are then combined with their complementary parts from the other parent, thereby producing two children. The offspring and their parents are then added to the next generation of reproducing algorithms. As the process repeats, the population's aptitude for solving the problem improves by way of evolution.[74]

Genetic programming is similar to genetic algorithms in that both approaches succeed in automating the trial and error process of evolution. However, with genetic programming, reproduction takes place at a higher level as algorithms mate at a functional level;[75] as algorithms can be arranged into decision trees (eg if x, do y; if not, do z), reproduction takes place by randomly swapping parts of each parent tree.[76] For example, if the father programme does x, followed by y, and the mother programme does a, followed by b, then mating will result in two children: one that does x, followed by b and another that does a, followed by y. This has the advantage of evolving algorithms based on what they actually do rather than randomly chosen parts of their binary code, which can sometimes ruin otherwise sound algorithms (ie if the bit string is broken at the wrong place).[77]

Neural networks and deep learning

This family of algorithms is modelled on the human brain. To understand how these work, it is useful to start with a basic exploration of how a brain's nerve cells (ie neurons) work. These contain three basic parts: the dendrites, the cell body and the axon.[78] The dendrites receive electrical signals into the cell body; the axon, which has a stem-like structure, sends electrical signals away from the cell body.[79] Neurons communicate via electro-chemical signals.[80] The cell body takes input from connected neurons via its dendrites until a certain chemical threshold is reached; when this happens, the neuron sends an electrical signal down its axon, on to other connected neurons.[81]

Neural networks mimic this process. These algorithms are made up of thousands, if not millions, of processing units modelled on brain neurons, which are arranged into layers. Each unit, called a node, takes input from the nodes in the preceding layer; when a node's input threshold is reached, it sends a signal to nodes in the next layer. If a node does not receive sufficient input to reach its threshold, it does nothing.[82]

Information flows through neural networks in the form of numbers. Each node multiplies its inputs by a weighting; when the sum of these weighted inputs exceeds a numerical threshold, the node sends information onwards to the next layer. Generally speaking, this means passing on the sum of the weighted inputs to downstream nodes.[83]

This process continues until the final layer, which contains a single node: if this node's input threshold is reached, it produces a 1; if the input threshold is not reached, it produces a 0.[84] In the context of a classification decision, such as identifying trees in images, 1 would mean 'tree', and 0 'no tree'. Such a decision is possible because images can be represented numerically.

For each correct classification decision, the algorithm is given a score of 1, while each incorrect classification earns it a 0. An average score is then calculated, whereby 1 denotes perfect accuracy; thus, the closer to 1, the better. The algorithm then attempts to boost this average by attaching greater weight to the preceding nodes that help the final node make a greater number of correct classification decisions. This process is known as back-propagation.[85]

Thus, the algorithm 'learns' to favour nodes that increase its overall accuracy. As different nodes take different inputs, back-propagation optimizes classification decisions by focussing the algorithm on the most relevant pieces of data. A tree-spotting algorithm, would, for instance, learn to pay more attention to nodes focussing on tree trunks as opposed to, say, bird feathers. Once an algorithm has been homed in on the most relevant data points, its proficiency can then be tested on an independent sample of data.

FIGURE 4.3 Basic neural network

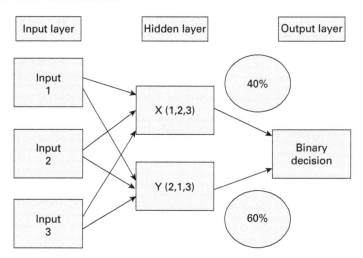

The first layer takes inputs; in the next layer, different nodes attach different weightings to each input. In this example, the X node favours input 1 over inputs 2 and 3 while the Y node favours input 2 over inputs 1 and 3. The decision node attaches a weighting to each of the preceding nodes: in this example, 40 per cent to X and 60 per cent to Y. In this way, the decision node expresses varying degrees of confidence in each of the preceding nodes, and ultimately, the underlying inputs when answering a binary classification question (eg 'A' or 'B'). The accuracy of this decision can be optimized by readjusting the relative weightings of nodes in each layer (ie back-propagation).

In its simplest form, a neural network only needs to contain two layers: an input layer and an output layer;[86] the former takes in data, while the latter provides a decision. However, advances in computing have enabled the inclusion of more intermediary layers, which is what makes these algorithms 'deep'.[87] In this way, a deep learning algorithm is really just a neural network with as many as 10, 20 or even 50 layers.[88]

Practical and ethical issues regarding AI

Whether one speaks of AI or ML, there are certain practical issues to consider when relying on algorithms for decision making. Because algorithms are often deployed within some sort of organizational context, it is pertinent to consider the surrounding governance and risk management frameworks.

As some algorithms lack transparency, it may be hard for human beings to ascertain how these come to their decisions, which makes them difficult to audit. This is of particular concern in regard to deep learning algorithms because they can be tens of layers deep and thousands of nodes wide.[89] This lack of algorithmic intelligibility, known as a 'black box', is a serious risk in situations where acting on an algorithm's decisions can have significant negative consequences for those involved.[90] As a result, some AI risk stems from its unwitting misapplication by people who do not understand how the underlying algorithms work.

Like other quantitative decision-making tools, AI is vulnerable to management bias: organizational politics and human psychology lead decision makers to favour data that yield the results they need,[91] whether they realize it or not. This is a problem at all levels of an organization, not just upper management. As a result, bias needs to be considered at all stages of the AI development cycle within organizations.

This starts with robust data management procedures. Because algorithms are only as good as their underlying data sets, these must be accurate, timely and relevant. As a result, data management is an ongoing process, which involves things such as data collection, data cleaning and integration with existing data sets.[92] In this way, the risk of biased algorithms can be mitigated by maintaining high-quality data sets under robust internal controls.

To further minimize the risk of bias, an algorithm can be reviewed by an independent person. Though the concept of independence is open to interpretation, it generally means someone other than the person who programmed the algorithm; in fact, the further removed the reviewer is, the better. For high-risk algorithms, independent review is imperative; in some cases, the reviewer may have to be someone from outside the organization, such as an IT specialist or auditor. Whoever the reviewer is, this person must have the skills and knowledge to conduct their review competently. This can be problematic on an industry level as there is a shortage of people with the requisite auditing skills who understand AI well enough to 'kick the tyres'. As a remedy, organizations could use the 'Extreme Programming' paradigm, whereby developers work in pairs, reviewing each other's work.[93] This approach also emphasizes automated software testing according to certain predefined performance requirements.[94] This in analogous to testing an algorithm's classification efficacy: this can be achieved by feeding an algorithm simulated data in order to ascertain that it performs as expected.[95]

In addition, AI-deploying organizations face the problem of concept drift, wherein the relationship between the input data and the classification target changes over time.[96] As a result, the algorithm's accuracy degrades as its decision-making rules no longer apply to the target population.[97] For example, an algorithm could 'learn' that online purchases of vitamin supplements are associated with mass purchases of toilet paper (ie as a result of the

COVID-19 outbreak); however, after the outbreak is over, this relationship may no longer hold. To address potential drift, an algorithm's performance will need to monitored on an ongoing basis and may need to be recalibrated with new data.[98]

With regard to ongoing review and validation of AI, fintechs can learn from the insurance sector as insurers build sophisticated quantitative models to forecast claims. The review and oversight procedures surrounding these models are integral to risk management within insurance companies.[99] As a result, these undergo stringent, and ongoing, validation processes, conducted by skilled staff who are independent from the construction of the model.[100] In addition, the model development and subsequent validation procedures are carefully documented and subjected to independent scrutiny.[101]

Despite adequate validation and review procedures, an AI may still exhibit bias. The issue of algorithmic bias is a cogent example of this: making decisions based on biased data can lead to discriminatory decisions. For instance, training a predictive policing algorithm on a sample of arrest records could lead police to target members of demographic groups overrepresented in the training sample.[102] After all, the algorithm does not know what it is being used for; it only classifies cases based on identified patterns in the training data.

One could address the problem of algorithmic bias by ensuring that the data in the training sample accurately reflects the algorithm's target population.[103] However, problems can also stem from a lack of diverse perspectives, which may result in group think.[104] These problems can be addressed by making AI teams more diverse; this goes beyond superficial characteristics, and can include diversity of personality types, data sets and modelling techniques.[105]

In addition to algorithmic bias, there are other potential sources of unfairness in the AI-based economy. One of these is the monopolization of data sets: large organizations have, on account of their greater scale, been able to gather large amounts of data; as algorithms require large data sets to hone their decision-making capabilities, this hands the advantage to established businesses.[106] By monopolizing their data sets, these organizations can entrench themselves, and make it harder for smaller firms to develop competing solutions.[107]

It would appear that policymakers are aware of this problem, and they have made attempts to ameliorate data monopolization. For example, in the European banking sector – where, perhaps, the problem has been particularly bad – this has been pursued via the Open Banking directive (see Chapter 1). By allowing bank customers to share their transactional data with fintech start-ups, this could foster greater innovation, and competition, in financial services.[108]

Furthermore, UK policymakers are looking at ways of facilitating data sharing across the economy via what it calls 'data trusts', which are frameworks for secure and ethical data sharing between different organizations.[109] In addition, the UK Government is making some publicly-owned data sets available in order to spur innovation.[110] Thus, it appears that the UK Government is attempting to replicate the Open Banking scheme in both public and private spheres.

As AI grows increasingly powerful, the question surrounding its values becomes ever-more pertinent.[111] Assuming it is possible to encode an algorithm with a code of ethics, how does one choose its underlying values? This question may be of limited consequence with regard to narrow AI systems. However, in the case of an all-powerful artificial generalized intelligence, it is of prime importance:[112] as values vary across different countries, cultures and religions, how do we decide which values to privilege over others; and who exactly gets to decide?

 CASE STUDY
ZOPA: Machine learning and credit risk

Founded in 2005, Zopa claims to have invented peer-to-peer (p2p) lending. The core idea was to connect borrowers and savers via its website in order to minimize overheads. As Zopa does not have branches, it has a leaner operating model which enables it to offer better rates to its borrowers and savers.[113]

The company's name appears to be an abbreviation of 'zone of possible agreement', a concept from micro-economics: in a negotiation, this is the range of agreements acceptable to both sides; in other words, the common ground on which a deal can be struck.[114] As a result, its name appears to be a nod to the company's role in connecting borrowers and savers.

Since its founding, the company has facilitated lending of more than £4 billion to *ca* 500,000 people.[115] The average borrower is 40 years old and has an income of around £40,000.[116] Zopa rejects 80 per cent of its loan applicants and focusses on borrowers who can demonstrate a history of paying back their debts.[117] In addition, customers are assured 'a fair deal as standard'.[118]

Unlike other p2p lenders, Zopa does not allow its users to lend directly. Rather, it splits each investment into £10 lots and lends these out across a portfolio of borrowers. The company classifies its borrowers into six different risk categories, in order to determine the interest rate they pay. Meanwhile, its savers choose between two lending options: a lower and higher risk. The former includes borrowers from the four lowest risk categories, while the latter contains borrowers from all risk categories. Naturally, savers who lend via the higher risk option are compensated with higher interest rates.[119]

In 2018, Zopa introduced an income verification feature for would-be borrowers that relies on Open Banking.[120] This allows borrowers to verify their incomes by connecting their bank accounts to Zopa, as opposed to manually uploading copies of bank statements.[121] Whilst this new feature may be more convenient for the company's customers, it is conceivable that customer transactions could also be used to assess creditworthiness on a more granular level.

Thus, Zopa could use Open Banking to build a richer picture of each customer's credit risk profile. Indeed, having access to a would-be borrower's bank account could give a potential lender valuable information about their spending patterns. With bank account data from enough customers – perhaps 15,000–20,000 – the company could employ machine learning algorithms to identify spending patterns that indicate a heightened risk of default.

To this end, risk factors could include the ratio of ingoings to outgoings, monthly income, how often the account is in debit, and so on. Besides helping the company screen out bad credit risks, machine learning may facilitate the prediction of defaults before they occur. If a borrower's spending habits start to resemble those of a bad credit risk, this could indicate an imminent default. Thus, the ability to predict defaults could allow a company like Zopa to take preemptive action to limit losses, such as by refusing to extend further credit. At the time of writing it is unclear whether Zopa uses machine learning as described above. However, the company does use machine learning: according to its blog, Zopa uses a decision tree-based approach to assess credit risk.[122]

What are some potential practical and ethical issues to consider regarding the use of machine learning for assessing credit risk in p2p lending?
(Suggested answer at the end of this chapter.)

Chapter summary

The growing interconnectedness of our world, combined with improvements in data gathering and processing capabilities, has widened the scope of applications for the family of algorithms known colloquially as 'AI'. Meanwhile, AI-based tools have become more accessible via cloud computing, cheap sensor technology and data-gathering apps. We can measure more now than ever before, and our processing capabilities are greater than ever.

What the public calls 'AI' is really just a set of algorithms known as machine learning. These algorithms inform their decision-making rules based on the weight of data they receive rather than expert judgement. Automation enables these algorithms to facilitate quantitative decision making based on large data sets containing many variables.

Though the mathematics and quantitative methods underlying these algorithms have advanced over the years, the most recent progress in AI has been achieved due to the falling cost of processing power: as machine learning algorithms are extremely computationally intensive, they were previously commercially unfeasible. Thus, today's boom in AI and machine learning has more to do with increasing accessibility of computer hardware than recent advancements in mathematics.

The public discourse surrounding AI goes through cycles of 'spring' and 'winter': periods of great hope and great expectations followed by periods of disillusionment and disinterest. At the time of writing we are in the midst of an AI spring, usually defined by news stories about exciting breakthroughs and hopes for the future.

Though the future for AI currently looks bright, we must not lose sight of the practical and ethical issues that its widespread application brings to the fore. For businesses that rely on AI to any significant degree, addressing these potential issues before they arise is paramount. This necessarily involves close integration with the governance, oversight and risk management functions of the business. Getting AI right should be the responsibility of all layers of the organization, not just the people who build the algorithms.

To some, this chapter may have felt excessively technical, especially when compared to prior chapters. Regretfully, there will be no let-up for these readers: in the next chapter we will go into similar levels of technical detail regarding blockchains and cryptocurrencies.

 KEY TAKEAWAYS

The three big ideas from this chapter are:

- AI is really just machine learning algorithms with a greater degree of autonomy.
- Greater connectivity and the falling cost of acquiring processing power has been, and continues to be, a key enabler of AI-based applications.
- Widespread use of AI has both ethical and practical pitfalls which may not be immediately obvious to the people building or implementing it; therefore, independent scrutiny is critically important.

SUGGESTED ANSWERS TO DISCUSSION POINTS

 Given the scaling factors in the table below, if the policy of an insurance company is to accept only those drivers with a risk below the national average, will the algorithm accept or reject a case that exhibits all of the factors in the table?

TABLE 4.2 Accident risk factors

Risk factors	Effect on accident risk
Always observes speed limit	40% reduction
Young driver	50% increase
Lives in an accident-prone area	20% increase
Drives outside rush hour but not at night	15% reduction

$$p(accident) = 0.35\% \times (1-0.4) \times (1+0.5) \times (1+0.2) \times (1-0.15)$$
$$= 0.32\%$$

Accident risk is lower than national average, therefore accept.

 What are some potential practical and ethical issues to consider regarding the use of machine learning for assessing credit risk in p2p lending?

If making automated decisions without human oversight, then a p2p lender like Zopa will need to consider the implications of GDPR, particularly in regard to seeking consent from customers in regard to making automatic decisions that affect them materially (see Chapter 8 for further detail). Processes (and staff) will need to be in place to address the customer queries that will inevitably arise as a result of lending decisions not going as customers expect. As a result, p2p lenders relying on machine learning may need more staff who understand machine learning well enough to be able to review lending decisions.

In addition, a p2p lender using Open Banking to build a database of customer transactions in order to inform its lending decisions will need to be transparent with its customers about this and make sure that they consent to this. Consent is a difficult area, because customers don't often read lengthy disclosures, when they can just tick a box to make it go away. As a result, any p2p lender wishing to demonstrate (perhaps to a regulator) that they have gained customer consent should think about how it is asked for via the user interface; are the most important terms and conditions unambiguously clear or is it just a tick-box exercise?

Finally, the lending algorithms need to be reviewed on a periodic basis to ensure that they are fit for purpose and/or not making discriminatory decisions. As a credit risk algorithm is material to the business of a p2p lender, its performance needs to be monitored as part of the company's risk management and governance process. To this end, the company needs to make sure that there are independent people 'kicking the tyres'.

References

1,6,8,9,13 McWaters, R J, Blake, M, Galaski, R, Chubb, C K, Uykur, D, Blickling, A and Münch, T (2018) The new Physics of Financial Services: How artificial intelligence is transforming the financial ecosystem, World Economic Forum, 15 August, www.wefo rum.org/reports/the-new-physics-of-financial-services-how-artificial-intelligence-is-transforming-the-financial-ecosystem (archived at https://perma.cc/35VS-Z7GA)

2 Turing, A M (1950) Computing Machinery and Intelligence, *Mind*, 59 (236), 433–60 (October)

3 Taylor, F W (1911) *The Principles of Scientific Management*, Harper & Brothers, New York

4 Yudkowsky, E and Harris, S (2018) AI: Racing Toward the Brink, Waking Up [podcast transcript], 28 February, intelligence.org/2018/02/28/sam-harris-and-eliezer-yudkowsky/ (archived at https://perma.cc/HK6P-FB6B)

5 Bostrom, N and Yudkowsky, E (2014) The Ethics of Artificial Intelligence, Machine Intelligence Research Institute, intelligence.org/files/EthicsofAI.pdf (archived at https://perma.cc/53Z2-LM8S)

7,30,31,33,36 The Royal Society (2017) Machine learning: the power and promise of computers that learn by example, royalsociety.org/~/media/policy/projects/machine-learning/publications/machine-learning-report.pdf (archived at https://perma.cc/N74C-N8E9)

10 Borowiec, S (2016) AlphaGo seals 4-1 victory over Go grandmaster Lee Sedol, *The Guardian*, 15 March, www.theguardian.com/technology/2016/mar/15/googles-alphago-seals-4-1-victory-over-grandmaster-lee-sedol (archived at https://perma.cc/D44G-XMRP)

11,12 Silver, D, Schrittwieser, J, Simonyan, K, Antonoglou, I, Huang, A, Guez, A, Hubert, T, Baker, L, Lai, M, Bolton, A, Chen, Y, Lillicrap, T, Hui, F, Sifre, L, van den Driessche, G, Graepel, T and Hassabis, D (2017) Mastering the game of Go without human knowledge, *Nature*, 550, 354–59

14 IBM Marketing Cloud & Comsense (2017) 10 Key Marketing Trends for 2017 and Ideas for Exceeding Customer Expectations, comsense.consulting/wp-content/uploads/2017/03/10_Key_Marketing_Trends_for_2017_and_Ideas_for_Exceeding_Customer_Expectations.pdf (archived at https://perma.cc/CHG7-BXGT)

15 Lohr, S (2013) The origins of 'big data': An etymological detective story, *New York Times*, 1 February, bits.blogs.nytimes.com/2013/02/01/the-origins-of-big-data-an-etymological-detective-story/ (archived at https://perma.cc/JLM7-9KPC)

16,19,34 Maltby, D (2011) Big Data Analytics, University of Texas at Austin, pdfs.semanticscholar.org/9f50/708abe1f28a8993bae362f1d30697b71a32e.pdf (archived at https://perma.cc/9MPY-STW5)

17, 91 PricewaterhouseCoopers (2016) The human factor: Working with machines to make big decisions, www.pwc.com/us/en/advisory-services/big-decision-survey/assets/the_human_factor_working_with_machines_to_make_big_decisions.pdf (archived at https://perma.cc/T4GW-DXBF)

18,20,21 Manyika, J, Chui, M, Brown, B, Bughin, J, Dobbs, R, Roxburgh, C and Byers, A H (2011) Big data: The next frontier for innovation, competition, and productivity, The McKinsey Global Institute, www.mckinsey.com/insights/business_technology/big_data_the_next_frontier_for_innovation (archived at https://perma.cc/AG3J-TAYX)

22,23,24 Dormehl, L (2017) *Thinking machines: The quest for artificial intelligence – and where it's taking us next*, Penguin Random House, New York, in AI in the UK: Ready, willing and able? House of Lords Select Committee on Artificial Intelligence, Report of session 2017–19, London, 16 April 2018, publications.parliament.uk/pa/ld201719/ldselect/ldai/100/10002.htm (archived at https://perma.cc/7GZK-5595)

25,27,28,106,107 House of Lords Select Committee on Artificial Intelligence (2018) AI in the UK: Ready, willing and able? Report of session 2017–19, 16 April, publications. parliament.uk/pa/ld201719/ldselect/ldai/100/10002.htm (archived at https://perma. cc/7GZK-5595)

26,32 Mitchell, T (1999) Machine Learning and Data Mining, *Communications of The ACM*, 42 (11), 31–35 (November)

29,35,77,84 Domingos, P (2015) *The Master Algorithm: How the quest of the ultimate learning algorithm will remake our world*, Penguin Books, London

37,38 Spector, P and Breiman, L (1995) Parallelizing CART using workstation network, University of California, Berkley, www.stat.berkeley.edu/~breiman/pcart.pdf (archived at https://perma.cc/74RT-MPSG)

39,41,43 Bacham, D and Zhao, J (2017) Machine Learning: Challenges, Lessons, and Opportunities in Credit Risk Modelling, Moody's Analytics Risk Perspectives (July, www. moodysanalytics.com/risk-perspectives-magazine/managing-disruption/spotlight/ machine-learning-challenges-lessons-and-opportunities-in-credit-risk-modeling (archived at https://perma.cc/R6GH-ZRXN)

40 Shang, N and Breiman, L (n.d.) Born again trees, University of California, Berkley, www. stat.berkeley.edu/~breiman/BAtrees.pdf (archived at https://perma.cc/849D-5DM4)

42,122 Galli, S (2017) Machine learning at Zopa: Looking at the trees and the forests, Zopa Limited, 13 February, blog.zopa.com/2017/02/13/Tree-MachineLearning-Post/ (archived at https://perma.cc/9AMY-FDZJ)

44,45 Liaw, A and Weiner, M (2002) Classification and Regression by randomForest, *R News*, 2 (3), 18–22 (December)

46 Bellhouse, D R (2004) The reverend Thomas Bayes, FRS: A Biography to Celebrate the Tercentenary of His Birth, *Statistical Science*, 19, 3–43

47,48 Jøsang, A (2016) Generalising Bayes' Theorem in Subjective Logic, in IEEE International Conference on Multisensor Fusion and Integration for Intelligent Systems, Baden-Baden (September)

49,50 Wiggins, C (2006) What is Bayes's theorem, and how can it be used to assign probabilities to questions such as the existence of God? What scientific value does it have?, *Scientific American*, 4 December, www.scientificamerican.com/article/what-is-bayess-theorem-an/ (archived at https://perma.cc/CT9B-WC38)

51 Spiegelhalter, D J, Myles, J P, Jones. D R and Abrams, K R (2000) Bayesian Methods in Health Technology Assessment: A Review, *Health Technology Assessment*, 4 (38), 5–15 (December)

52,53 Reuters (2016) Facebook stymies Admiral's plans to use social media data to price insurance premiums, 2 November, www.reuters.com/article/us-insurance-admiral-facebook-idUSKBN12X1WP (archived at https://perma.cc/5BE4-59RJ)

54,55 Admiral Group plc (2020) Black Box, www.admiral.com/black-box-insurance (archived at https://perma.cc/ZN4G-DDWQ)

56 McClenahan, C L (2001) Ratemaking, in *Foundations of Casualty Actuarial Science*, 4th edition, Casualty Actuarial Society, Arlington, VA

57,59,60 Hollis, A and Strauss, J (2007) Insurance Markets when Firms are AsymmetricallyInformed: A Note, www.researchgate.net/publication/4822341_Insurance_Markets_When_Firms_Are_Asymmetrically_Informed_A_Note (archived at https://perma.cc/7VEB-GVCF)

58 RAC Motoring Services (2019) A Guide to Black Box Car Insurance, www.rac.co.uk/insurance/black-box-insurance/guide-to-black-box-insurance (archived at https://perma.cc/6M4D-EQTG)

61 Collinson, P (2019) Average UK car mileage falls again on back of higher petrol prices, *The Guardian*, 14 January, www.theguardian.com/money/2019/jan/14/average-uk-car-mileage-falls-again-on-back-of-higher-petrol-prices (archived at https://perma.cc/5NM2-PDR6)

62 Department of Transport (2019) Reported road casualties in Great Britain: 2018 annual report, assets.publishing.service.gov.uk/government/uploads/system/uploads/attachment_data/file/834585/reported-road-casualties-annual-report-2018.pdf (archived at https://perma.cc/E7UA-DS7P)

63 Admiral Group plc (2019) Home to the UK's safest drivers, 10 September, London, https://www.admiral.com/press-office/london-home-to-the-uks-safest-drivers (archived at https://perma.cc/LG4L-RLX4)

64 Zhang, H (2004) The Optimality Naive Bayes, in Proceedings of the Seventeenth International Florida Artificial Intelligence Research Society Conference, www.cs.unb.ca/~hzhang/publications/FLAIRS04ZhangH.pdf (archived at https://perma.cc/4XRV-ZSGT)

65 Domingos, P (2015) The Master Algorithm, Talks at Google [Video], www.youtube.com/watch?v=B8J4uefCQMc (archived at https://perma.cc/Y3V8-FM88)

66,70,71 Crammer, K and Singer, Y (2001) On the Algorithmic Implementation of Multiclass Kernel-based Vector Machines, *Journal of Machine Learning Research*, 2, 265–92

67 Cortes, C and Vapnik, V (1995) Support vector networks, *Journal of Machine Learning*, 20, 273–97

68 National Health Service (2019) What is the body mass index (BMI)?, www.nhs.uk/common-health-questions/lifestyle/what-is-the-body-mass-index-bmi/ (archived at https://perma.cc/Q57A-NSE5)

69 Adams, R, McIntyre, N and Weale, S (2019) GCSE results: girls fare better than boys under more rigorous courses, 22 August, www.theguardian.com/education/2019/aug/22/gcse-results-more-rigorous-courses-appear-to-benefit-girls (archived at https://perma.cc/75J7-JWVE)

72,73,74 Holland, J H (n.d.) Genetic Algorithms, Iowa State University, www2.econ.iastate.edu/tesfatsi/holland.gaintro.htm (archived at https://perma.cc/L2CY-MLB3)

75,76 Walker, M (2001) Introduction to Genetic Programming, Montana State University, www.cs.montana.edu/~bwall/cs580/introduction_to_gp.pdf (archived at https://perma.cc/L87P-RHZW)

78,79 Chudler, E H (2019) Types of neurons (Nerve Cells), University of Washington, faculty.washington.edu/chudler/cells.html (archived at https://perma.cc/TH4F-RPKE)

80,81 University of Bristol (2011) Brain basics: The fundamentals of neuroscience, 27 September, www.bris.ac.uk/synaptic/basics/basics-0.html (archived at https://perma.cc/S3FJ-LU5Q)

82,83,87,88,89 Hardesty, L (2017) Explained: Neural networks, MIT News, 14 April, news.mit.edu/2017/explained-neural-networks-deep-learning-0414 (archived at https://perma.cc/2Y69-LTW8)

85 Rojas, R (1996) *Neural Networks – A Systematic Introduction*, Springer, Berlin

86 Microsoft Azure (2019) Deep learning vs. machine learning, 8 July, docs.microsoft.com/en-us/azure/machine-learning/service/concept-deep-learning-vs-machine-learning (archived at https://perma.cc/QMW3-HUTU)

90 Babel, B, Buehler, K, Pivonka, A, Richardson, B and Waldron, D (2019) Derisking machine learning and artificial intelligence, McKinsey & Company, www.mckinsey.com/business-functions/risk/our-insights/derisking-machine-learning-and-artificial-intelligence (archived at https://perma.cc/US7E-TYBY)

92 Gandomi, A and Haider, M (2015) Beyond the hype: Big data concepts, methods, and analytics, *International Journal of Information Management*, 35, 137–44

93,94 Jeffries R (2011) What is Extreme Programming? 14 March, ronjeffries.com/xprog/what-is-extreme-programming/ (archived at https://perma.cc/6M6Q-RFWV)

95,102,103,104,105 London, S, Chui, M and Wigley, C (2019) The ethics of artificial intelligence [interview], McKinsey & Company, www.mckinsey.com/featured-insights/artificial-intelligence/the-ethics-of-artificial-intelligence (archived at https://perma.cc/V5Y8-5LYA)

96,97,98 Gama, J, Žliobaitė, I, Bifet, A, Pechenizkiy, M and Bouchachia, A (2014) A survey on concept drift adaptation, *ACM Computing Surveys*, 46 (4), (March)

99,100,101 Stricker, M, Wang, S and Strommen, S J (2014) Model Validation for Insurance Enterprise Risk and Capital Models, Casualty Actuarial Society, Canadian Institute of Actuaries & Society of Actuaries Joint Risk Management Section, www.soa.org/globalassets/assets/Files/Research/Projects/research-2014-model-valid-ins.pdf (archived at https://perma.cc/SC4G-GJCW)

108 Deloitte LLP (2017) How to flourish in an uncertain future: Open Banking and PSD2, www2.deloitte.com/uk/en/pages/financial-services/articles/future-banking-open-banking-psd2-flourish-in-uncertainty.html (archived at https://perma.cc/4VDT-AZXY)

109,110 HM Government (2018) Government response to House of Lords Artificial Intelligence Select Committee's Report on AI in the UK: Ready, Willing and Able, www.parliament.uk/documents/lords-committees/Artificial-Intelligence/AI-Government-Response2.pdf (archived at https://perma.cc/FEN2-8CSR)

111,112 Soares, N (2016) The Value Learning Problem, in Ethics for Artificial Intelligence Workshop at 25th International Joint Conference on Artificial Intelligence, Machine Intelligence Research Institute, intelligence.org/files/ValueLearningProblem.pdf (archived at https://perma.cc/K9CW-N2PC)

113,115 Zopa Limited (2019) Our story, www.zopa.com/about/our-story (archived at https://perma.cc/CW5T-ABU7)

114 Halton, C (2019) Zone of Possible Agreement (Zopa), Investopedia, 14 June, www. investopedia.com/terms/z/zoneofpossibleagreement.asp (archived at https://perma.cc/ AS8V-LWUQ)

116,117,119 Zopa Limited (2019) Peer-to-peer investing, www.zopa.com/invest (archived at https://perma.cc/N38C-VFXZ)

118 Zopa Limited (2019) About Zopa, www.zopa.com/about (archived at https://perma. cc/6V78-YUT2)

120,121 Steinthaler, M (2018) Whose data is it anyway? Open Banking, PSD2 and what it means for you, Zopa Limited, 12 January, blog.zopa.com/2018/01/12/whose-data-anyway-open-banking-psd2-means/ (archived at https://perma.cc/637Y-MHVR)

05

Bitcoin, blockchain and cryptocurrencies

The applications of distributed ledger technology in finance

LEARNING OBJECTIVES

This chapter aims to help you understand:

- How blockchain technology works and why it is useful.
- How this technology can be leveraged with smart contracts.
- Some of the practical considerations concerning the use of blockchain.

Introduction

The terms blockchain, cryptocurrency and Bitcoin entered the mainstream of public discourse sometime around the year 2016. Like AI and machine learning, these terms are readily thrown around by pundits, business leaders and policymakers alike, often with very little understanding of their meaning. As a result, the public conversation surrounding blockchain is, at best, facile.

As a remedy, this chapter seeks to help the reader build a foundational understanding of blockchain technology, how it works and why it is useful. To this end, we will examine Bitcoin at great length: as of 2019, Bitcoin was the most widespread and well-known example of blockchain technology in use. As a digital currency system, Bitcoin is a monetary application of blockchain technology.

In this way, Bitcoin is to blockchain what neural networks are to machine learning: in seeking a thorough understanding of the sub-category (ie Bitcoin, neural networks), one implicitly gains some knowledge of the wider domain (ie blockchain, machine learning). This is not to say that everything concerning Bitcoin is directly relevant to all blockchain applications. Rather, a firm grasp of Bitcoin will give the reader the basic knowledge, and crucially, the confidence to learn more about other blockchain systems.

When learning about blockchain, most non-technical readers find themselves frustrated by jargon, or worse, code that they do not understand. The aim of this chapter is to remove some of these stumbling blocks. In this way, the reader's curiosity is not frustrated at the outset, thereby facilitating the journey of learning.

One of the first stumbling blocks on this journey is the overlap in meaning of the following terms: blockchain, Bitcoin, distributed ledger and cryptocurrency. To be clear, blockchain and distributed ledger technology (DLT) mean the same thing. For this reason, they are often used interchangeably, which can be confusing; as this chapter progresses the origin of each term will become clear.

As previously mentioned, Bitcoin is an example of blockchain technology used as a currency system; this application is known as a cryptocurrency, which takes its name from cryptography, the technology underpinning the security, privacy and integrity of these systems. Of the few thousand cryptocurrencies in existence today, Bitcoin is the largest, by market capitalization, as well as the most widely traded.[1]

The genesis of Bitcoin

In the autumn of 2008, someone by the name of Satoshi Nakamoto published an online paper called *Bitcoin: a peer-to-peer electronic cash system*.[2] This paper, which has become known as the Bitcoin White Paper, would become seminal not only to Bitcoin, but blockchain technology itself. To this day, the identity of Nakamoto remains uncertain, and it is not officially known whether the Bitcoin White Paper was authored by a single individual or a collective.

The Bitcoin White Paper was published at the height of the 2007–09 financial crisis, a time when a failing banking system, plain for all to see, threatened to collapse the global economy. Indeed, Nakamoto makes passing references to some of the banking system's inherent flaws (see below). However, most of the ideas contained in the White Paper were not new. Rather, Bitcoin is an amalgamation of economics, computing and cryptography. Thus, Nakamoto merely combined these to create an alternative currency system.

By inventing Bitcoin, Nakamoto conceptualized a decentralized record-keeping system, which has become known as a blockchain. Though it is the case for Bitcoin, the information stored on a blockchain does not need to concern financial transactions. Thus, the key difference between Bitcoin and non-currency blockchain systems is that Bitcoin is used to transfer digital representations of value between users. This point and its significance are elaborated on below (see 'From Bitcoin to blockchain').

Following the publication of the Bitcoin White Paper, an open source community of cryptographers and software engineers came together to develop Bitcoin, which was launched in 2009. The first real-world purchase using Bitcoin is said to have occurred in May 2010, when a software developer paid a friend 10,000 Bitcoins in exchange for two pizzas.[3] Since then, Bitcoin has appreciated significantly, reaching an all-time high just below $20,000 in December 2017.[4]

Bitcoin has gone through several boom–bust cycles over the years. Since its 2017 peak, the price of Bitcoin fell below US$3,200 in December 2018[5] – a decline of *ca* 84 per cent in the space of a year. Despite this volatility, Bitcoin remains the most liquid and widely used cryptocurrency.[6]

Furthermore, individual Bitcoins can be sub-divided as far as eight decimal places.[7] This means the last decimal place would represent US$1 if the price per Bitcoin were US$100 million. As a result, higher Bitcoin prices do not matter so much, as users can simply transact in progressively smaller denominations as Bitcoin prices rise; in addition, if Bitcoin's price were to reach unusable levels, the number of decimal places could be increased via a network update.[8]

A decentralized currency system

To understand how Bitcoin works, it is best to start by contrasting it with the current banking system. Within this system, most significant transactions are digital, certainly in developed countries; cash is still used, of course, but this tends to be for smaller, relatively immaterial transactions, or for transactions where a physical good or service is rendered on, or before, payment, such as when buying a coffee or getting a haircut.

Unlike cash payments, digital transactions are intangible: at their core, digital transactions involve no more than changing numbers on a screen. When you send money to someone, you're not actually sending them anything; rather, you are increasing the balance in their bank account via the transmission of electrical signals.

For the sake of the financial system's integrity, no one can be allowed to spend their digital currency more than once (which is akin to sending the same email to multiple people); for this reason, the financial system relies on intermediaries to regulate and verify transactions between its users.[9] For example, when a business pays a supplier, it has proof, in the form of a bank statement, that payment has been made. At the same time, the supplier can confirm receipt of the payment by checking its bank accounts.

Consider then, what happens in the absence of banks. When the business makes a payment, how can it prove that this has been made? What is stopping the supplier from claiming, falsely, that payment has not been received? Why should the different parties trust one other?

In this way, the system is dependent on banks acting as trusted intermediaries:[10] though neither party in a transaction may trust the other, both trust that their respective banks will resolve disputes quickly and fairly. To this end, banks have inter-bank mechanisms for resolving disputes, which greatly increases the degree of confidence that both transacting parties can place in their respective bank statements.

Just as businesses look to their banks for transaction verification, banks rely on central banks to verify inter-bank transactions.[11] Banks have accounts with their respective country's central bank, which allows them to settle inter-bank transactions on behalf of their customers on a net basis.[12] As a result, the responsibility of verifying transactions ultimately falls on the central bank.

Nakamoto recognized that this degree of centralization places a significant amount of power in the hands of one entity, which controls 'the fate of the entire money system… with every transaction having to go through them'.[13] They saw this centralization as problematic,[14] presumably because such concentration of power can lead to corruption and policy errors which can adversely affect the entire financial system: indeed, the first mined block of Bitcoin (see explanation below) contained the following text: 'The Times 03/Jan/2009 Chancellor on brink of second bailout for banks' – a reference to the financial crisis via the front page of *The Times* on the date that Bitcoin was born.[15]

As a remedy, Nakamoto proposed a currency system wherein users transact over a decentralized network: rather than relying on banks – and by extension, central banks – to act as trusted intermediaries, this system would rely on a software protocol.[16] Simply put, a software protocol is a framework, enshrined in code, that governs interactions between network participants. Consenting to these rules is easy: as Bitcoin is an open-source network, one can participate by downloading and running the Bitcoin protocol.[17]

The code that runs the Bitcoin and the network's transaction history are freely accessible via the internet.[18] As a result, the network's users can observe the rules that govern their interactions. Thus, no one can falsely claim that they have sent, or not received, a payment if the network's transaction history indicates otherwise. This transparency means that users rely on the integrity of the system for transaction verification rather than financial intermediaries. Such transparency is paramount in all blockchain networks.

Bitcoin is a peer-to-peer network.[19] Structurally, this means that it is similar to an online file-sharing network. Such networks enable its users to download content, such as music and video files, from the computers of other connected users. These networks have proven difficult to shut down because the same files are stored in many different locations on each network:[20] if one attempts to download a file from a location that goes offline, the download simply continues from another location.

Blockchain networks are similarly distributed.[21] The Bitcoin network stores all its transactions in one database across multiple locations throughout the world. In this way, blockchain networks are distributed. Thus, the banking system would be comparable to Bitcoin if banks were to combine their books (aka their ledgers) into one database, and then each hold a copy of this same ledger separately. Such a system can be described as a distributed ledger, which is synonymous to a blockchain;[22] the etymology of this term will become clearer as we go.

Bitcoin transactions in practice

To send and receive Bitcoin, users do not need to install and run the Bitcoin software. Instead, they can download what's called a wallet app, which interacts with the network on their behalf.[23] A multitude of cryptocurrency wallets are available, developed independently from the Bitcoin community; often, these are designed to hold multiple cryptocurrencies.

A cryptocurrency wallet functions much like an email application.[24] Whereas, e-mail users send messages to each other's e-mail addresses, Bitcoin users send funds to each other's *public addresses*. To authenticate messages, an e-mail user enters a password; similarly, a Bitcoin user authenticates transactions with a private key. Thus, transacting in Bitcoin is comparable to sending money via e-mail.[25] This comparison is particularly cogent because similar cryptographic methods underpin both e-mail and blockchain technology.

As Bitcoin users transact over a network (as opposed to relying on an intermediary), it is more cash-like than other digital payment solutions.[26] This is further underpinned by the fact that Bitcoin transactions are, by and large, irreversible:[27] once you hand over cash, it is up to the recipient whether they return it to you, just as getting Bitcoin returned to the sender relies on the good will of the recipient. As a result, transacting in Bitcoin is akin to transacting in cash. When paying someone in cash, you have to be almost certain that they will render the product or service as promised because the transaction is difficult to reverse. Similarly, transacting in Bitcoin puts an onus on the buyer to conduct proper due diligence before surrendering their Bitcoin. In practice, this is less severe than it sounds. For example, when buying a coffee in a cafe, one can observe the barista making the coffee.

Authenticating Bitcoin transactions

Each private key is known only to its user and is linked to the user's public address. However, there is no way of using the public address to obtain the private key. This is because the public address is generated from the private key via a computational process known as hashing (see box below).[28] As hashing processes are irreversible, users can share their public addresses without fear of revealing their private keys.

Private keys are used to authenticate transactions, and so controlling a private key determines ownership of the Bitcoin in its associated address. If you forget or lose your private key, it cannot be recovered, and the Bitcoin is lost;[29] likewise, if someone discovers your private key, they can steal your Bitcoin by sending it to a public address that they control. Worse yet, they can do so anonymously because each public address is merely a string of number and digits, without any personal information attached to it.

The non-recoverability of private keys makes Bitcoin transactions similar to physical currency, in that the person who holds the private key owns the Bitcoin. As a result, the private key is, in essence, an authentication mechanism, which allows users to confer ownership of their funds onto other users: when sending Bitcoin, users sign over control of their funds to a recipient, as identified by a public address. This effectively puts a lock on the Bitcoin, which can only be unlocked (and therefore spent) by the user who has the private key associated with the receiving address.[30] In this way, when sending Bitcoin to someone's address, a user is really saying 'if you have the private key associated with your address, you can spend the Bitcoin'.

The sender affixes a unique signature to each transaction, which is generated by hashing together: the sender's private key, the recipient's address, the sender's address and, crucially, the signature pertaining to the transaction which conferred the Bitcoin onto the sender.[31] This establishes a chain of ownership between the current owner and all previous users of the Bitcoin,[32] which underpins its value: just as establishing the provenance of an artwork helps prove its authenticity, linking one's Bitcoin to a chain of previous owners via the signature mechanism helps prove its scarcity, and thereby its value.

HASHING AND ITS ROLE IN CRYPTOGRAPHY

The branch of mathematics concerned with obscuring information in order to keep it secure is known as *cryptography*. Its name is derived from Greek and means 'hidden writing'.[33] Thus, the basic meaning of related words like encryption and its inverse, decryption, become clear: hiding and unhiding.

Hashing is a core part of many cryptographic processes because it enables users to share certain pieces of information without revealing linked pieces of private information, such as a public address and its associated private key. This has to do with the fact that hashing processes are irreversible.[34]

To understand why, it is best to start with an analogy. Simply put, hashing is a mathematical way of turning a string of characters (ie information) into a completely unrecognizable string of characters. However, there is no way of devising the input from the output. This makes hashing analogous to making a pancake: once the pancake is made, it is effectively impossible to turn it back into its original ingredients (milk, flour, eggs, etc).

In addition, a hashed output is the same length regardless of the length of the input. For example, the Secure-Hash-Algorithm (SHA) 256, which is a core part of Bitcoin's encryption processes,[35] returns a string of 64 characters.[36] In this way, whether you input a single letter or Tolstoy's *War and Peace* (a very long book), the hashing algorithm returns a string of 64 characters. Furthermore, if you change so much as a comma in *War and Peace*, the hashed output will look entirely different from that of the original book. Thus, the hashed output tells us nothing about its input.

As a result, there is no way of using the output of a hashing algorithm to find the original input. In fact, guessing is the most efficient way of finding the input, computationally speaking. In the context of Bitcoin, this makes it (nearly) impossible to find the private key given the public address: as the randomly generated private key contains 64 characters (A–F, 0–9),[37] it is said that there are more private key combinations than the number of atoms in the universe.[38] As a result, guessing someone's private key is much, much more difficult than finding a needle in a haystack. Even with a supercomputer, this would take an unfathomable amount of time to find,[39] making it onerously expensive and so effectively impossible, economically speaking.[40]

As mentioned above, the irreversibility of hashing processes is what enables a Bitcoin user to share their public address and transaction-specific signature without revealing the private key from which both were derived. Thus, the integrity of the Bitcoin network relies on users' ability to authenticate transactions without sharing their private keys.

Also important is the fact that each user's signature and public address have, as part of their genesis, the user's private key in common. Given that each hashed output is unique to its input, each transaction can thus be verified by proving that a signature–public address pair were generated using the same private key.[41] In other words, the signature mechanism allows users to prove that they are in possession of the private key linked to a public address, without revealing said key.[42]

This process relies on advanced algebra: in essence, the public address and signature will only fit into the same mathematical proof if they come from the same private key.[43] How this works is beyond the scope of this book (for more information see Antonopoulos (2017). Computationally speaking, this process makes it easy for the Bitcoin network to verify transactions as fake signatures are readily identifiable.

Thus, hashing algorithms are an important component of the encryption processes underpinning both e-mail and blockchain technology; of course, most e-mail users are unaware of this because their private keys lie hidden beneath a user interface. This is because the e-mail application stores each user's private key, which is what allows users' passwords to be recovered if lost; similarly, many cryptocurrency wallets have password recovery features enabled by the application storing its users' private keys. This makes transacting in cryptocurrency somewhat more user-friendly as users can, and will, lose their passwords, and thus will need to reset them from time to time.

How the Bitcoin network reconciles differences

Blockchain networks are maintained by a multitude of computers, known as network nodes. In the context of Bitcoin, these nodes, which log the network's transactions and maintain an up-to-date copy of its ledger, are known as miners.[44] As blockchain networks are distributed geographically, different users transact concurrently in different parts of the network. Without some reconciliation mechanism, this means that different ledgers will emerge in different parts of the network. As a remedy, transactions are stored in batches, called 'blocks' which are arranged chronologically.[45] This puts the word 'block' into blockchain.

In theory, different miners could take turns adding the next block; that is, if they were to trust each other completely, which is the case in some private blockchain networks. However, in open-source blockchain networks, like Bitcoin, this is not the case: as these networks allow anyone to join,[46] they require a mechanism for establishing trust; in the context of Bitcoin, this mechanism relies on the assumption that individual miners are self-serving. In this way, the Bitcoin network maintains its integrity (and thereby user trust) via the alignment of the system's incentives such that individual miners keep an accurate and up-to-date ledger as a by-product of pursuing their own interests.[47]

In the context of Bitcoin, miners reconcile their ledgers by competing for the right to add the next block of transactions to the blockchain.[48] To win this right, a miner needs to generate a hashed output that begins with a certain number of zeros.[49] As part of this, the miners combine their logged transactions, a hash of the previous block, plus a random input, and run these through a hashing algorithm.[50] As the hashed output changes according to each new input, the miner's best hope, computationally speaking, is to repeat this process as many times as possible by guessing randomly.

In addition, an output preceded by, say, 10 zeros, takes more guesses to generate, than one preceded by two zeros. For a demonstration of this, try

FIGURE 5.1 Blockchain linkages

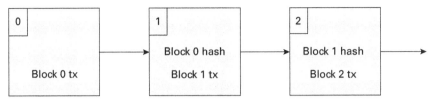

As each block in the blockchain contains a hash of all the information in the previous block, it is impossible to change anything in the transaction history without changing all subsequent hashes.

typing random strings of text into an online hashing generator, and see how long it takes you to produce just two or three zeros in a row. Thus, generating the required output consumes a significant amount of processing power.

The more computing power a miner has, the more hashes it can make, and so the greater its likelihood of adding the next block. As a result, miners that expend more energy are more likely to add each new block, and thereby more likely to build the longest chain. Of course, this expense is not for naught: when a miner adds a new block, it is rewarded with newly issued Bitcoins. This is why the network-maintaining computers are called miners; because their activities are akin to gold miners who consume energy and hardware (ie 'work') in search of a financial reward: as a result, the hashed output that allows a miner to add their block to the blockchain is called a *proof of work*.[51]

The proof-of-work mechanism ensures that each block contains a hash of the information in the previous block, including that block's proof of work.[52] This ensures that each new block – and by extension, each new transaction – is consistent with all prior transactions; thus it becomes impossible to change anything about the network's transaction history without alerting the rest of the network, as changing so much as a comma will make all subsequent hashes look completely different.[53] In this way, the linking of blocks via hashes puts the 'chain' into blockchain.

How the Bitcoin network stays honest

When a miner finds a proof of work, it announces this to the rest of the network. The other miners must then verify the transactions in the miner's block: if each transaction contains a valid public address–signature pair, the miner is allowed to add their block to the blockchain.[54]

Before they can go on to look for the next proof of work, each competing miner must verify the transactions in the winner's block.[55] As stated above, this is done by proving that the signatures and public addresses for each transaction fit together, algebraically speaking; any invalid transactions will cause the entire block to be rejected,[56] which results in the 'winner' foregoing the financial reward of adding their block to the blockchain.

Thus, there is an incentive on the part of miners to log only valid transactions, lest they lose out, financially speaking, when they find a proof of work. Furthermore, there is an onus on competing miners to verify the winning miner's block quickly and truthfully, as they want to get on to looking for the next proof of work; if they waste time disputing valid transactions, the honest miners will get ahead of them in the race to find the next proof of work. As a result, honest nodes are incentivized to log and verify only valid transactions, knowing that other nodes are subject to the same incentives.

The importance of self-interest in maintaining the integrity of the system becomes clearer when viewed in the context of the Bitcoin network's core principle: that the longest chain is the valid one.[57] On the surface, this notion may seem absurd. What if someone builds a fraudulent, yet longer chain?

To do so, one would need to command a majority of the network's computing power. This would make a dishonest node more likely to mine a succession of proofs of work, thus enabling it to stack blocks of fraudulent transactions and build the longest chain; if one does not control the majority of the network's processing power, the honest nodes are simply more likely to build and maintain the longest chain.[58]

The reason the longest-chain principle is so powerful is that, even if a miner were to gain control over a majority of the network's processing power, it would still be incentivized to remain honest.[59] To understand why, let's consider what would happen if someone were to acquire a majority of the network's computing power in order to steal everyone's Bitcoin: 1) all Bitcoin would become worthless overnight as the currency's value rests on the integrity of the network; and 2) the value of the expensive, and over-specialized, hardware used to subvert the system would be significantly impaired. Thus, the longest-chain principle ensures that miners with enough processing power to subvert the system also have the most to lose by doing so, and therefore have more to gain by defending the integrity of the system.[60]

Alternative reconciliation mechanisms

As an incentives-based system, proof of work is necessary in the context of Bitcoin because network participants – nodes and users alike – do not trust each other. This is because Bitcoin is a permissionless blockchain; an open-source blockchain network which anyone can join. Thus, in the complete absence of a vetting mechanism, individual nodes cannot be trusted to act in any other way than that which serves their financial interests.

Alternatives to proof of work do exist for permissionless blockchain networks. For example, under the proof-of-stake model, nodes gain the right to add blocks by vesting cryptocurrency within the system;[61] thus, if your stake amounts to 5 per cent of the cryptocurrency vested, you get to mine 5 per cent of the blocks. In this way, nodes with a greater financial interest in maintaining the integrity of the system are able to exercise a greater degree of control over the evolution of the ledger.

As there are many different blockchain networks and cryptocurrencies in existence, hybrids of these two models do exist – along with a few other, alternative approaches. Crucially though, all permissionless blockchain protocols attempt to align the interests of their users (eg network integrity, security, etc) with the financial interests of the nodes maintaining the network (ie the miners).

The potential conflict of interest between users and nodes is less of a problem in private blockchain networks, the so-called permissioned systems. In these networks, the nodes trust one another, and so there is no need for incentives-based reconciliation mechanisms. This is because the permissioned blockchain networks are managed professionally, usually by a consortium of management consultancies, technology companies and banks. By working together, the sponsoring firms trust the consortium just as they would trust a bank or IT vendor.

As a result, individual nodes in a permissioned network do not need a direct financial incentive to stay honest; rather the participants in the system provide sufficient scrutiny to maintain the network's integrity.[62] In this way, the network does not need to expend resources on a reconciliation mechanism and can thus devote more processing power to verifying and logging transactions. A good example of this is RippleNet, a blockchain network run by Ripple, a start-up backed by the likes of Accenture, Santander and Standard Chartered.[63] As RippleNet is a trust-based network, it can support 1,500 transactions per second, which is multiples of Bitcoin's 3–6 transactions per second.[64]

Why Bitcoin is useful as a cryptocurrency

Though the above provides an explanation of *how* Bitcoin works, it may still be unclear to the reader *why* it works. Learning about Bitcoin is a bit like assembling a jigsaw puzzle; by combining the individual pieces – each easily understood on their own – the bigger picture starts to make sense. To this end, it is useful to summarize:

- The distributed structure of the network helps ensure its robustness and integrity by virtue of having no nexus of control.
- As no one controls the network, it is difficult to corrupt or attack.
- The network's transaction history and source code are freely available for all to see online, which ensures its transparency.
- This transparency means that participants can observe (and thereby trust) the network's rules as opposed to relying on intermediaries.
- It also means that users cannot falsely claim that they have not sent or received a payment.
- Secure authentication mechanisms allow users to approve transactions without compromising their privacy.
- As a result, network participants rely on the integrity of the system rather than the good faith of their counterparties.
- This integrity is maintained by incentive structures that align miners' financial interests with activities that promote the network's integrity.

These facets allow Bitcoin users to transact digitally as if they were transacting in cash. Thus, Nakamoto's description of Bitcoin as an electronic cash system[65] is cogent: Bitcoin is useful because, like cash, it gives its users the option of transacting, and indeed, storing their wealth, outside the financial system.

People living in countries with relatively low inflation and stable national currencies, may not see the attraction of this. However, for residents of countries suffering from hyperinflation, such as Venezuela,[66] holding Bitcoin may have clear benefits. In such circumstances, storing your savings in Bitcoin becomes preferable to suffering inflation rates above 300,000 per cent,[67] even when Bitcoin's market value declines more than 80 per cent in the space of year, as was the case during 2018.[68]

Furthermore, human rights activists, freelance journalists and other political dissidents living under kleptocratic and authoritarian regimes, might find a use in Bitcoin as it allows them to transact outside their countries' financial systems. In this way, those seeking to curtail their activities cannot eliminate their access to finance. In addition, the inherent anonymity of Bitcoin allows these dissidents to keep their financial activities hidden from their governments; after all, the only thing linking a person to their Bitcoin address is knowledge of their private key: to protect their anonymity, privacy-minded users can use new addresses for every transaction.[69]

Finally, Bitcoin, and by extension, cryptocurrencies, has the potential to promote greater financial inclusion as it enables anyone, anywhere with an internet connection to transact globally. For the estimated 2 billion people without access to formal financial services, this can facilitate greater access to economic opportunities, and thus reduce poverty in developing countries.[70]

From Bitcoin to blockchain

The shorthand description of Bitcoin as 'money by e-mail'[71] is telling, not only because each technology relies on similar cryptographic methods, but also because it touches on an important truth: that financial transactions are merely transfers of information. When we send someone an e-mail, we are, in essence, adding information to their inbox; similarly, when we send Bitcoin, or indeed any blockchain-based digital currency, we are merely adding to the recipient's balance.

Thus, Bitcoins do not, in fact, exist. Rather, what does exist, is the network's record of transactions. Thus, the only transfer that takes place is a transfer of information. Because computers can process vast quantities of information, the technology has applications in domains which require secure, yet transparent authentication mechanisms, which broadens the scope of blockchain's potential applications to areas such as insurance and capital markets.[72]

Smart contracts

As blockchain transactions are, fundamentally speaking, information transfers, the technology has use-cases in domains that are not, strictly speaking, financial; in this way, there is no need for blockchain tokens, such as Bitcoin, as these are merely artefacts of user transactions. Instead, the transparency, secure authentication mechanisms and robustness of blockchain networks can facilitate all manner of user interactions. Specifically, blockchain technology may find use-cases in areas involving information transfers.

In this regard, smart contracts appear particularly promising. A smart contract is a programme that carries out the terms of a legal contract, if and when its provisions are met. Thus, a smart contract is, in essence, a self-executing legal contract. This idea is not new; in fact, many people engage with smart contracts on a regular basis. The vending machine is a commonplace example of this: it takes payment and, subject to receiving the requisite amount of money, renders the product to the consumer.[73]

Smart contracts can be combined with blockchain technology to enhance the transparency, security and integrity of information transfers between users. Just as people rely on cryptocurrencies to transact financially, the same underlying blockchain technology enables them to transact informationally. In the context of smart contracts, this means that users can confirm that contractual provisions have been met with their private keys, thereby triggering the execution of the contract.

Thus, if there is a routine process, which relies on one or more signoffs, lacks transparency and is time-consuming, then it can likely be facilitated by a blockchain-based, smart contract. As a result, there are potential applications in areas such as securities trading, regulatory reporting and risk management.[74] In addition, Blockchain-enabled smart contracts could disrupt clerical sectors such as law, accountancy and finance by reducing the amount of professional time required for intermediary-based processes.[75] By one estimate, this could reduce the overall cost base in banking by 27 per cent.[76]

Smart contracts are not without their pitfalls. As blockchain applications allow users to transact anonymously over the internet, this limits the enforceability of smart contracts via the courts. In addition, as these contracts are self-executing, there is a question surrounding their applicability in cases of fraud or error: if a private key is stolen and used to trigger a contract, is the victim still bound by the contract? Thus, the widespread use of smart contracts will require updates to existing contract law.[77]

This raises an important point in regard to new technologies: they do not exist in isolation. As a result, they cannot be applied in a business context without considering the surrounding legal and regulatory context. As these are still evolving, it is likely that the first applications of blockchain-enabled smart contracts will be within organizations, or between organizations working cooperatively behind the scenes. In other words, in domains with considerably less legal and reputational risk than customer-facing areas.

CASE STUDY
Generali Group: Blockchain-based insurance

The Generali Group is a global insurance company headquartered in Italy. It has *ca* 61 million customers. Generali's core business is in life, property and casualty insurance. In 2018, it collected insurance premiums amounting to 67 billion euros.[78]

One of the group's subsidiaries, Generali Employee Benefits (GEB), specializes in work-based insurance solutions for multinational companies. GEB helps these companies provide their employees with insurance including life, accident and health cover. Generali is a global leader in this sub-sector: it has *ca* 1,500 multinational clients and is active in more than 100 countries.[79]

As part of its offering, GEB provides captive insurance services. To aggregate and provide for the risks facing their subsidiaries, international companies form internal insurance companies, called *captives*. By catering exclusively to its own group of companies, a captive enables more cost-effective and flexible insurance cover for the group's employees. In addition, insurance captives allow their parent companies to retain underwriting profits and gains on invested reserves.[80]

Furthermore, captives enable groups to pool their employees' risks, thereby achieving economies of scale.[81] In this way, they protect individual subsidiaries from unpredictable increases in the cost of providing insurance cover. In the wake of a workplace accident, such as a factory fire killing several employees, the individual subsidiary would be faced with significantly higher insurance premiums. However, for a large multinational, a localized event like this would make little difference to the overall cost of insuring its employees on a global scale: the losses stemming from freak accidents would likely be offset by lower than expected accident rates in other areas.

Running an insurance company with tens, if not hundreds, of thousands of insured people, spread across multiple jurisdictions is not an easy task. In addition, multinationals specializing in non-financial sectors may not have the expertise, or inclination, to manage their own insurance captives. As a result, they employ companies like GEB to do it for them.

In practice, GEB's captive insurance service works as follows: the client's subsidiaries buy insurance on behalf of their employees from local insurance companies affiliated with GEB.[82] Then, Generali takes on the risks of these policies by undertaking to pay their claims in exchange for their premiums.[83] In this way, the local insurers effectively manage each policy (a service for which they receive a small part of the premium), while the insurance risk is ceded back to Generali. This process is known as reinsurance.

GEB pools the insurance policies into a global book, collecting premiums and recompensing local insurers for claims paid. On a periodic basis, Generali pays the captive a dividend, provided that premium income exceeds claims and other expenses; if claims exceed certain pre-defined thresholds, they are charged against captive's capital.[84] This means that the insurance risk ultimately sits with the client's captive, and not GEB.

According to Generali, its captive insurance solution has more to offer than economies of scale and convenient access to insurance expertise: GEB consolidates information about underlying policies and reports this back to the insurance captive.[85] In theory, this allows clients to detect global patterns and identity outliers, which, in turn, should facilitate better oversight, risk management and sharing of best practice.

In 2019, Generali announced the launch of a blockchain-based captive insurance solution with the expressed aim of streamlining GEB's operating model by integrating different stakeholders' systems, data and processes. This announcement followed a successful prototype, developed in conjunction with Accenture, which involved Syngenta, a multinational agriculture company, and local insurers in Serbia, Spain and Switzerland.[86]

Speaking of the solution, Andrea Pontoni, GEB's Chief Operating Officer, said: 'The use of this technology eliminates the need for a central authority or intermediary to process, validate or authenticate data exchanges... [it] enables the stakeholders... to share and synchronize both contractual agreements and underlying data.'[87]

Generali's solution is inspired by B3i, a collaborative effort led by a collection of large insurance companies with the aim of exploring applications of blockchain technology.[88] Set up in 2018, B3i is owned by a group of insurance market participants from around the world, which includes Generali.[89] It aims to enable 'frictionless risk transfer' in an insurance industry still held back by legacy work-flows dominated by e-mail and telephone-based processes.[90]

In 2019, B3i launched a blockchain-based reinsurance solution for catastrophe insurers that enables them to: negotiate and structure reinsurance contracts; send messages; share documents; and, track their status and surrounding workflows.[91] These features are important because insurance obligations (and premiums) are often shared between multiple reinsurers. B3i estimates that this solution could reduce the e-mail flow surrounding reinsurance transactions by as much as 90 per cent.[92]

How can the various facets of blockchain technology facilitate GEB's captive reinsurance processes?
(Suggested answer at the end of this chapter.)

Practical issues regarding blockchain and cryptocurrencies

Although blockchain technology holds great promise, there are several big-picture practical issues that must be addressed before rolling out a solution in a consumer or business context. In both domains, these primarily have to do with the usability and usefulness of blockchains. That said, there are also regulatory issues regarding their use, particularly in regard to money laundering and financing of terrorism[93] (for more on this, refer to Chapter 8).

As private keys cannot be reset, blockchains, at least in their purest form, are not consumer friendly. Consequently, bare-bones blockchain applications are probably more useful behind the scenes, away from the consumer, who can, and will, make mistakes. That said, irreversible hashes underpin e-mail technology, and yet we can reset e-mail passwords: this is because the private key is hidden beneath a user interface. Rather than trusting the consumer with a private key, the e-mail application stores it for us. When we lose our password, we can reset it via a quick message to our mobile phone or an alternative e-mail address.

In this way, e-mail user-interfaces are designed to prevent us from losing access permanently; after all, we humans are fallible. As a result, fintechs would do well to build their blockchain applications accordingly, and design them to assist users *when* they make mistakes, or, better yet, prevent them from making said mistakes in the first place. Thus, it is incumbent on any blockchain solution intended for mainstream use to have foolproof security processes, and an intuitive user interface (see Chapter 3).

The tendency of consumers to err is perhaps why so many of the enterprise blockchain applications seen before 2020 were deployed behind the scenes. For most organizations, consumer-facing areas are inherently risky as mistakes can come with a reputational cost. As a result, large organizations appear to be experimenting with blockchain technology for internal or behind-the-scenes applications first, as can be seen in the case study above. Similarly, in 2018, HSBC announced that it had successfully used blockchain to facilitate a trade finance transaction; crucially, the prototype transaction was a letter of credit concerning two subsidiaries of the same multinational client:[94] in other words, in a paper-laden area where the stakes were comparatively lower than its more consumer-facing business lines.

Although the usability of blockchain solutions can be enhanced somewhat by designing better user interfaces, there are issues regarding the *usefulness* of cryptocurrencies for mainstream adoption. The idea of an open-source, private currency system like Bitcoin is compelling because of its inherent monetary discipline: if there is no central authority to control the issuance of a currency and the laws concerning its use, its supply cannot be increased without its users switching into other, less inflationary, forms of money.[95] Therefore, if issuance exceeds the natural demand for a currency, its price will drop. That Bitcoin is a fixed-supply currency is perhaps a result of this reality. New issuance will cease once the supply of Bitcoin reaches 21 million:[96] at this point, the network's upkeep will be funded via transaction fees.[97]

Unfortunately, Bitcoin and its cryptocurrency peers have yet to reach mainstream adoption. This is not a failure of the free market; rather, it is because no functional cryptocurrency alternative to mainstream fiat currencies (ie dollars and euros) has emerged. For any asset to be useful as money, it must fulfil three functions: a medium of exchange, a unit of account, and a store of value.[98]

Cryptocurrencies are extremely volatile. This volatility gets in the way of their usefulness as money. If the value of an asset can change in the time between one agrees to a transaction and its completion, such as ordering pizza in a restaurant and paying for it post consumption, then it is not useful as a medium of exchange or, for that matter, a unit of account. Of course, dollars and euros are volatile as well. However, their volatility is much lower and generally goes unnoticed by day-to-day consumers as they get paid and have most of their expenditures in the same currency.

This leaves one monetary function for cryptocurrencies, as a store of value. In this regard, the usefulness of cryptocurrencies depends on two things: the users' holding period; and, the users' surrounding economic circumstances. For users who live in countries with stable countries, holding cryptocurrencies as a short–medium store of value may not appear attractive. However, as cryptocurrencies can be removed from the financial system, this gives them safe-haven properties, in that they are likely to hold value during times economic uncertainty. This effect was observed during the 2010–2013 Greek and Cypriot financial crisis, which saw an increase in local Bitcoin prices.[99]

As a result, there may be a case for holding cryptocurrencies on a long-term basis, as a hedge against economic, market and political uncertainty. This notion appears to be supported by empirical evidence, which suggests that Bitcoin, as a safe-haven asset, is something of a hybrid between gold and the dollar.[100] As a result, there may be a place for cryptocurrencies as part of a diversified portfolio of assets, on the assumption that troubled times will continue to produce volatile, yet upward increases in cryptocurrency values.

In theory, the volatility of cryptocurrencies should decline with more users and increasingly liquid markets. In the context of Bitcoin, this appears to be happening, in that its average volatility has come down somewhat since its inception.[101] That said, this volatility remains high: broadly speaking, the rolling 30-day average volatility has fluctuated between 1 per cent and 15 per cent since 2013.[102]

To reduce the volatility of a cryptocurrency, one could back its value with a more stable asset, such as gold. As a cryptocurrency is only ever worth what someone else is willing to pay for it, doing so would likely put its volatility on a par with that of the underlying asset. In this way, an asset-backed cryptocurrency would be akin to an exchange-traded fund (ETF), because this derives its value from its underlying assets.[103]

Moreover, asset-backed cryptocurrencies would have an inherent advantage over conventional asset-backed currencies in that they can be digitally sub-divided into smaller parts – unlike their underlying assets. In theory, this should prevent asset-backed currencies from becoming impractical to use if the value of their underlying assets rises faster than the price of goods and services. In these circumstances, users of an asset-backed cryptocurrency would merely need to transact in lower denominations in order to preserve their liquidity.

Asset-backed or not, permissionless (aka open-source) cryptocurrencies rely on a cohesive community of users, miners and developers. To implement network updates, a community must be able to align the interests of these stakeholders – in other words, it must have some modicum of governance. Unfortunately, the governance surrounding many cryptocurrencies has been lacking. As the largest cryptocurrency, Bitcoin is perhaps the most striking of example of this; over the years, network updates have been impeded by conflicts between miners, users and open-source developers.[104] As a result of such governance issues, the community has struggled to adapt the network to accommodate the increasing volume of users, which led to the separation of Bitcoin into two separate cryptocurrencies in 2017.[105]

The community politics and slow pace of change exhibited by some permissionless networks accentuate the appeal of permissioned systems: as centrally run private networks, they are run like IT vendors, complete with professional management, user support and periodic of software updates. R3 is a good example of such a network; as the firm behind Corda, an enterprise-level blockchain, it is run by 180 professionals who are supported by more than 2,000 technology, financial and legal experts.[106] These are drawn from R3's supporting institutions, which comprise organizations from various industries, as well as the public sector.[107]

Permissioned systems have an additional advantage in that they are more energy efficient than permissionless systems. It has been estimated that the Bitcoin network consumes as much electricity as the Republic of Ireland.[108] As this estimate is from 2014, it is likely that this footprint has since increased significantly. Trust-based permissioned systems do not have this problem as they do no need to invest energy in computationally intensive reconciliation processes such as proof of work.[109] Consequently, permissionless systems will require more energy-efficient reconciliation mechanisms to be sustainable in the long run; otherwise, they risk being swept aside by permissioned networks offering faster, cheaper transactions and lower carbon footprints.

Regardless of their reconciliation mechanism or governance structures, blockchain networks are at risk of being misused by bad actors. In the context of cryptocurrencies this means fraud, money laundering and/or the financing of terrorism.[110] This puts an onus on organizations deploying blockchain solutions to consider how they can be abused – which is not always obvious – and implement preventative measures into existing anti-money laundering and data protection processes; these will be further addressed in Chapters 7 and 8.

CASE STUDY
Facebook and the Libra cryptocurrency

In 2019, Facebook announced that it was working on a cryptocurrency called Libra. Unlike many other cryptocurrencies, Libra is a stable coin, meaning that it is backed by a reserve of financial assets, such as mainstream fiat currencies and short-term government bonds.[111] The supply of Libra is not fixed; as a result, the issuance and redemption of Libra tokens entails cash flows in and out of its reserve.[112]

The Libra blockchain was conceived as a permissioned network managed by the Switzerland-based Libra Association. This organization is a non-profit funded by interest income on assets in the Libra reserve. Though it is Facebook-led, Libra is independent of Facebook's core business; rather, the Libra Association is backed by organizations from a diverse array of sectors, ranging from finance and technology, to non-profits and academic institutions. It has *ca* 100 founding members, which include the likes of Uber, Vodafone, Spotify and Coinbase.[113]

The Libra network is maintained by a collection of validator nodes, each controlled by a founding member.[114] Thus, rather than putting their trust in the system's incentive structures – as they would do with Bitcoin – users trust Libra's governance structures and those of its founding members. This removes the need for computationally intensive reconciliation mechanisms, which should make for faster transactions and lower energy costs.

In addition, the asset reserve protects Libra's value from speculative swings, which should increase its liquidity.[115] In this way, Libra addresses some of biggest drawbacks of Bitcoin – namely its volatility, slow transaction speeds and environmental footprint – thus making it more useable.[116]

Libra is intended to facilitate greater financial inclusion by connecting the world's unbanked to the global financial system.[117] This cuts both ways: whilst Libra enables entrepreneurs in developing countries to access capital cheaply and easily, it also allows savers in low-growth economies to access investment opportunities anywhere in the world. In this way, the 'global, open, instant, and low-cost movement of money will create immense economic opportunity and more commerce across the world'.[118]

That said, Libra is by no means an exclusively charitable endeavour: during a conference call with investors, Facebook CEO Mark Zuckerberg said that Libra is 'really just one of a set of things – everything from Instagram Shopping, which is going to help people connect to brands and emerging creators, to Facebook Marketplace which is more consumer-to-consumer paying and buying and selling used goods, or things like WhatsApp Business, which is more about connecting with small businesses.'[119]

After the release of the Libra White Paper in 2019, concerns were raised regarding its global impact. For example, significant uptake in any one country, particularly a smaller one, may take monetary policy out of the hands of the central bank as users can simply take to transacting in Libra rather than their local currency. In addition, it is feared that global uptake will create distortions in the capital markets pertaining to Libra's underlying assets.[120]

Furthermore, in 2019, the United States Treasury Department stated that the Libra Association would be subject to a wide-ranging set of laws and regulations, including those concerning privacy, anti-money laundering (AML) and countering the finance of terrorism (CFT). Moreover, the Treasury stressed that organizations facilitating the trade of the Libra cryptocurrency would be subject to the same AML/CFT controls as conventional financial institutions.[121]

In addition, concerns have been raised regarding Facebook's role in leading a global currency project like Libra.[122] Over the years, the company's reputation has suffered due to a number of scandals involving user data. Most notably, it was censured for its role in the Cambridge Analytica scandal, in which millions of users' personal data was allegedly used by third parties without their knowledge.[123] This resulted in an investigation by the US Federal Trade Commission, culminating in a US$5 billion penalty and an undertaking by Facebook that it would overhaul its framework for protecting user privacy.[124] According to FTC Chairman Joe Simons, these measures were put in place 'to change Facebook's entire privacy culture to decrease the likelihood of continued violations'.[125]

This was not the first time that Facebook has been punished for failing to protect user privacy. In 2018, the Information Commissioner's Office in the UK fined Facebook £500,000 for failing to obtain clear and informed consent when sharing users' data with third parties between 2007 and 2014. This fine was the maximum allowable under UK law, pre-GDPR.[126]

According to regulatory disclosures from Facebook Inc, the company views adverse changes in regulation as one of the risks facing its business model. In addition, the company notes that its over-reliance on advertising revenue means that maintaining the quality and relevance of the data it collects from its users is a core element of monetizing its properties, which besides Facebook, includes WhatsApp and Instagram. To this end, maintaining user trust is paramount in facilitating data collection.[127]

If you were a regulator, what potential reservations might you have about allowing Libra into your jurisdiction?
(Suggested answer at the end of this chapter.)

Chapter summary

This chapter was intended to give the reader a basic understanding in crypto-currencies and blockchain technology as well as to understand how and why blockchain-based applications are useful in a non-currency context. As discussed above, blockchain is, to a large degree, an agglomeration of existing technologies such as cryptographic hashes and peer-to-peer networks. In this way, blockchain is, in many ways, analogous to e-mail technology.

When combined with smart contracts, blockchain's potential uses expand significantly. This is because a cryptocurrency, like Bitcoin, is no more than a decentralized database of a network's transactions: its secure authentication protocols, transparency, decentralized control and robust reconciliation mechanisms make the underlying blockchain technology useful in domains that involve approval processes, and information transfers contingent thereon. In this way, blockchain could be used to optimize many back-office processes and lead to significant cost savings.

 KEY TAKEAWAYS

The most important points from this chapter are:

- A transaction on a blockchain is a transfer of information.
- Blockchain enables parties to transact without intermediaries due to its authentication mechanisms and transparency.
- It has potential time-saving applications in routine processes that lack transparency and require multiple layers of approval.
- A foolproof user interface is required if blockchain solutions are ever to succeed with consumers because private keys are not recoverable.

SUGGESTED ANSWERS TO DISCUSSION POINTS

 How can the various facets of blockchain technology facilitate GEB's captive reinsurance processes?

As GEB's business involves transferring risks and rewards pertaining to insurance agreements passed between at least three parties (the local insurer, Generali and the client's captive), blockchain could be useful in several ways, for example:

- The network's transparency could replace conventional communication mechanisms (e-mail, phone) for keeping track of who owes whom what.
- Payments could be automated subject to proper authentication on the blockchain.
- Agreements could be standardized (with sufficient modularity for dates, client addresses, premium amounts, etc) which would enable them to be checked automatically rather than reviewed by costly lawyers/auditors.

- All stakeholders may be able to view the status of the insurance agreements in real time. For GEB, this could mean being able to consolidate the latest information about its entire captive business and feed this into its management information systems, thereby enabling better oversight and risk management.

- Stakeholders may be able to authenticate information transfers on the blockchain rather than signing contracts. This would eliminate the need for paperwork, which would reduce the risk of contract/policy errors.

 If you were a regulator, what potential reservations might you have about allowing Libra into your jurisdiction?

A financial regulator, or indeed a policymaker, might have the following reservations about allowing Libra into their country:

- As with other financial innovations, there is a risk that Libra could be used by criminals and terrorists for transferring funds.

- Facebook's business model relies on harvesting user data. Even though it has committed to maintaining Libra as a separate entity, controlled by its member organizations, it is likely that allowing Libra into the Facebook ecosystem will enable it to harvest user data. No other financial institution has this level of information on their users. Does this give Facebook too much power and/or an unfair competitive advantage?

- Given Facebook's record on handling user data, there is a question to be answered on whether it can be trusted with users' financial transactions.

- If the Libra reserve grows very big, might this give the Libra Association extraordinary power over smaller countries if their currencies are included in the reserve? For example, if a small country like Denmark has its currency included, might this create distortions in the market for Danish kroner? Also, with the implied threat of being ejected from the Libra reserve, there is a risk that authorities in smaller countries like Denmark might feel pressured to neglect enforcing local laws against Facebook and members of the Libra Association.

References

1,6 CoinMarketCap (2019) All Cryptocurrencies, 16 November, coinmarket cap.com/all/ views/all/ (archived at https://perma.cc/4456-ZP6Mc)

2,9,10,13,14,16,31,32,47-52,54-60,65,69,97 Nakamoto, S (2008) Bitcoin: A Peer-to-Peer Electronic Cash System, bitcoin.org/bitcoin.pdf (archived at https://perma.cc/ CJZ4-SHNS)

3 Caffyn, G (2014) Bitcoin Pizza Day: Celebrating the Pizzas Bought for 10,000 BTC, Coindesk, 22 May, www.coindesk.com/bitcoin-pizza-day-celebrating-pizza-bought-10000-btc (archived at https://perma.cc/Y22T-5YJT)

4,5,68 CoinMarketCap (2019) Bitcoin price charts, 16 November, coinmarketcap.com/ currencies/bitcoin/ (archived at https://perma.cc/9UZ2-79GS)

17,18,23,24,30 Antonopoulos, A (2017) *Mastering Bitcoin: Unlocking Digital Cryptocurrencies*. O'Reilly Media, Sebastopol, CA.

7,8,96 Bitcoin Wiki (2019) Bitcoin FAQ, 17 June, en.bitcoin.it/wiki/Help:FAQ (archived at https://perma.cc/82D9-KRXD)

11,12 Bank of England (2020) Payment and settlement, 9 March, www.bankofengland.co. uk/payment-and-settlement (archived at https://perma.cc/WV8D-ETSB)

15 Bitcoin Wiki (2017) Genesis block, 30 November, en.bitcoin.it/wiki/Genesis_block#cite_note-block-1 (archived at https://perma.cc/YJ2T-K6Y4)

19,20,21,22,27 Brito, J and Castillo, A (2013) Bitcoin: A Primer for Policymakers, George Mason University, www.mercatus.org/system/files/Brito_BitcoinPrimer.pdf (archived at https://perma.cc/42S7-5UNE)

25,26,71 Antonopoulos, A (nd) Bitcoin 101 – Introduction to the future of money [video], https://aantonop.com/videos/ (archived at https://perma.cc/DKG8-3VBA)

28 Bitcoin Wiki (2019) Technical background of version 1 Bitcoin addresses, 28 March, en. bitcoin.it/wiki/Technical_background_of_version_1_Bitcoin_addresses (archived at https://perma.cc/G7BA-QQXL)

29 Eskandari, S, Barrera, D, Stobert, E and Clark, J (2018) A First Look at the Usability of Bitcoin Key Management, arxiv.org/pdf/1802.04351.pdf (archived at https://perma. cc/47TT-UFTG)

33 Merriam-Webster (2020) Cryptography, 24 March, www.merriam-webster.com/ dictionary/cryptography (archived at https://perma.cc/555C-NS5Q)

34,40,53 Di Pierro, M (2017) What is the blockchain? *Computing in Science & Engineering*, 2017, 19 (5), 92–95 (September–October)

35 Bitcoin Wiki (2016) SHA-256, 29 January, en.bitcoin.it/wiki/SHA-256 (archived at https://perma.cc/5YCH-5FA5)

36 National Institute of Standards and Technology (2015) Secure Hash Standard (SHS), FIPS PUB 180-4 (August)

37 Bitcoin Wiki (2019) Private key, 4 May, en.bitcoin.it/wiki/Private_key (archived at https://perma.cc/N2QU-CN2V)

38,39 Sedgwick, K (2019) How hard is it to brute force a Bitcoin private key? Coinnews Telegraph

41,42,43 National Institute of Standards and Technology (2013) Secure Hash Standard (SHS), FIPS PUB 186-4 (July)

44,45,46,61,62,72,109 Eyal, I (2017) Blockchain Technology: Transforming Libertarian Cryptocurrency Dreams to Finance and Banking Realities, *Computer*, 2017, 50 (9), 38–49

63 Ripple (2019) Our company, www.ripple.com/company (archived at https://perma.cc/8TL6-5JBT)

64 Ripple (2019) XRP: A digital asset built for global payments, www.ripple.com/xrp (archived at https://perma.cc/M7AE-ZSBD)

66,67 Trading Economics (2019) Venezuela – Economic Indicators, tradingeconomics.com/venezuela/indicators (archived at https://perma.cc/EKA7-EMJ6)

70 Larios-Hernandez, G J. Blockchain entrepreneurship opportunity in the practices of the unbanked, *Business Horizons*, 2017, 60 (6), 865–74 (November–December)

73 Szabo, N (1996) Smart Contracts: Building Blocks for Digital Markets, www.fon.hum.uva.nl/rob/Courses/InformationInSpeech/CDROM/Literature/LOTwinterschool2006/szabo.best.vwh.net/smart_contracts_2.html (archived at https://perma.cc/K77F-VU8V)

74 Financial Conduct Authority (2017) FS 17/4: Distributed Ledger Technology – Feedback Statement on Discussion Paper 17/, www.fca.org.uk/publication/feedback/fs17-04.pdf (archived at https://perma.cc/3LK7-5K6S)

75,77 Giancaspro, M. Is a 'smart contract' really a smart idea? Insights from a legal perspective, *Computer Law & Security Review*, 2017, 33, 825–35

76 Accenture Consulting (2017) Banking on blockchain, www.accenture.com/us-en/_acnmedia/Accenture/Conversion-Assets/DotCom/Documents/Global/PDF/Consulting/Accenture-Banking-on-Blockchain.pdf (archived at https://perma.cc/SY8C-N29K)

78,79 Generali Group (2019) Media Kit, September, www.generali.com/media/media-kit (archived at https://perma.cc/SY4Q-8FDR)

80,81,82,83 Generali Group (2017) Reinsurance to Captive, geb.com/sites/default/files/2017-08/CAPTIVE%20_A4_ART_WEB_opt_0.pdf (archived at https://perma.cc/S84Q-YTRQ)

84,85 Generali Group (2017) The Generali LifeCycle Pooling Approach, April, geb.com/sites/default/files/2017-08/GEB_Factsheet_Generali_Lifecycle.pdf (archived at https://perma.cc/6DNS-CY2N)

86,88 Accenture (2019) Accenture and Generali Employee Benefits Apply Blockchain Technology, Aiming to Transform the Reinsurance Process for Captive Services, 16 April, newsroom.accenture.com/news/accenture-and-generali-employee-benefits-apply-blockchain-technology-aiming-to-transform-the-reinsurance-process-for-captive-services.htm (archived at https://perma.cc/WZ82-FAWE)

87 Generali Group (2018) Blockchain 'firsts' at GEB: For the employee benefits industry & for the network, April, www.geb.com/through-our-world/news/blockchain-firsts-geb-employee-benefits-industry-network (archived at https://perma.cc/J2DU-Y89L)

89,90 B3i Services AG (2019) About us, b3i.tech/who-we-are.html (archived at https://perma.cc/G8MC-9LUR)

91,92 B3i Services AG (2019) Cat XoL product deployed to customers' production environments, 15 October, https://b3i.tech/news-reader/cat-xol-product-deployed-to-customers-production-environments.html (archived at https://perma.cc/TY8D-4AJW)

93,110 Bank of International Settlements (2018) Cryptocurrencies: looking beyond the hype, BIS Annual Economic Report, www.bis.org/publ/arpdf/ar2018e5.htm (archived at https://perma.cc/BB68-N2YB)

94 HSBC Holdings plc (2018) *HSBC and ING execute groundbreaking live trade finance transaction on R3's Corda Blockchain platform*, www.hsbc.com/media/media-releases/2018/hsbc-trade-blockchain-transaction-press-release (archived at https://perma.cc/T4ZW-484Z)

95 Hayek, F A. Toward a Free-Market Monetary System, in: Gold and Monetary Conference, New Orleans Gold: *The Journal of Libertarian Studies*, 1977, 3, 1–8

98 Lo, S and Wang, J C (2014) Bitcoin as Money? Current Policy Perspectives, No. 14-4. Federal Reserve Bank of Boston, www.bostonfed.org/-/media/Documents/Workingpapers/PDF/cpp1404.pdf/ (archived at https://perma.cc/M7C7-79MU)

99 Bouri, E, Gupta, R, Tiwari, A and Roubaud, D. Does Bitcoin Hedge Global Uncertainty? Evidence from wavelet-based quantile-in-quantile regressions, *Finance Research Letters*, 2017, 23, 87–95 (November)

100 Dyhrberg, A. Bitcoin, gold and the dollar – A GARCH volatility analysis, *Finance Research Letters*, 2016, 16, 85–92 (February)

101,102 Buy Bitcoin Worldwide (2019) The Bitcoin volatility index, www.buybitcoinworldwide.com/volatility-index/ (archived at https://perma.cc/2EHU-WRRA)

103,120 G7 Working Group on Stablecoins (2019) Investigating the impact of global stablecoins, October, www.bis.org/cpmi/publ/d187.pdf (archived at https://perma.cc/7FXR-DRGT)

104 Odell, M (2015) A Solution to Bitcoin's Governance Problem, TechCrunch 21 September, techcrunch.com/2015/09/21/a-solution-to-bitcoins-governance-problem/ (archived at https://perma.cc/B5K8-HT3B)

105 Lee, T B (2017) Why the Bitcoin network just split in half and why it matters, arsTECHNICA, 2 August, arstechnica.com/tech-policy/2017/08/why-the-bitcoin-network-just-split-in-half-and-why-it-matters/ (archived at https://perma.cc/RCX3-Q55F)

106,107 R3 (2019) Corda Enterprise: The blockchain platform built for business, www.r3.com/wp-content/uploads/2019/05/CordaEnterprise_FS_May2019.pdf (archived at https://perma.cc/B4VQ-N84G)

108 O'Dwyer, K A and Malone, D (2014) Bitcoin Mining and its Energy Footprint, in IET Irish Signals & Systems Conference, Limerick: Hamilton Institute, National University of Ireland Maynooth, www.researchgate.net/publication/271467748_Bitcoin_Mining_and_its_Energy_Footprint (archived at https://perma.cc/6GZT-QHW4)

111,113,114,116,117,118 Libra Association (2019) An introduction to Libra: White Paper, libra.org/en-US/wp-content/uploads/sites/23/2019/06/LibraWhitePaper_en_US.pdf (archived at https://perma.cc/AN2E-CHQW)

112,115 Catalini, C, Gratry, O, Hou, J M, Parasuraman, S and Wernerfelt, N (2019) The Libra Reserve, Libra Association, libra.org/wp-content/uploads/2019/06/TheLibraReserve_en_US.pdf (archived at https://perma.cc/U4K6-DZZ4)

119 Facebook Inc. (2019) Second quarter 2019 results conference call, 24 July, investor.fb.com/investor-events/event-details/2019/Facebook-Q2-2019-Earnings/default.aspx (archived at https://perma.cc/DF7L-PS9E)

121 United States Department of the Treasury (2019) Response to Representative Cleaver, 21 October, cleaver.house.gov/sites/cleaver.house.gov/files/Treasury%20Facebook%20 Response.pd (archived at https://perma.cc/6FQN-C342)

122 Congressman Emanuel Cleaver, II. (2019) Treasury Agrees to Cleaver's Call For Federal Investigation Into Libra, 22 October, https://cleaver.house.gov/sites/cleaver.house. gov/files/Treasury%20Facebook%20Response.pdf (archived at https://perma.cc/ C4DE-MUVA)

123,124,125 Federal Trade Commission (2019) FTC Imposes $5 Billion Penalty and Sweeping New Privacy Restrictions on Facebook, 24 July, www.ftc.gov/news-events/ press-releases/2019/07/ftc-imposes-5-billion-penalty-sweeping-new-privacy-restrictions (archived at https://perma.cc/M858-SP24)

126 Information Commissioner's Office (2018) ICO issues maximum £500,000 fine to Facebook for failing to protect users' personal information, 25 October, ico.org.uk/ about-the-ico/news-and-events/news-and-blogs/2018/10/facebook-issued-with-maximum-500-000-fine/ (archived at https://perma.cc/62J5-WLCD)

127 Facebook, Inc. (2018) Form 10-K: Annual report pursuant to section 13 or 15(d) of the Securities exchange act of 1934 for the fiscal year ended December 31, 2018, United States Securities and Exchange Commission, 31 January.

06

Digitizing the price mechanism

The impact of automation and social media on financial markets

---

LEARNING OBJECTIVES

This chapter will help you understand:

- Why prices transmit information.
- How markets aggregate data.
- How digitization is changing financial markets.

Introduction

What is the economy? What is the internet? These questions have, at least, two answers in common: the first is that they are both networks; the second is that they are both markets. Whereas the web is a marketplace for information, the economy is a marketplace for goods and services. The transactions in either sphere are, in essence, signals: internet users transact via clicks and messages, while consumers communicate with their wallets.

Thus, web browsing and transacting financially both entail a transfer of information. In this chapter, we examine how the confluence of these data flows is affecting the financial system. As part of this, we explore how the web and the global financial system are merging: as overlapping networks, these are connected via the transmission of electrical signals, and more abstractly, price movements in financial markets.

Prices as a communication tool

A user's browsing data can illuminate their interests, beliefs and emotional state. Meanwhile, financial transactions can provide insight into what that user has bought and – if there is a discernible pattern – what they might buy in the future. Hence, both types of data have commercial value.

However, making a payment forces an individual to weigh up their needs and preferences in a way that browsing the web does not. The decision made at the point of sale represents the net result of this exercise. Consequently, people's transactions can be seen as expressions of their most important needs, preferences and values at the time of the transaction.[1]

When making transactions, individuals and businesses convey their preferences to the rest of the economy. The sum of this information manifests in the prices set according to supply and demand: high prices indicate unmet needs while low prices signal abundance. In this way, prices act as signalling mechanisms for the allocation of resources.[2]

Thus, the price mechanism – like the internet – is a two-way communication system. Internet users convey information with clicks and messages; participants in the market economy do so via prices.[3] As prices are quantified in monetary terms they make the costs of different options comparable, thereby helping consumers prioritize their expenditures: for example, it would be difficult to decide between going on holiday or buying a car without prices.

In addition, prices help producers direct resources towards their most profitable use.[4] In many enterprises, this tends to be towards the supply of goods and services that generate the highest profit. Though it may not be feasible for producers to ascertain the preferences of each individual consumer, they can observe overall shifts in consumer behaviour via changing market prices.[5] This, in turn, facilitates decision making as each business decision can be evaluated with a simple question: does it make money?

Therefore, the price mechanism is effectively an information conduit between consumers and producers.[6] On one hand, prices aggregate and convey consumer needs to producers; on the other, prices help producers communicate the cost of meeting these needs back to consumers. In this way, prices help both parties prioritize their spending.

Mean estimates

Broadly speaking, producers behave in similar ways in that they pay close attention to market signals in order to maximize profits. The same cannot be said for consumers, who can exhibit vastly different spending patterns: while some people never drink alcohol, others may spend hundreds of thousands of pounds on champagne in a single night.[7]

However, as a group, consumer preferences tend toward those of the average person. For every millionaire buying bucketloads of champagne, there are many more people who never drink or only do so on special occasions. As a result, the average champagne consumption per person will be somewhere in between these extremes, closely resembling that of a great number of consumers. This is because each person's spending is, in effect, their vote on what the average person's consumption ought to be. In large groups, extreme preferences – both high and low – tend to occur to the same degree on either side of the population mean (aka the average): like a perfectly balanced tug of war, these extremes tend to offset each other. As a result, they do not affect the mean itself.

This phenomenon can be seen in many areas of life with large numbers of people making choices independently. For example, the statistician Francis Galton famously observed that 800 or so farm show attendees were, as a group, able to guess the weight of an ox: though individual guesses varied widely, the average guess was within 1 per cent of the ox's true weight.[8] How could this be?

The answer lies in the fact that estimation errors (ie extreme guesses) tend to cancel each other out; while some estimates are too high, others are too low. However, given a sufficiently large group of people, the most inaccurate guesses cancel each other out, thereby leaving better-informed estimates to form the group consensus (ie the mean estimate). Though statisticians have known about this phenomenon for some time, it has been popularized as the *wisdom of crowds*.[9]

This effect is also present in financial markets. To understand how, we must look at the mechanics of transacting in financial markets. For the purposes of this discussion, all traded instruments (eg stocks, bonds, derivatives, etc) shall be referred to generically as *securities*.

Liquidity in financial markets

Trading in financial markets is a tug of war between buyers and sellers. On one side, buyers want to pay the lower price, called the *bid*; on the other, sellers want to receive the higher price, known as the *offer* or *ask*.[10] The difference between the two prices is called the spread.[11]

The first party to give in crosses the spread and accepts the other side's best price. For example, when buying a security, you would have to accept the seller's offer and pay the higher price. All else being equal, if you were to sell the security in the same instant, you would receive the buyer's bid price, less than what you initially paid. Thus, the spread is a transaction cost.

As a result, neither bid nor offer prices reflect a security's true value. Rather, the average of the two prices, called the *mid-price*, can be taken as a more accurate estimate of a security's true worth in the eyes of both buyers and sellers. All else being equal, if a buyer and seller were to transact at the mid-price, they would effectively share the cost of the spread. In this way, the market mid-price reflects all information, both positive and negative, relevant to determining the security's value.

In practice, market participants do not have to transact at the prevailing bid–offer prices. Rather, these prices tend to be for unsophisticated investors transacting with the market maker, who earns the spread by simultaneously transacting on both sides of the market.[12] Generally speaking, transacting at the prevailing bid–offer spread ensures that one's trade is completed, albeit at the cost of the spread; this compensates the market maker for providing *liquidity* to the market.

In general, the more liquid a security, the easier and cheaper it is to trade. Thus, the concept of liquidity explains the positive correlation between the number of market participants and the cost and ease of transacting in a market; in this way, a market with a greater number of buyers and sellers is more liquid. This can be explained by the intra-group competition that exists on both sides of the spread.

Securities trading commonly takes place via protocol known as a central limit order book. As seen in Figure 6.1, this system entails ranking proposed trades in terms of their acceptability, pricewise, to the other side of the market.[13] In this way, the highest bid and the lowest offer prices will be adjacent in the order book. To jump to the front of the queue, a trader must submit a price that is higher than the highest bid, if buying, or lower than the lowest offer, if selling; for a transaction to occur, someone must cross the spread and accept a proposed trade from the other side of the market.

When the number of market participants increases, the greater degree of competition narrows the spread as both buyers and sellers compete amongst against each other to transact with the other side. In this way, individual

FIGURE 6.1 A central limit order book

	Price	Size
	124.05	4
	123.95	10
	123.78	17
Lowest offer	123.50	20

Highest bid	123.20	34
	123.15	21
	123.00	5
	122.94	11

Trades are ranked according to their acceptability to the other side. This means higher bids (ie proposed buys) and lower offers (ie proposed sells) go to the front of the queue. When a buyer crosses the spread, they will receive the highest offer; if their purchase is larger than the size of the best offer, it will be topped up with securities from the second-best offer. For example, if someone were to buy 25 securities in the order book above, they would purchase 20 securities at 123.5 and 5 securities at 123.78.

buyers attempt to outbid each other in order to make their proposed trades more attractive to potential sellers, thereby pushing up the bid price. Meanwhile, a similar competition between sellers drives down the offer price. Consequently, a greater number of market participants narrows the spread, thereby making it easier and cheaper to transact. Similarly, reducing the number of market participants would widen the spread, thereby increasing the cost of transacting.

Over the last few decades, financial market liquidity has increased in tandem with greater connectivity and advances in technology. For example, forex (foreign exchange) spreads have fallen notably since the digitization of currency markets in the 1990s.[14] In this way, technological advancement has improved access to financial markets and lowered transaction costs; this, in turn, has enabled progressively smaller transactions.

As a result, the pool of market participants has grown which, combined with freer information flows, has increased the efficiency of financial markets.[15] In this way, better informed – and more plentiful – market participants facilitate the accurate pricing of securities. That is to say, liquid securities trade at market prices that generally reflect all information relevant to their accurate valuation.

As a market for a security is effectively a poll of buyers and sellers regarding its value, each completed trade represents a consensus opinion regarding its value at a given point in time. The word 'consensus' is important because the transacting buyer and seller did not reach this agreement in isolation. Rather, a multitude of potential buyers and sellers voted with their bids and offers to frame the trade in a narrow price range that was agreeable to both sides of the transaction. Thus, while only two parties transacted financially, a multitude of parties transacted informationally.

In this way, it is the accumulated knowledge and intentions of competing market participants, expressed through their bids and offers, that collectively decides on a security's price. As market prices are established by the continuous trading of buyers and sellers, each completed trade represents the market's consensus estimate of a security's value at a given point in time; as new information comes out, the combined reactions of market participants ensure that this consensus shifts accordingly. Thus, a security's market price should, at all times, reflect all known information relevant to its value; when this is the case, the market can be said to be efficient.[16]

While academics have been arguing for decades over the extent of financial market efficiency, it appears that the greater connectivity and information flow enabled by the internet has accelerated the assimilation of knowledge into security prices: this is not surprising given that universal access to information combined with a large pool of market participants are key prerequisites for market efficiency.[17] This, in turn, is reshaping the relationship between financial markets and the web. To understand how, it is necessary to examine how markets assimilate information in the context of the *efficient market hypothesis* (EMH).[18]

Market efficiency and passive fund management

By forcing buyers and sellers to compete, the bid–offer mechanism ensures that prices in liquid financial markets generally reflect all relevant information. In order to transact, buyers and sellers must arrive at a price that is acceptable to both sides of the spread. Therefore, they must settle on a price that reflects both the optimistic and pessimistic perspectives on the security; in other words, one that simultaneously reflects reasons for buying and selling the security. As market participants do not want to give the other side an unduly favourable price, they compete to value the security more accurately than their counterparties. Because buyers and sellers approach this problem from opposing perspectives, this competition ensures that all information pertaining to the security's value is included in its price.

As an example, consider the following question: what is the most you would pay to purchase a five-dollar bill? If you are rational, the answer is US$5 because you know exactly what the piece of paper is worth. Now, consider the opposite proposition: what is the lowest price you would accept for selling a five-dollar bill? Again, the answer should be the same as before: exactly $5. Of course, there is no market for five-dollar bills. This is because all information pertaining to its value (ie $5) is known, and so no profit can be made from having better information.

In financial markets, things are not as straightforward. Though information about a given security may be widely available, it generally yields a more nuanced, and sometimes contradictory, picture of the security's value. This leads to different market participants arriving at different valuations. They settle these disagreements via the market, hoping to edge out a profit at the expense of their counterparties by valuing the securities more accurately.

In theory, this competition should ensure that a security's market price never strays too far from the price that reflects all information pertaining to its value.[19] To understand why, consider what happens when a market participant submits a trade that is too far removed from prevailing bid–offer prices: either the trade is not accepted because its price is worse than those of other trades on the same side of the spread; or, if the trade goes too far into enemy territory (ie by being unduly favourable to the other side), it quickly gets snapped up by more savvy traders. In this way, market participants who consistently misprice securities remove themselves from the market, either by never trading or losing all of their money.

As a result, it is not necessary for all market participants to possess all information relevant to valuing a security. Rather, all that is required is a sophisticated core of rational investors who do. Consequently, as long as there is enough liquidity to hold the centre around the bid–offer spread, trades that deviate too far from the market consensus will not affect prices significantly.

When new information is released, the tug of war between buyers and sellers quickly establishes a new consensus price to reflect the market's newfound knowledge. Any new information relevant to the value of a security affects its supply and demand. This, in turn, upsets the balance of bids and offers, moving the mid-market price. Given free-flowing and widely available information, such changes can happen almost instantaneously as buyers and sellers readjust their expectations concurrently.[20]

In theory, an efficient market ensures that security prices adjust instantaneously in response to new information. This renders securities trading a futile exercise: as the market mechanism ensures that prices reflect all relevant information, it should therefore be impossible to consistently make investment returns above the market average, by any means other than chance.[21]

In practice, however, some investors do consistently make returns above the market average. However, this tends to be the domain of professional investors as the required labour – in the form of research, market analysis and trading – makes this endeavour a full-time job. As a result, the above-average returns accruing to these highly sophisticated investors can be seen as their reward for maintaining the efficiency of the market.

In markets that are efficient or nearly efficient, the unsophisticated investor can benefit from the work of sophisticated investors by adopting a passive investment strategy. As part of this, the investor does not attempt to outperform the market by picking individual securities. Rather, they put their money into funds that track well-known market indices such as the FTSE 100, which is comprised of the 100 largest companies by market capitalization trading on the London Stock Exchange.[22] As the FTSE 100's constituent securities are widely traded and well known (that is to say, liquid), the investor is, on the whole, buying a basket of securities that are priced accurately. This is not a bad trade: very few investors can outperform the market consistently and a passive investment strategy removes the risk of underperforming the market to any significant degree.

Crucially, the investor can achieve this without putting in the time and effort required to analyse and trade individual securities. In this way, passive investment strategies optimize returns for the time required for their implementation. Indeed, these strategies can be automated with applications that recommend fund allocations based on an individual's risk appetite. These applications, known as robo-advisers (see the case study in Chapter 2), effectively allow people to put their investment strategies on autopilot, thereby minimizing the time cost of investing.

As it has become increasingly difficult to outperform market indices via conventional investment strategies,[23] more and more investors are turning to passive investment. For example, in 2016 the *Financial Times* estimated that a third of all money held in US mutual funds was invested passively; three years before, this figure had been around 25 per cent.[24]

Passive investment funds typically have lower management fees than active funds do. After all, a passive investment strategy is relatively easy to automate as it is rules based (eg 'buy all stocks in the FTSE 100 in proportion to their market capitalization'). As a result, passive investment funds are much cheaper to run than actively managed funds (which incur research costs, for example). Ultimately, this translates into lower charges against the assets in passive funds. As fees are predictable, while investment returns are not, the leaner fee structures of index funds underpin the growing popularity of passive investment strategies. In turn, this trend is putting pressure on fee revenue across the investment management industry.[25] Thus, asset managers find themselves pushed towards greater technology application in their operations in order to realize efficiencies as a way of making up for declining fee revenue.

Sentiment mining with natural language processing

As passive investment grows in popularity, more sophisticated investors find themselves in a race to profit from having more up-to-date information than their competitors. To acquire this information, some investors turn to social media in the hope of finding patterns in user posts to serve as indicators of market sentiment, and thereby predict price movements.[26]

These investors use sophisticated computational techniques, known as natural language processing (NLP), to gather and analyse vast quantities of user posts on social media platforms. The tone and volume of user posts can be used to capture overall market sentiment or, indeed, sentiment with regard to a particular security.[27] For example, a programme may detect an uptick in the volume of posts containing negative adjectives about a company's products: for example, a technology company's latest mobile phone may described in user posts as being 'useless', 'slow', or 'rubbish', which could indicate disappointing sales in the future. When a shift in market sentiment is identified, the programme makes an automated trade in response. In this way, sophisticated investors are able to trade before this information is fully assimilated into market prices, thereby profiting from being ahead of the market.

NATURAL LANGUAGE PROCESSING

NLP can be described as the intersection of linguistics and artificial intelligence.[28] NLP enables computers to translate human language into computer language. In this way, human communications can be compiled and analysed by computers to identify problems and offer solutions. The applications of NLP are manifold, including automation of customer support centres, translation, text suggestion features and legal contract analysis.

During the infancy of the field, it was thought that NLP should take a rules-based approach to computerizing human language.[29] However, writing a rule for every circumstance is labour intensive and difficult to scale. As language is constantly evolving and used in different ways by different people, there are many subtleties which are hard to codify as computers take everything literally: puns, specialist jargon, things unsaid and words whose meanings are context-dependent, such as spirit (which can, among other things, be used to refer to a person's soul or an alcoholic substance).[30]

This is where machine learning (ML), more commonly known as artificial intelligence, comes in. ML is a probabilistic approach to decision making that uses large quantities of data to inform NLP algorithms (for more on this, see Chapter 4).[31] Instead of using experts to write hard and fast rules, NLP employs ML to make probabilistic inferences based on the data captured from user behaviour. For example, a text-suggestion algorithm may detect that the word 'cat' is most often associated with the adjective 'cute'; then, when someone types 'The cat is', the algorithm may recommend completing the sentence with 'cute'. If the user ignores this suggestion and starts the next word with an 'f', the algorithm may recommend completing the word with 'funny' – having detected that a word beginning with 'f', when associated with 'cat', is likely to be the adjective 'funny'. Regardless of the user's ultimate choice, the algorithm uses this input, along with that of thousands, if not millions, of other users, to inform future recommendations.

To make sense of user input, NLP algorithms employ a set of computational techniques known as lexing and parsing. This starts with the lexing process, which takes user inputs, in the form of a strings of characters, and distils these into individual units of meaning, known as tokens.[32] As part of this process, the lexing algorithm matches each input against a library of examples in order to find its meaning; when an input matches an example, the now identified token is sent to the parsing algorithm.[33]

Then, the parsing process seeks to establish relationships between tokens.[34] It does this by matching the structure of the tokens against examples of known patterns. When supported by ML, the parsing algorithm's choices are dictated by the weight of data, and therefore represent the most likely, rather than perfect, matches.[35] Thus, by establishing a pattern, the computer is able to classify the user's input into a decision tree and respond accordingly.

The growth in web-connected consumer devices – such as laptops and smart-phones – coupled with increases in computing power has greatly facilitated data gathering via social media platforms and content-rich websites such as wikipedia.[36] Consequently, the writing of the rules for NLP algorithms has become crowdsourced: rather than relying on experts, the task of computerizing meaning from language has been outsourced to millions of brains via the internet.

Thus, social media platforms have effectively become polling tools.[37] However, unlike a direct survey, social media users do not know they are taking part. As a result, their input will not be biased by the knowledge that they are being polled. This is a common problem in direct surveys, where respondents may be tempted to give the answer that they think the interviewer wants to hear, rather than what they actually think.

That said, social media posts contain other forms of noise: user ignorance, hype, malicious posts and typos. For this reason, predictability can be improved by tracking only high-profile users, according to a study of Stocktwits, an investment-focussed social media platform.[38] Users with larger followings, more likes and a history of successful predictions exhibited greater prediction accuracy; by harvesting posts from these 'smart' users, researchers were able to predict short-term price movements in high-profile US stocks (eg Apple, Amazon, etc) with a degree of accuracy that was *ca* 10 per cent higher than the platform average.[39]

In addition, research suggests that sentiment mining is better at predicting price movements for stock indices, as opposed to individual securities.[40] This could be the result of greater data availability: at any given time, it is likely that there are more users posting about a multitude of stocks, the economy and the stock market as a whole rather than any stock in particular. As a result, there is a greater weight of data to inform predictions about stock market indices.

Thus, it can be said that social media functions as a mirror, which reflects the general mood of markets, the economy and society. By the same token, sentiment mining represents a conduit between the web and the financial system, which enables social media content to be expressed in market prices.

Curiously, there is evidence to suggest that negative sentiment is a better predictor of market movements than positive sentiment.[41] Again, part of this phenomenon may be explained by greater data availability: as newspaper editors have known for centuries, negative news stories capture the reader's attention. As a result, social media users may be more likely to make posts about bad news, thereby providing more data for the NLP algorithms to process.

In addition, some of the sentiment-price effects could be self-fulfilling:[42] on account of their large followings, high-profile users could cause many people to replicate their trades, thereby affecting market sentiment via changing prices and/or social media activity. As sentiment-trading tends to be automated, this could create feedback loops, especially if a growing number of market participants use social media to inform their trading decisions. A spike in negative sentiment could set off a downward price spiral, whereby market participants – or rather, their trading algorithms – sell securities, causing prices to decline, thereby worsening market sentiment which would then trigger further selling.

Of course, sentiment mining could exacerbate market swings either way; positive price spirals are also possible. However, given that negative sentiment offers greater predictability,[43] negative price spirals appear more likely. Such effects may already be prevalent in markets. For example, the Dow Jones's descent into a bear market in the spring of 2020 – defined as a decline of more than 20 per cent off its peak – was the fastest in stock market history, taking just 20 trading days; on average such declines take 255 sessions.[44]

However, market declines can be much faster as a result of algorithmic price spirals (aka flash crashes): on the afternoon of 6 May 2010, the US stock market fell 5–6 per cent in a matter of minutes. However, the average decline masks the volatility of the day: while the Dow Jones Industrial Average – comprised of large, well-known securities – fell by about 2.5 per cent, more than 300 securities fell by at least 60 per cent. Prices recovered almost as quickly as they had fallen, and, by the end of the day, they had recovered most, if not all, of their losses.[45]

This flash crash was triggered by a trader in London submitting an unusually large sell order for S&P 500 futures that he never intended to complete; in essence, creating a self-fulfilling bet that the S&P 500 index would fall while being in position to profit from lower prices.[46] This spike in selling volume triggered some trading algorithms to sell, which, in turn, triggered further selling, which had a snowball effect on the entire market and led prices to fall rapidly. The algorithms, seemingly, had a mind of their own.

The risks associated with yielding agency to increasingly sophisticated trading algorithms have been dramatized in *The Fear Index*,[47] a thriller set during the events of 6 May 2010: in the story, a scientist builds a programme that predicts future events by scouring the internet for data, only to realize later that the programme has a hand in precipitating these events.

Though this story is fiction, it may, to some degree, have been eerily prescient: in 2017, it was estimated that the number of web-connected devices would more than double to around 20 billion by 2020.[48] By the time you read this, this figure will likely have been surpassed. Thus, one may wonder whether the growth in connectivity actually increases the risk of more severe flash crashes in the future.

In an ideal world, NLP algorithms would search the web and trade in response to even the smallest changes in sentiment or new information. Price changes would be instantaneous and incremental, taking market efficiency to even greater heights. However, the road to more efficient markets may be full of bumps as exposing trading algorithms to the emotional vicissitudes of social media users may cause dangerous price spirals. Regardless, the increasing prevalence of NLP-enabled trading algorithms is likely to push a growing number of retail investors towards passive investment strategies. The time, expense and skill required to compete with high-tech, sophisticated investors will likely make it too difficult for retail investors to do otherwise.

CASE STUDY
Stocktwits: A social medium for investors

Stocktwits is a micro-blogging platform for investors, traders and financial market professionals.[49] Its features and functionality are similar to those of Twitter. This interface, along with the obvious nod to Twitter posts (ie 'Twits') in its name, is no accident: Stocktwits started life as an application built on Twitter, though it has since migrated to its own platform.[50]

Users on Stocktwits can use up to 1,000 characters in their posts; far more than Twitter's 280 characters. These posts are pinned to individual securities by using a cash-tag – ie the $ sign – in front of the security's ticker symbol:[51] thus, Microsoft becomes $MSFT. Just like hashtags (eg #microsoft) on Twitter, cash-tags help users identify trending topics on Stocktwits. Unlike Twitter, however, trending items are shown horizontally on a tickertape.

Furthermore, the platform has a sector-based heat-map feature. This helps identify stock sectors that users have been posting about over the preceding 1, 6, 12, and 24 hours. The greater the volume of user posts concerning stocks in a particular sector, the more space that sector takes up in the heat-map. Users can zoom in by clicking on each sector to reveal the constituent stocks driving the conversation. As at sector level, the stocks with the greater volume of posts take up more space on the heat map. Stocks that have increased in price are shown in green, while red indicates declines; clicking on a stock takes the user to a dedicated page showing a price chart as well as the latest posts relating to the stock.

It is not hard to see how a platform like Stocktwits is useful to investors seeking to gauge the mood of the market, especially as it facilitates volume-based sentiment analysis. Indeed, research conducted on user posts of Yahoo! Finance, a finance-focussed messaging board, and Stocktwits rival, suggests that large increases in the volume of posts concerning a particular stock, when associated with significant changes in sentiment, can be used to predict extreme price moves – changes of at least 15 per cent.[52]

Founded in 2008, Stocktwits aims to 'connect regular investors and traders with each other so they can profit, learn, and have fun'.[53] Clearly, there is an emphasis on building relationships and being different from the rest of the investment industry. This is evident in the musings of one of the company's founders, Howard Lindzon – an outspoken blogger and investor – who in 2016 wrote: 'In my industry (venture capital and asset management) there seems to be no humanity left.'[54]

Perhaps then, it is no surprise that Stocktwits appeals to people who have lost faith in mainstream financial institutions. According to the company's CEO, Ian Rosen, people have become reluctant to entrust individual financial experts with their money since the global financial crisis of 2007–09. Instead, they turn to networks of people they trust to help inform their financial decisions.[55]

In addition, Stocktwits focusses on attracting younger investors, who are digitally savvy and more open to online collaboration.[56] This approach appears to be working: 80 per cent of Stocktwits users are under the age of 45, and, on average, they are getting progressively younger.[57]

Posts on Stocktwits are heavily moderated in order to prevent abuse. To this end, the platform enforces stringent house rules to keep posts 'respectful, spam-free and on-topic'.[58] This helps ensure quality content while encouraging users to be friendly and collegiate.[59] The emphasis on building a healthy community of users who produce and share quality content appears to be working: at the time of writing, Stocktwits had around 2 million users.[60] These users are highly engaged, spending an average of 51 minutes a day on the platform.[61]

Stocktwits is heavily reliant on advertising, which accounts for *ca* 60 per cent of its revenue.[62] That said, the company is diversifying its revenue base: in 2018, it launched a premium rooms feature: for a monthly fee, users gain access to exclusive content from high-profile users via private chat rooms.[63] The value proposition is clear: research indicates that such high-profile users are better at predicting stock price movements than the average user on the platform.[64] In addition, the premium rooms feature enables high-profile users to monetize their content,[65] thereby incentivizing them to stay on the platform and create quality content.

The company followed this with another innovation: in 2019, it announced the launch of a commission-free trading app, which enables users to trade shares without paying brokerage fees.[66] Though other transaction costs, such as taxes and market spreads, still apply,[67] this radically lowers total transactions costs for smaller investors. In addition, the app permits fractional share trading, which allows users to invest in much smaller amounts.[68]

The Stocktwits platform has had trading functionality for a number of years via its integration with the no-commission trading app Robinhood.[69] This has enabled users to share their trades with the Stocktwits community,[70] thereby helping successful traders build credibility with their followers. In this way, the launch of Stocktwits' own trading app appears to be an effort to further diversify its revenue base: indeed, no-commission trading apps can monetize their user base by earning interest on customer deposits and charging for additional services such as leveraged trading.[71]

How might the growing popularity of platforms such as Stocktwits affect stock market efficiency?
(Suggested answer at the end of this chapter.)

Prediction markets

As information travels across the web, it manifests as price movements in securities markets. With every new piece of information, expectations about the future change, which causes prices to change. Traders do not know for sure if prices will go up or down. As a result, they are willing to transact – at the right price – because there is always some degree of uncertainty about the future.

The connectivity of the web has facilitated the securitization of this uncertainty, enabling market participants to trade predictions about future events, such as election outcomes or weather conditions. This trading takes place on platforms known as prediction markets. If a user believes that an event will happen, they buy that event; if they believe that the event will not happen, they sell it. Trading on prediction markets is very similar to trading on financial markets, complete with a bid–offer spread.[72]

Depending on the market, participants trade using real or virtual money. In either case, the party that correctly predicts the outcome of the traded event wins money from the other side, virtual or real: if you buy an event, you win money from the seller if the event occurs; as the seller, you would win money from the buyer if the event does not occur.[73]

'Shares' in traded events are typically quoted at a price between 1 and 100 cents.[74] The magnitude of the final cash flow between buyer and seller is determined by the difference between the traded price and 100 cents.[75] For example, if you buy a share in an event for 55 cents and the event happens, you would receive 45 cents from the seller; if the event does not occur, you would pay 55 cents to the seller.

As in all markets, prices fluctuate according to the balance of buyers and sellers. In this way, the price of an event goes up or down in tandem with the market's degree of certainty in its future occurrence, just as a stock price reflects market expectations about the underlying company's financial prospects. Consequently, a prediction market is effectively an opinion poll expressed through the price mechanism. When speculating on future events, a user 'puts their money where their mouth is'. As a result, they are likely to gather more information and consider their decisions more carefully than when answering a survey.

Thus, these markets help capture and distil dispersed information as the price mechanism aggregates information about the likelihood of traded events: the tug of war between buyers and sellers should ensure that all relevant information is reflected in the price, while savvy traders ensure that outlandish estimates (ie trades too far removed from the market mid-price) do not change the market consensus. As a result, prediction markets can be used as forecasting tools, by using market prices as consensus probability estimates:[76] if a particular event has a market price of, for instance, 58 cents, it means that the market believes that said event has a 58 per cent probability of occurring.

The efficacy of using prices as prediction tools can be explained by the fact that markets force buyers and sellers to concur. As buyers believe a traded event will happen, they may be biased in favour of it; by the same token, sellers may be biased against the event. The market mechanism pushes buyers and sellers into a compromise, thereby counterbalancing their respective biases, thus letting only relevant information dictate the price.

For this reason, prediction markets are remarkably proficient at predicting future outcomes. For instance, they have been shown to outperform opinion polls 74 per cent of the time when used to predict the outcome in US presidential elections.[77] Furthermore, prediction markets have been used internally by Microsoft to estimate such things as project completion times and the number of software bugs.[78] This is not surprising as research on sales forecasts at Hewlett Packard indicates that prediction markets can outperform conventional forecasting tools up to 75 per cent of the time.[79]

Whereas users of conventional forecasting tools have to weigh up contra-dictory pieces of evidence to arrive at a prediction, no such process is necessary when relying on a prediction market. Rather, the price action reveals the final result: if the weight of evidence in favour of a prediction is stronger, the price will rise above 50 cents as buyers outweigh sellers, and vice versa. In addition, market prices offer a more nuanced and probabilistic perspective: if the price moves far in either direction, this suggests that the weight of evidence strongly favours one side of the argument. On the other hand, if price action is marginal, the issue at hand may perhaps be more nuanced and difficult to judge.

Thus, prediction markets can help aggregate dispersed, and often complex, information.[80] As a result, they help prevent information bottle-necks (ie 'paralysis by analysis'). As the market mechanism ensures that only relevant and important pieces of information are reflected in the price, it helps filter out noise. This effect is similar to the role of prices in a market economy, in that they help facilitate resource allocation: without external price signals, management would find it difficult to gather and quantify all information relevant to making business decisions.[81] Thus, prediction markets enable management to use the price mechanism within their organ-izations, for decisions that do not strictly pertain to supply of goods and services. In this way, prediction markets allow management to synthesize and quantify internal information more readily than when using other decision-making tools.

Furthermore, the price mechanism provides a layer of anonymity which enables employees to express information that is otherwise confidential, unpleasant to hear or not known to management. In this way, a prediction market can function as a bottom-up feedback mechanism, from the front-line to senior management. In theory, prices should adjust to new information as it becomes known to market participants. As a result, inter-nal prediction markets allow management to capture 'changes on the ground' in a way that is potentially much faster than when using other corporate oversight tools.[82]

In a prediction market that is efficient, non-trading observers can gather information based on the trading of others. For example, an insurer could, in theory, use prediction markets to estimate the likelihood of risks which would otherwise be hard to quantify, such as operational risk ('op risk') events: when things go wrong within a company because of failings in a company's people or its processes, it tends not to be publicized widely. As a result, there is very little data available regarding the general occurrence of op risk events. Thus, it is difficult for insurers to estimate their probability which complicates the calculation of insurance premiums.

To gather op risk data, an insurer might ask the following question via an internal prediction market open to staff at one of their corporate clients: *over the next 12 months there will be an accident within my organization resulting in losses of more than US$1m.* In this way, an employee-facing prediction market could help an insurance company estimate the likelihood and possible impact of op risk events. Moreover, the insurer could invite several of its clients to take part in the same prediction market, thereby increasing sample size and enabling better estimates of op risk in its client base. The upside to the insurer's clients should be clear: better information helps the insurer estimate risks more accurately which should translate into more competitive insurance premiums. In addition, by analysing the responses from each participating organization, the insurer could help its clients understand where they stand in relation to their peers, thus encouraging high-risk clients to take preventative action.

While internal markets can be used to predict, and therefore mitigate risk, external prediction markets could, in theory, also be used for risk management. Because they are open to a potentially larger pool of participants, external prediction markets should, in theory, be more efficient than internal markets. As a result, real-money external markets may one day be used by insurers for do-it-yourself risk mitigation: for example, an auto-insurer could use an external prediction market to buy above average rainfall during the half year from September through March in order to mitigate the risk of greater than expected car accidents due to poor weather conditions. If there is less rainfall than anticipated, the insurer makes a loss in the prediction market but is compensated for this via lower insurance claims; if there is more rainfall than expected, the insurer makes a profit in the prediction market, which compensates it for greater than expected insurance claims.

In this way, companies could use *external prediction markets* to mitigate some risks. However, not all risks can be traded on external prediction markets as these require an objective benchmark for determining the outcome of each traded event: in the market for average rainfall, for example, the outcome can be independently verified by reference to meteorological authorities. When dealing with more specific risks, such as accidents within an organization, no objective benchmarks exist, and therefore op risk events are generally unsuitable for real-money trading on external markets.

As a tool for mitigating risk, external prediction markets are very similar to futures markets, which have been around for decades. A future is a security that derives its value from the price of another asset or commodity (and so futures are a common type of 'derivative' security). As a result, futures allow market participants to speculate on the future price of an asset or commodity without holding said underlying asset or commodity. As a result, businesses can use these markets to mitigate risk: for example, a large manufacturer of chocolate bars could buy cocoa futures to hedge against an increase in cocoa prices. If cocoa prices fall, the manufacturer loses on the futures position but benefits from lower input costs in the form of cheaper cocoa; if cocoa prices rise, the higher raw material costs should be offset by the profit on the futures position.

Granted, futures are not perfect as they tend to be standardized into large contract sizes, and so are only really useful as risk mitigation tools to large organizations: as the contract size for cocoa futures on the Intercontinental Exchange is 10 metric tonnes,[83] it is useless for smaller chocolate manufacturers. Therefore, if you need 15 tonnes of cocoa to make chocolate bars, you can either use one or two futures contracts to offset the risk of rising prices. In either case, you'd still be at the mercy of price swings in the cocoa market as the size of the futures position either does not offset the costs of your purchase or significantly overshoots it.

A situation like this arises when we cannot fully offset a real-world business risk against a synthetic financial risk because the risk management tool itself (ie the futures contract) is too blunt and instrument. To remedy this, companies could mitigate their risks by creating and trading more bespoke predictions via prediction markets. In this way, such markets could be used by smaller companies to mitigate risks on a more granular basis. Therefore, the greater openness and reach of the internet has the potential to allow companies to employ more precise, and smaller-scale, risk-mitigation tools than those offered by mainstream financial markets.

In spite of their promise, prediction markets are not yet widely used for risk mitigation. Without a large pool of market participants, these markets are not as liquid as mainstream financial markets, which diminishes their appeal as risk-mitigation tools. Perhaps what is needed, then, is for large social media or e-commerce platforms to enter the space with a user base large enough to ensure requisite market efficiency.

CASE STUDY
Augur: A decentralized prediction market

Augur is a peer-to-peer (p2p) prediction market governed by an open-source protocol – software that dictates how different computers interact. The platform is hosted on a multitude of independent servers around the world connected via a p2p network. As a result, it is decentralized.[84]

Trades are settled in cryptocurrency – digital tokens that allow users to transact online without intermediaries (see Chapter 5). The Augur platform does not handle user funds. Rather, it enables users to transact directly within a binding framework. When users trade an event, they stake their funds within the network: Augur protocol facilitates the transfer of funds between the users subject to the outcome of the traded event. This allows anyone to participate in Augur's prediction markets anonymously.[85]

Trades are settled in Ether, a popular cryptocurrency that is independent of the Augur platform. Other transactions on the network, such as the payment of bonds and fees (see below), are settled in the Augur token, known as Reputation.[86] Both tokens are traded against Bitcoin – the best known and most liquid cryptocurrency – on a multitude of cryptocurrency exchanges, and are therefore ultimately convertible into conventional fiat currencies (ie dollars, euros, etc).

Anyone can create a market for a prediction. At the outset, a market creator posts a bond which is returned, plus a creator's fee, once the traded event has been successfully settled: in other words, when either the buyers or sellers have won. If the outcome cannot be verified, the creator forfeits their bond. Thus, creators are incentivized to set up markets for events which are unambiguous and time constrained, and whose outcomes can be objectively verified.[87]

As part of the market-creation process, the creator nominates an independent source, such as a mainstream news site, which will later be used to verify the outcome of the traded event. The task of verifying event outcomes then falls on a group of users known as reporters. Again, this can be anyone; the key requirement is that each reporter posts a bond at the outset.[88]

The verification process works as follows: after trading has ended – which happens when an event has either occurred or failed to occur within the required timeframe – the reporters vote on the result by staking their bonds on the side of the market that correctly predicted the outcome. Reporters on the wrong side of the market forfeit their bonds, which is redistributed among the reporters on the right side of the market. In return for their services, these reporters receive a fee.[89]

Thus, there is an incentive for reporters to tell the truth and, perhaps more implicitly, only agree to report on events which can be objectively verified. Furthermore, the risk of collusion between traders and reporters is minimized as the Augur community has a window of seven days to dispute any reporting decision: parties who successfully challenge a reporting decision are rewarded financially.[90] This openness, combined with strong incentives to be honest, helps ensure the robustness of the outcome-verification mechanism.

As the Augur protocol is open source, the code that runs the network is in the public domain: the Forecast Foundation, a non-profit organization, maintains a copy of this code and publishes improvements to it in response to feedback from the Augur community. However, the Forecast Foundation does not host the Augur platform. Rather, Augur is hosted on a multitude of computers around the world, whose owners are incentivized by the issuance of cryptocurrency.[91]

As it is open source, Augur does not rely on anything other than an active community of users and developers to perpetuate its existence. In theory, the Forecast Foundation could disappear without significant disruption to the network: as long as the Augur protocol is available online and there is a financial incentive to host it, the platform is likely to continue existing.

Questions have been raised in regard to Augur's legality. As it allows users to wager on yes or no outcomes, this makes its similar to a binary options market. In the United States, these must be approved by the Commodities and Futures Trading Commission (CFTC). As this is not the case and Augur does not prevent US residents from using its platform, there are concerns that it may be in violation of both federal and state laws.[92]

However, the Forecast Foundation claims that it cannot control who uses the platform: as an open-source network anyone with the Ether cryptocurrency can access its markets.[93] As a result, there is no way of limiting access to US residents. However, this may not be good enough for the regulators. In 2018, a CFTC spokesperson said that 'facilitating a product or activity by way of releasing code onto a blockchain does not absolve any entity or individual from complying with pertinent laws or CFTC regulations'.[94]

In this way, Augur presents a conundrum for regulators: as its creators have no way of removing the platform from the internet, the CFTC cannot stop US residents from using it. In this regard, Augur is similar to online file-sharing networks in that their decentralized structure prevents regulators from shutting them down.[95]

Therefore, a softer regulatory approach may be more feasible. In the context of real-money prediction markets, this is not without precedent: in 2014, the CFTC issued a *letter of no action* to PredictIt, a non-profit prediction market based at the University of Wellington.[96] This eliminated the risk of prosecution in exchange for certain concessions on the part of PredictIt: the maximum stake per user for each market was limited to US$850; and, each market was limited to 5,000 users.[97] Like Augur, PredictIt is run on a non-profit basis.[98] As a result, making similar concessions to the CFTC in exchange for regulatory forbearance must appear tempting to the creators of Augur.

**If Augur were to apply restrictions similar to those of PredictIt
in order to secure a no-action letter from the CFTC, how
might this affect trading on the platform?**
(Suggested answer at the end of this chapter.)

Chapter summary

Since the 1990s, the web has enabled more people to access financial markets and armed them with better information. This is making it increasingly difficult to outperform the market. As a result, average investors find themselves drawn toward passive investment strategies, which, somewhat absurdly, rely on sophisticated investors to keep the market efficient for them.

To stay ahead, some investors use natural language processing (NLP) algorithms to harvest data from social media in the hope of detecting shifts in market sentiment before these manifest as price changes. At the same time, other high-profile investors seek to monetize their expertise by disseminating their insights via investment-focussed social media platforms.

Thus, a core of well-informed influencers can help shape the market consensus: while large algorithmic investors dominate the market via trading, high-profile influencers help shape market sentiment – and by extension, price action – via social media platforms. In this way, these platforms are fast becoming a key information conduit between the real world (as reflected in social media) and financial markets. In time, this should, in theory, make financial markets more efficient, by way of democratizing access to financial market expertise (via social media) and shortening the time it takes for new information manifest in market prices (via NLP-driven trading algorithms).

That said, social media content is no different from any other market information in that it is often inconclusive, contradictory and, at times, misleading. Given this inherent uncertainty, it is unlikely that a perfectly efficient market will ever exist as long as online information remains so riddled with imperfections.

In spite of this, it appears that the web and the financial system are merging: in the past, one had to phone a broker in order to invest – there was a clearer demarcation between financial markets and the rest of life. Nowadays, this line is becoming increasingly blurred as the financial system connects to more and more devices (laptops, phones, tablets, etc).

Furthermore, the web is slowly decentralizing the financial system by enabling individuals to transact directly, via a multitude of web-based intermediaries. This has increased liquidity in the financial system while broadening the scope of securities on offer. This change is evident in the advent of prediction markets, which enable investors to securitize and trade uncertainty. One day, companies could use these markets to manage risks in a way that is more bespoke and granular to their businesses than when using conventional financial instruments.

However, this is likely to be some way off. Current platforms are not sufficiently popular or liquid: in other words, these markets are not yet sufficiently efficient to be useful for risk mitigation purposes.

At the beginning of this chapter, we proposed that the economy and the internet are similar in that they are both markets. After all, prices are information conduits; as are websites and messaging apps. In the next chapter we shall look at some of the cybersecurity implications of the increasing digitization of finance.

 KEY TAKEAWAYS

The most important ideas in this chapter are:

- Digitization is enabling more liquid and efficient financial markets.

- Social media and securities markets are an information conduit between the web and the financial system.

- This is giving rise to new ways of investing and managing risk, such as social media sentiment analysis.

 SUGGESTED ANSWERS TO DISCUSSION POINTS

(A) How might the growing popularity of platforms such as Stocktwits affect stock market efficiency?

Stocktwits is an example of how greater connectivity has enabled more people to access financial markets. The free flow and exchange of information via platforms like Stocktwits has made investment research more accessible. In this way, it has effectively crowdsourced financial punditry.

As a large number of users and free-flowing information are key prerequisites for stock market efficiency, the greater popularity of platforms like Stocktwits could facilitate greater market efficiency. By connecting investors who are interested in the same securities, platforms such as Stocktwits facilitate the gathering and dissemination of price-relevant information. In theory, this should help ensure that market prices reflect all relevant information, as Stocktwits users should effect these price changes through their trading.

Furthermore, this effect could be strengthened by an increase in the number of no-commission trading apps that offer integration with financially focussed social platforms. These apps could help increase market liquidity by lowering transaction costs and position sizes for smaller investors, thereby expanding the pool of market participants.

Unfortunately, platforms such as Stocktwits could also help create dangerous feedback loops. If there is an uptick in volume and sentiment (positive or negative) regarding a particular stock and this is picked up by a trading algorithm, the increase in price action (up or down) could exacerbate the existing sentiment and set off more trading algorithms, thereby increasing market volatility. As a result, the growing popularity of platforms such as Stocktwits poses both benefits and risks to market efficiency and stability.

(A) If Augur were to apply restrictions similar to those of PredictIt in order to secure a no-action letter from the CFTC, how might this affect trading on the platform?

In the short term, the positive publicity that is likely to be associated with a no-action letter from the CFTC might grow the user base, which would improve liquidity on the platform. Furthermore, having its activities implicitly countenanced by a regulatory authority is likely to enhance the platform's appeal and attract more users. In the best-case scenario, this could have a snowball effect on the number of users: as more users join the platform, its markets become more liquid, which, in turn, draws more users to the platform.

In the long term, however, any restrictions on position sizes and the number of users in each market could limit its appeal to larger players. As a result, the platform may prove less useful for corporates looking to use it as a tool for risk management.

Finally, the question remains whether it is technically feasible to restrict user transactions on Augur. As an open-source platform, the software is on the internet for all to see, and use. As a result, platform restrictions may well provide an impetus for copycat platforms to spring up. As a result, the cat may already be out of the bag. Perhaps it is too late for regulators to do anything about decentralized prediction markets, and Augur is merely the first to appear?

References

1 Worldpay (2018) Global payments report: The art and science of global payments

2,3,4,5,6,81 Hayek, F A (1945) The Use of Knowledge in Society, *The American Economic Review*, 35 (4), 519–30 (September)

7 MailOnline (2018) British millionaire spends £330,000 on a single round of champagne… and needed 12 staff to help him serve it, 9 September, www.dailymail.co.uk/news/article-2332675/British-millionaire-spends-330-000-single-round-champagne--needed-12-staff-help-serve-it.html (archived at https://perma.cc/L76G-8LHL)

8 Galton, F (1907) Vox populi, *Nature*, 75, 450–51 (March)

9 Surowiecki, J (2004) *The Wisdom of Crowds: Why the many are smarter than the few and how collective wisdom shapes business, economies, societies and nations*, Random House, New York

10,11,12 Chen, J (2018) Bid and Ask, Investopedia, 4 August, www.investopedia.com/terms/b/bid-and-ask.asp (archived at https://perma.cc/J2ZC-PBNH)

13,15 Markets Committee (2018) Monitoring of fast-paced electronic markets, Bank for International Settlements, www.bis.org/publ/mktc10.pdf (archived at https://perma.cc/H9NR-P4U9)

14 Ding, L and Hiltrop, J (2010) The electronic trading systems and bid-ask spreads in the foreign exchange market, *Journal of International Financial Markets, Institutions & Money*, 20 (4), 323–45 (October)

16,17,18,19,20,21 Fama, E (1970) Efficient Capital Markets: A Review of Theory and Empirical Work, *Journal of Finance*, 25 (2), 383–417

22 FTSE Russell (2020) FTSE 100 Index, 30 April, research.ftserussell.com/Analytics/FactSheets/Home/DownloadSingleIssue?issueName=UKX (archived at https://perma.cc/EQJ5-Z6RR)

23,25 McWaters, R J, Blake, M, Galaski, R, Chubb, C K, Uykur, D, Blickling, A and Münch, T (2018) The New Physics of Financial Services: Understanding how artificial intelligence is transforming the financial ecosystem, World Economic Forum, 15 August, www.weforum.org/reports/the-new-physics-of-financial-services-how-artificial-intelligence-is-transforming-the-financial-ecosystem (archived at https://perma.cc/B4EH-LRKM)

24 Marriage, M (2016) Passive funds take third of US market, *Financial Times*, 11 September, www.ft.com/content/4cdf2f88-7695-11e6-b60a-de4532d5ea35 (archived at https://perma.cc/V6X8-8FXE)

26,27,37,52 Al-Ramahi, M, El-Gayar, O, Liu, J and Chang, Y (2015) Predicting big movers based on online stock forum sentiment analysis, in Twentieth Americas Conference on Information Systems, Savannah, USA

28,30,35 Nadkami, P M, Ohno-Machado, L and Chapman, W W (2011) Natural language processing: An introduction, *Journal of the American Medical Informatics Association*, 18 (5), 544–51 (September)

29,31,34,36 Otter, D W, Medina, J R and Kalita, J K (2018) A Survey of the Usages of Deep Learning in Natural Language Processing, University of Colorado Springs, 27 July, arxiv.org/abs/1807.10854 (archived at https://perma.cc/XMZ2-UC4Z)

32,33 Might, M (2015) What is parsing? [video], www.youtube.com/watch?v=V6LiAtG_0QI (archived at https://perma.cc/RMH6-RD4F)

38,39,64 Coyne, S, Madiraju, P and Coelho, J (2017) Forecasting stock prices using social media analysis, in IEEE 15th International Conference on Dependable, Autonomic, and Secure Computing, Orlando, USA

40,41,42,43,49 Deng, S, Huang, Z, Sinha, A and Zhao, H (2018) Can social media affect stock market performance? [Blog], London School of Economics, 19 September, blogs.lse.ac.uk/businessreview/2018/09/19/microblogging-sentiment-and-stock-returns/ (archived at https://perma.cc/6CQS-7TKC)

44 Winck, B (2020) The Dow plunged into a bear market in just 20 days – the fastest 20% drop in history, Business Insider, 12 March, markets.businessinsider.com/news/stocks/dow-index-bear-stock-market-20-days-fastest-history-coronavirus-2020-3-1028989775?op=1 (archived at https://perma.cc/7EVG-9Z2Z)

45 U.S. Commodity Futures Trading Commission & U.S. Securities & Exchange Commission (2010) Findings regarding the market events of May 6, 2010: Report of the staffs of the CFTC and SEC to the Joint Advisory Committee on Emerging Regulatory Issues, 30 September

46 The United States Department of Justice (2016) Plea agreement: United States v. Navinder Singh Sarao, 9 November. Court docket number 1:15-CR-00075-1

47 Harris, R (2011) *The Fear Index*, Random House, New York

48 Gartner (2017) Gartner says 8.4 billion connected 'things' will be in use in 2017, up 31 percent from 2016, 7 February, www.gartner.com/en/newsroom/press-releases/2017-02-07-gartner-says-8-billion-connected-things-will-be-in-use-in-2017-up-31-percent-from-2016 (archived at https://perma.cc/U4HB-T3TW)

50,53,60 Stocktwits (2019) About us, about.stocktwits.com/ (archived at https://perma.cc/M5VR-LS3B)

51,57,59,61,62 Archer, S (2017) A company that's trying to teach millennial 'noobies' how to invest is growing like crazy, Markets Insider, 6 September, markets.businessinsider.com/news/stocks/stocktwits-ian-rosen-teach-millennial-noobies-how-to-invest-2017-9-1002346294 (archived at https://perma.cc/2GEV-PKSK)

54 Lindzon, H (2016) The Future of Asset Management...the State of Venture Capital... and Goldman Sachs is Spamming me [Blog] Howard Lindzon, 11 April, howardlindzon.com/the-future-of-asset-management-the-state-of-venture-capital-and-goldman-sachs-is-spamming-me/ (archived at https://perma.cc/Q8JZ-9THX)

55,56 Chowdhry, A (2017) How Stocktwits is building upon its social platform for millennials, *Forbes*, 10 October, www.forbes.com/sites/amitchowdhry/2017/10/10/how-stocktwits-is-building-upon-its-social-platform-for-millennials/#76ce8cf921b4 (archived at https://perma.cc/X3Z7-JTU5)

58 Stocktwits (2019) ST rules, stocktwits.com/st/rules (archived at https://perma.cc/XJ7M-MQ79)

63,65 PRNewswire (2018) Stocktwits to announce groundbreaking premium rooms at Stocktoberfest West to connect users with industry leaders, Yahoo! Finance, 23 October

66,68,69 Muhn, J (2019) Stocktwits Launches Free Online Trading, Finovate, 18 April, finovate.com/stocktwits-launches-free-online-trading (archived at https://perma.cc/WY7F-8LWG)

67 Stocktwits (2019) Trade App Commissions and Fees, content.stocktwits.com/Commissions and Fees.pdf (archived at https://perma.cc/K686-94TL)

70 Stocktwits (2015) We Teamed Up with Robinhood to Bring True Social Trading to the Stocktwits Community, The Stocktwits Blog, 20 November, blog.stocktwits.com/we-teamed-up-with-robinhood-to-bring-true-social-trading-to-the-stocktwits-community-3c52a909f6aa (archived at https://perma.cc/E9PG-TNFY)

71 Cheng, E (2018) How commission-free trading app Robinhood tries to make money, CNBC, 11 May, www.cnbc.com/2018/05/11/how-commission-free-trading-app-robinhood-tries-to-make-money.html (archived at https://perma.cc/ACQ3-9ELE)

72–76 Yeh, P F (2008) Using prediction markets to enhance US intelligence capabilities: A 'Standard & Poors 500 Index' for intelligence, Central Intelligence Agency, 26 June

77 Berg, J E, Nelson, F D and Rietz, T A (2008) Prediction market accuracy in the long run, *International Journal of Forecasting*, 24 (2), 285–300 (April–June)

78 Berg, H (2007) Prediction Markets at Microsoft [Lecture], Microsoft Corporation, 1 November, users.wfu.edu/strumpks/PMConf_2007/HenryBerg(PredictionPoint%20 KC%20071101).pdf (archived at https://perma.cc/W5MB-ZVN3)

79 Chen, K Y and Plott, C R (2002) Information aggregation mechanisms: Concept, design and field implementation for a sales forecasting problem, California Institute of Technology, Social Science Working Paper 1131 (March)

80,82 O'Leary, D (2011) Prediction Markets as a Forecasting Tool, *Advances in Business and Management Forecasting*, 8, 169–84

83 Intercontinental Exchange (2019) ICE futures US: Cocoa Futures, www.theice.com/products/7/Cocoa-Futures (archived at https://perma.cc/C3S6-7KPF)

84,85,86,91,93 Forecast Foundation (2019) Frequently asked questions, www.augur.net/faqs (archived at https://perma.cc/7VFK-LUVK)

87,88,89,90 Peterson, J, Krug, J, Zoltu, M, Williams, A K and Alexander, S (2018) Augur: a Decentralized Oracle and Prediction Market Platform (v2.0), Forecast Foundation, 12 July, www.augur.net/whitepaper.pdf (archived at https://perma.cc/2X7K-MN2E)

92,95 Orcutt, M (2018) This new blockchain-based betting platform could cause Napster-size legal headaches, MIT Technology Review, 2 August, www.technologyreview.com/s/611757/this-new-ethereum-based-assassination-market-platform-could-cause-napster-size-legal/ (archived at https://perma.cc/27QC-ARZT)

94 Leising, M (2018) Crypto Prediction Market on Blockchain Raises Regulatory Concerns, *Insurance Journal*, 27 July, www.insurancejournal.com/news/national/2018/07/27/496202.htm (archived at https://perma.cc/U6ST-MKJT)

96,97,98 U.S. Commodity Futures Trading Commission (2014) CFTC letter no. 14-130: No-action, 29 October

07

Financial crime, cybersecurity and risk management

Pitfalls and opportunities in fintech

LEARNING OBJECTIVES

By the end of this chapter you will understand:

- How new technologies and innovation can be a source of risk.
- That risk management systems must be both adaptive and forward looking.
- Why risk should be at the heart of every business model.
- How culture shapes risk management, and how to get it right in a fintech context.

Introduction

This chapter surveys the technology-enabled risks that financial institutions face. Its main focus is especially pertinent to fintech: data security in the context of cloud computing. In addition, this chapter examines some of the advantages and disadvantages of using algorithmic mitigation tools for the purposes of preventing and detecting cybercrime.

It is widely recognized that, before the global financial crisis of 2007–09, there was a disparity between the risks taken by financial institutions and those monitored in board rooms across the industry; thus, this failure in governance can be seen as a contributing factor to the crisis.[1] As a result, risk management in financial services has seen a period of increasing sophistication in terms of expert staff, systems and governance. Financial services institutions, big and small, can no longer afford to get risk management wrong. This is because criminals constantly innovate in order to exploit security vulnerabilities in businesses. As a result, the threats facing financial institutions are evolving at a greater pace than ever before.

With this in mind, it is hoped that the reader will gain a newfound appreciation of risk management in a fintech context: as a core part of the business model, and not an afterthought. Of course, this relies on a key ingredient: an organizational culture that is risk aware. For this reason, this chapter will finish by exploring the role that this plays within risk management.

At this stage it should be noted that the term 'bad actors' does not describe high school drama teachers, but is instead used as a catch-all for all manner of criminals; in short, those that seek to use technology to disrupt financial institutions, steal from them or their customers or otherwise damage society. Thus, this group comprises fraudsters, money launderers, terrorists, hackers and other undesirables.

Technology risk and opportunity

Greater global connectivity is laden with opportunity, and risk. Whilst economic liberalization from the 1980s onwards expanded international commerce and increased prosperity around the world, it also opened up new avenues for criminals and other bad actors to ply their trade, aided by advancements in technology which have made it easier for them to operate across jurisdictions.[2]

The boiler room, which refers to a scam operating out of a call centre, is a good example of this. Herein, call-centre staff apply high-pressure sales tactics to lure their victims – who are often elderly or otherwise vulnerable – to buy worthless or, at best, overvalued investments.[3] Despite enforcement action, extensive media coverage and multiple Hollywood movies about these scams, boiler rooms continue to exist. Within the EU, for example, they commonly operate out of countries in Eastern or Southern Europe, employing native English speakers to prey on the naivety and greed of investors in the UK and Ireland.

Boiler rooms are difficult to combat because they tend to prey on people living in different jurisdictions from those in which they operate;[4] this allows them to evade the attention of local authorities, at least initially. When enforcement does happen, it tends to involve police from multiple jurisdictions, which is resource intensive. In this way, criminals are exploiting the free movement of people and capital for nefarious ends; while using communications technology to reach their victims, they take advantage of geographical distance to shield themselves from scrutiny and enforcement action.

Of course, none of this would be possible without cheap and accessible communications technology; like start-ups, criminals seek to leverage technology in order to exploit gaps, not in the marketplace, but in human psychology, law and security systems. Thus, what is an opportunity for some can be a risk to others.

Furthermore, criminals innovate; they adapt their tactics in response to new business models and technologies in order to exploit them. As a result, fintech start-ups, which are often desperate for customers, could easily find themselves in the crosshairs of bad actors. These know that fintechs' security and risk management systems are unlikely to be as advanced as those of large banks. As a result, start-ups must be vigilant from day one; whilst more established organizations may be attractive targets on account of their size, small start-ups are attractive because of their perceived vulnerability.

In some ways, technology has lowered the barriers to entry in the criminal sector.[5] In the past, committing theft would necessitate leaving one's home. No more: nowadays, bad actors can do so digitally, from the other side of the world. Just as the internet has made it easier for fintechs to reach potential customers, it has also made it easier, and more cost effective, for criminals to connect with potential targets.

In contrast, it is not cheap to fight cybercrime;[6] the more bad actors that enter the space, the more resources have to be devoted to fending them off. Moreover, financial institutions and law enforcement do not have unlimited resources. This is made worse by the fact that these organizations compete in the same labour pool for talent to combat cyberthreats. In this way, it can be said that cybercriminals have a cost advantage over the good actors.

As a result, there is an onus on law enforcement agencies and the financial sector to unite, to fight off all manner of bad actors: from terrorists and money launderers, to fraudsters and hackers.[7] As in all wars, one gains the upper hand by forming alliances and being one step ahead of the enemy. Unfortunately, this is a war without end; though all bad actors cannot be eradicated, they can be pre-empted, frustrated and contained. To even stay in the fight, however, the good actors must address the threats posed in adaptive and innovative ways – in other words, evolve with their adversaries.

Why care about risk management and financial crime?

It is estimated that cybercrime costs the global economy *ca* US$600 billion per year;[8] for individual businesses, cybercrime can impact the bottom line significantly. This can come in the form of remedial expenses, audit costs and litigation.[9] Moreover, cybercrime comes with significant opportunity costs, as the need to invest time and money in cybersecurity on an ongoing basis prevents firms from putting these resources to productive use elsewhere in the business.[10] In addition, any customer-specific breach, such as a data loss, can damage a company's reputation and brand, whilst inconveniencing customers. This makes fintech start-ups that are centred around the customer experience especially vulnerable. As a result, risk management needs to be at the core of their business models.

In addition, regulatory intervention is another potential downside of taking a cavalier approach to risk management. Under GDPR, for example, firms in the EU and UK can be fined up to the greater of €20 million or 4 per cent of their worldwide revenue for failing to protect customer data.[11] For instance, in 2019, the UK Information Commissioner's Office announced that it would seek to fine British Airways £183 million for vulnerabilities in its website which enabled the theft of 500,000 customers' personal details.[12]

Furthermore, in many jurisdictions it is becoming more difficult for senior management to hide behind their organizations: in the UK, for example, senior management are held accountable for regulatory failings within their firms via the Senior Management and Certification Regime.[13] This puts pressure on senior managers to take personal responsibility for their firm's compliance with laws and regulations in a proactive manner. A similar dynamic can be seen in global anti-money laundering (AML) regulations; though regulations may differ across jurisdictions, individuals can commonly be held criminally responsible for failing to report suspicious transactions, for example.

Finally, there is a moral imperative for fighting crime. Whether in the digital or physical realms, crime degrades the social fabric of societies and, if it gets out of control, this can undermine political and democratic institutions. Moreover, crime harms individuals: the octogenarian grandmother who loses her life savings to a scammer is someone's grandmother – she could be yours! As a result, one might say there is a moral argument for preventing harm to others, to the extent that it is practicable.

Security weaknesses in cloud systems

Cloud solutions are favoured by many fintech start-ups because they offer flexible access to computing resources. As small fintechs often operate on shoestring budgets, relying on cloud-based infrastructure may not be optional. However, like most technologies, cloud computing comes with risks of its own.

Reliance on cloud services has become near-ubiquitous: one survey of IT professionals in North America, Asia and Europe found that the proportion of organizations storing data on the cloud, of which the majority was sensitive, grew from *ca* 50 per cent to around 70 per cent between 2018 and 2019.[14] However, this is not without risk; by outsourcing parts of their systems, they are creating more doors for criminals to break through.[15]

In addition, there seems to be a widespread lack of awareness regarding the extent of cloud usage in industry. One survey asked IT professionals across 11 countries to estimate the number of cloud-based solutions used within their organization; the average estimate of 31 grossly underestimated the true average of 1,935. Though this number may seem surprisingly high, it becomes increasingly plausible when one considers that many mainstream applications are in some way cloud-based. Prime examples include social media (eg Facebook), email (eg Gmail), collaboration (eg Microsoft OneDrive), and file storage solutions (eg Dropbox), in addition to any number of less obvious solutions within the Everything-as-a-Service (XaaS) paradigm.[16]

The lack of awareness regarding cloud solutions can create vulnerabilities in organizational systems. An organization with limited oversight of its cloud usage risks deploying cloud-based applications that are inconsistently configured across different business units, departments and users. This can leave gaps in applications' security settings, which can be exploited by bad actors.[17]

Thus, what is essentially a governance flaw (ie lack of oversight) increases risk in a way that would perhaps not be possible without the fast-growing rollout of cloud services. Given that an estimated 83 per cent of cloud-using organizations store sensitive data on the cloud,[18] it is imperative that businesses treat their cloud solutions as part of their cybersecurity remit.

Relying on cloud computing comes with unique risks. By placing different organizations' data on the same server, there is a risk that these may get mixed up, and thereby corrupted. In addition, though data may be deleted from a server, it can leave an imprint. Without adequate countermeasures, these inherent vulnerabilities can be exploited by bad actors.[19]

When customers trust organizations with their data, few, if any, go as far as considering their cloud providers. Thus, when organizations use cloud services they place trust in external organizations on behalf of their customers. In this way, there is a chain of reliance which compels organizations to take a systemic view of their use of cloud services:[20] in other words, as part of the business and therefore subject to the oversight.

This means holding cloud providers to the risk management and security standards that organizations hold themselves to. Organizations need to ask themselves how and why they trust cloud providers with their customers' data.[21] This necessitates ascertaining that solution providers have fit-for-purpose security systems and that they employ best-practice data protection measures.[22]

Unfortunately, cloud providers' systems have different levels of security. For example, it is estimated that less than 1 in 10 providers encrypt data *stored at rest* (ie data that is not in use or transit).[23] This highlights that service providers can, and will, take shortcuts, despite competitive pressures: given the overarching need to keep customer data secure, one might otherwise think that maximum security should be a matter of course in a business model like cloud computing.

Relying on cloud solutions also has implications for business continuity planning:[24] how will business be disrupted if a business-critical cloud provider goes down, even temporarily? What back-up measures can be put in place? These questions need to be considered as part of, and ideally in advance, of deploying a cloud solution. Thus, business-critical cloud providers must be viewed as key suppliers and treated accordingly.

Furthermore, detecting potential threats within cloud-reliant organizations is made inherently difficult because of the high amount of noise within these systems: on average, such organizations generate 3.2 billion unique transactions (eg document edits, user logins, file downloads, etc) per month.[25] Out of these, roughly 31 are threats; as the rest are benign, this yields a signal to noise ratio of 1 to 100 million,[26] which makes threat detection a far more difficult problem than looking for the proverbial needle in a haystack.

Thus, without automation, detection systems would get clogged up due to the volume of data.[27] In addition, bad actors often attempt to hide their actions by mimicking normal user behaviour.[28] To address this, organizations deploy machine learning algorithms to detect the small anomalies that identify bad actors.

Combatting cybercrime with machine learning

The volume of transactions and increasing sophistication of bad actors imposes detection costs on financial institutions:[29] just as there is a cost of failing to detect financial crime, false positives inconvenience customers and waste staff time. As a result, organizations turn to automation in order to maximize detection of bad actors whilst minimizing false alarms.

Thus, financial institutions deploy machine learning and data mining algorithms as sorting mechanisms, whereby obviously malevolent transactions are dealt with automatically, leaving more complex cases for human review.[30] In this way, automation helps organizations sift through large volumes of data and deploy staff time more efficiently.

That said, the low signal to noise ratio of malicious transactions to benign transactions can be problematic as the small sample of true positives makes it difficult for the algorithms to identify consistent patterns.[31] Thus, there is a strong argument for deploying supervised algorithms (ie human and machine) rather than algorithms that learn autonomously. In fact, the combination of unsupervised and supervised algorithms has been shown to be more effective in detecting credit card fraud than either approach on its own.[32]

Unfortunately, financial institutions often have incomplete information with regard to attacks suffered. For example, if a customer's computer has been hacked to perpetrate a fraud, it is unlikely that the bank will have much information beyond the data captured at its end. Thus, financial institutions must learn how such attacks differ from regular customer interactions. For example, an automated attempt at stealing customer funds may follow the normal customer journey, such as checking the account balance before transferring money out; however, if this process takes just a few seconds, impossible for any human to complete in the same time, the attack identifies itself.[33]

In this way, gathering richer and more detailed data is an integral part of fighting cybercrime. Moreover, once an attack happens, the target will invariably suffer some loss: in cases of online banking fraud, for example, recovering lost funds is both difficult and costly.[34] Though early detection can minimize losses, prediction can prevent them. Therefore, it is imperative to calibrate detection algorithms towards predicting attacks.[35]

Algorithms have been demonstrated to be effective against the constantly evolving tactics of bad actors.[36] This is because they can spot small anomalies in large data sets,[37] and thereby flag potential 'innovations' on the part of cybercriminals; as the number of nefarious transactions is low in relation to total transaction volume, it is expedient to focus on identifying anomalies as well as known patterns of attack.[38] Of course, these tasks needn't be performed by the same algorithm.

In practice, a balance needs to be struck between spotting anomalies and pattern recognition; in other words, prevention and detection. Moreover, as different organizations have different business models, and therefore different vulnerabilities, their preventative measures need to be tailored according to the degree of risk they face.[39]

Though algorithms can be effective in detecting, and even pre-empting, malevolent transactions, the good actors need to stay one step ahead. One way of achieving this is by deploying so-called 'ethical hackers': good actors who attempt to breach organizations' systems in order to expose vulnerabilities in them. Though commonly deployed in the domain of cybersecurity, there is no reason ethical hackers can't be employed to expose vulnerabilities within financial institutions' anti-fraud or AML procedures, for example.

In addition, hackers do not necessarily have to deploy 'high-tech' methods. In a world of rapidly evolving cyberthreats, it is easy to overlook more down-to-earth vulnerabilities. For example, ethical hackers were able to install *key-logging* software within one organization's IT department by mailing company-branded USB sticks to its Chief Technology Officer (CTO), who then passed these to members of the technology team. This is an example of 'social hacking' because the intruders exploited the authority of the company's brand and its CTO to overcome potential suspicions; it is conceivable that security concerns might have been raised if the USB sticks had not been company-branded.

Whilst predictive algorithms and ethical hacking may help prevent attacks, these are mere tactical interventions. In order to further insulate themselves from potential attackers, financial services institutions need to take the higher ground by approaching data security from a holistic perspective: the underlying data flows need to be structured so that they are harder to breach. As part of this, firms anonymize data in order to mitigate the negative effects of potential data losses.

Anonymization and data security

This term refers to a set of techniques that serve to protect an individual's privacy by concealing certain aspects of their personal data.[40] For example, a person's medical record may omit their name, address and date of birth. In this way, anonymization enables organizations to share customer data with third parties.[41] Data anonymization techniques can include the following:[42]

- Aggregation: whereby all data is shown as totals (or averages) so that no individual can be identified (eg disclosing average customer income).

- Partial data removal: whereby certain details that enable a person to be identified are left out (eg sharing a customer's age instead of their date of birth).

- Pseudonymization: using a coded reference or pseudonym in place of other data (eg using numbers to refer to individuals instead of names).

The list is not exhaustive and there are variants to each of the techniques highlighted above. However, regardless of the technique used, those that deploy them are subject to the same trade-off: that of data usability vs privacy.[43] The more detailed a data set is, the more useful it is; however, the more granular the data, the greater the risk of de-anonymization.[44] That is to say, if an anonymized data set contains sufficiently granular information it may allow bad actors to identify individuals by piecing together individual data points.[45]

Generally speaking, bad actors seek to de-anonymize personal data by matching it to data about an individual already in the public domain.[46] For example, when the State of Massachusetts made summaries of state employees' hospital visits available to researchers in the 1990s, an academic was able to identify the governor's records using only his city of residence, date of birth, sex and ZIP code.[47] This illustrates that de-anonymization can be achieved with surprisingly little data. Indeed, according to a study of 1.1 million people's credit card transactions, 90 per cent of people can be identified using the dates and locations of just four transactions.[48] Thus, data that may not appear to be personal, may nonetheless be sensitive because it can be used to de-anonymize personal data.[49]

The risk of de-anonymization has increased as the internet has broadened the availability of data while advances in computing have made sifting through large data sets easier.[50] When assessing the risk of de-anonymization, an organization has to gauge the risk of a bad actor successfully matching the anonymized data to publicly available information. With the advent of social media, this has become increasingly difficult, as it has become increasingly difficult to judge the extent to which personal information pertaining to individuals in the data set is already in the public domain.[51]

Thus, it makes sense for organizations to take a prudent approach to releasing anonymized data. As the risk of de-anonymization can never be completely eliminated, the issue is not whether de-anonymization is possible, but whether a bad actor can feasibly de-anonymize it given any supplementary information they conceivably may have. As a result, some organizations employ third-party consultants that attempt to de-anonymize data in order to ascertain the robustness of anonymization before it is released publicly.[52]

Though it is widespread, anonymization is not the only way of pre-empting bad actors. Tokenization is another preventative measure against attackers. As part of this, customer data is protected at the point of sale by obscuring it in advance of the transaction.

SECURING CUSTOMER DATA WITH TOKENIZATION

One of the inherent problems concerning credit and debit card transactions is that the customer has to present both their card number and some form of unique information (eg a PIN in-store or the number on the back of card online) to the merchant in order to authenticate a transaction at the point of sale. If a bad actor can intercept these two pieces of data, then the card can be misused.

This problem can be addressed via tokenization. Under this security paradigm, a third party, such as a digital wallet provider, stores the user's card number securely and provides the customer with a stand-in number known as a *token*.[53] At the point of sale, the user presents this to the merchant instead of their actual card number. As part of the transaction authentication process, the merchant's system queries the wallet provider's system to ascertain that the token is legitimate; the wallet provider confirms this by matching the token against the user's card number within its own system.[54]

Thus, security is maintained strategically as the merchant's system never sees the user's actual card number.[55] As a result, an attack on the merchant's system would be incomplete as the attacker would not obtain users' card numbers. In this way, the merchants' systems become somewhat less attractive as potential targets for hackers as the focus shifts to the token providers.[56] However, this degree of centralization can be a weakness as it only takes one breach to affect many customers; however, it can also be a source of strength as the organizations providing the tokens tend to have greater resources and sophistication for fending off attacks.

Colloquially speaking, the idea of risk is taken to mean something bad; however, quantitatively speaking, risk can mean both positive and negative outcomes – upside as well as downside. For example, a new product may increase profits if it becomes popular with customers. On the other hand, it could flop and thereby cause the business to lose money. At the same time, protecting customer data from cyberattacks protects an organization's reputation, and thereby its ability to generate revenue; failing to do so could cause revenues to decline.

Thus, there are revenue-generating risks and revenue-losing risks. In essence, a business model is merely a structured approach to managing a given set of risks. Just as different businesses have different brands, products, and customers, they also have slightly different approaches to managing each type of risk. In this way, businesses can find a competitive advantage in managing risks more effectively than their competitors.[57]

Risk management in a fintech context

In the years leading up to the GFC, there was a focus on revenue generation in the financial industry, wherein risk managers had limited influence on business decisions. The relegated role of risk functions within banks' governance structures, along with the incentives therein, are widely seen factors to the financial crisis of 2007–09.[58]

However, in a dynamic risk environment, financial institutions cannot afford to treat risk management as a box-ticking exercise, and even less so in the case of cyberrisk: according to one estimate, the average cost of cybercrime to large corporates was US$13 million in 2018.[59] Of course, these costs can vary widely. In 2017, the shipping giant Maersk incurred losses amounting to US$450 million as a result of a cyberattack disrupting its shipping activities for 10 days.[60]

Unlike large, established institutions, fintech start-ups are in a unique position with regard to risk management. As they do not have the scale and sophistication of large banks, they are starting with a blank slate. By building their businesses from the ground up, they have the opportunity to embed risk management into the DNA of their organizations, rather than treating it as an add-on. This means placing risk management at the centre of business planning to inform both short- and long-term decision making.[61]

Because of their small size, fintechs have a unique opportunity in that revenue-generating and revenue-preserving staff often work side by side. This enables fintechs to bridge the gap between these two groups more effectively than large financial institutions can. As the business grows, management needs to work toward preserving this connection. Otherwise, there is a risk that individual teams get stuck in a silo mentality, only focussing on things within their remit and losing sight of the bigger picture. This can be damaging because fintechs tend to have a bias towards innovation and growth, and, consequently, they may overlook the risk-based interventions that preserve what is being built.

To manage risk effectively, financial institutions need to deploy risk and compliance teams as business planning tools for taking calculated risks. Just as a new product innovation can be costed and assessed on its advantages and disadvantages, organizations need to consider potential risks when making strategic business decisions. In other words, ask themselves: is it worth it?

Just as managing user engagement on a mobile application relies on gathering data, effective risk management in a financial services context hinges on capturing relevant and timely information about the risks facing the business. This allows countermeasures to be put in place and tracked. Fintechs are in a unique position in this regard because they can build their organizations to facilitate better, and richer, data capture.

Regardless of the amount and quality of data captured, most businesses need to have clear and well-defined risk appetites.[62] For a company's management, this means quantifying potential – and acceptable – losses from the crystallization of each risk.[63] For example, the organization could state how much it is willing to lose per year as a result of fraud. In addition, risks should be quantified in terms of their likelihood.[64] In this way, risks can be prioritized in terms of their likelihood and impact. Furthermore, quantification enables management to impose the potential losses from uncrystallized risks as costs in manager/team budgets, and thereby incentivize mitigation.

Granted, such an exercise may be difficult for fintechs because, as new organizations, they may have very little experience, and thus data, regarding the risks they face. This problem is compounded by the fact that there is very little industry-level data available. This phenomenon is not confined to financial services, because very few organizations are keen to publicize their risk events/mistakes for fear of damaging their reputations.

However, there are signs that the fintech sector is trying to do things differently in order to overcome the lack of relevant organizational experience concerning risk events and security breaches. The Fintech Fincrime Exchange (FFE) is a good example: as an international forum for fintech businesses to share information and experiences regarding the fight against bad actors, it helps disseminate best practice in the fintech sector.[65] In this way, fintechs are able to adapt more quickly to criminal innovations. This speaks to the sector's collaborative ethos; after all, most firms do not compete explicitly on their ability to prevent online fraud, for example. Rather, fintech customer value propositions focus on convenience, experience and price. As a result, it makes sense for fintechs to share best practice with one another as each breach has the potential to harm the industry's reputation as a whole.

Forward-looking risk management

At the bare minimum, a risk management function must ensure that its organization complies with applicable laws and regulations, operates effectively, and implements effective preventative measures.[66] In addition, there must be processes for validating the effectiveness of its approach to risk management; after all, the risk function must evolve with the changes in the risk environment.[67]

Calibrating an organization's approach to risk management in a dynamic environment can be problematic because risk management metrics are inherently backward looking. This is because quantitative measures tend to capture what has happened, rather than what will happen. Thus, the newer the data, the better. However, even real-time data is technically past data. As a result, excessive focus on quantitative metrics can lead organizations to overlook emerging risks, especially in a fast-moving sector like fintech.

This myopia is one reason that financial regulators now mandate that banks conduct stress testing. As part of this, banks model the impact of plausible, yet severe, scenarios on their balance sheets.[68] In this way, it is intended to force banks to look to the future and consider how certain risks could affect their business; and, in doing so, go beyond merely reacting to current risks.

In addition, many financial regulators take a forward-looking approach to supervision. For example, the UK's Financial Conduct Authority attempts to 'pre-empt or address poor conduct so that the risk and any associated harm does not materialise' and, when things go wrong 'ensure it does not cause significant harm to consumers or markets'.[69]

Therefore, in order to pre-empt regulatory intervention, financial institutions need to be able to demonstrate – and document – that they themselves make forward-looking and risk-based decisions. In practice, this means using the organization's own risk management processes to inform business planning, capital allocation and contingency planning. Furthermore, these activities are not exclusively quantitative: thus, even though small fintechs may not have the sophistication required to deploy advanced forecasting models, there is nothing stopping them from looking ahead on a qualitative basis.

The focus on linking risk management with business planning stems from risk-based regulation: the idea that regulators and businesses have limited resources and so must therefore focus their resources on preventing their most significant risks from crystallizing. Thus, by taking a cue from regulation, fintechs can employ a similarly rational approach to risk management; acting under limited resources, they must focus on the most promising opportunities while, at the same time, addressing their largest and most pressing risks. In this way, risk management is a balancing act between revenue-generating and revenue-preserving activities.

CASE STUDY
RiskGenius: An 'insurtech' for insurers

The insurance industry has long been plagued by inefficient behind-the-scenes processes. For example, contract-renewal negotiations for catastrophe insurance have historically been conducted via email: this comes with both risks and inefficiencies concerning version control, data integrity and document management, not to mention security.[70]

The manual nature of the insurance industry's back-office processes leaves loopholes in many companies' risk management systems that bad actors can exploit. This can significantly impact the bottom line. For instance, it has been estimated that insurance fraud costs the UK insurance industry £50 per policyholder every year.[71] In spite of this, many insurers report underusing anti-fraud software packages due to their cost and incompatibility with existing systems.[72]

Thus, the insurance industry's outdated systems and inefficient processes are contributing to the cost of providing insurance cover. This means higher insurance premiums; after all, it is ultimately the customers who bear the cost of insurance fraud. However, the real tragedy is that this prices some people out of the market. In this way, financially vulnerable people are prevented from getting insurance cover they may need.

Unless established insurers update their risk management and IT systems, they may soon find themselves losing customers to smaller, and more tech-savvy, competitors, known as 'insurtechs'. Indeed, if these firms are better at detecting insurance fraud, they may well be able to undercut their larger competitors. In addition, large corporates, dissatisfied with the lack of bespoke cover from large insurers, are now looking towards insurtechs for more customer-centric insurance solutions.[73]

Not all insurtechs are, strictly speaking, insurance companies. RiskGenius (RG) is one such firm. This insurtech is in fact a service provider to the insurance industry, which believes in 'connecting insurance professionals to digital knowledge'.[74] In this way, RG appears to be facilitating digital transformation in the insurance industry as opposed to competing directly with established insurers.

RG was founded in 2012 by two claims attorneys in the United States. Its founders' shared dislike for 'messy insurance documents' was part of RG's genesis. To address this problem, the company applies machine learning to insurance contracts to automate workflows across the insurance industry.[75]

In some wholesale insurance businesses (eg brokers and reinsurers) an insurance contract is usually 'vaulted' after it has been agreed and signed; in other words, stored away securely, on a hard disk or in a file cabinet. In this way, it becomes difficult for insurance companies to extract and aggregate information across different policies.

Indeed, review processes often rely on pen and paper and/or manual keyword searches, which impedes oversight.[76]

This can be remedied using machine learning: natural language processing (NLP) algorithms are deployed to sift through large volumes of text to find policy wording inconsistencies and flag areas requiring further attention; these are then reviewed by a highly skilled employee who can recommend an intervention, such as a policy wording update. In this way, NLP enables insurance companies to deploy professional time more efficiently.[77]

RG uses machine learning to help insurers identify 'silent' exposures:[78] insurance risks that arise when policy wording has not been adapted to changes in the risk environment. For example, the company helped one of its clients scan 100,000 policies for the word 'environment',[79] presumably to identify insurance risks related to climate change. In this way, RG helps insurance companies identify emerging risks.[80] This is important as insurers could otherwise be charging insufficient premiums for unwittingly covering certain risks and/or face having to pay out unforeseen claims due to the lack of oversight. Speaking on this point, RG's CEO and founder Chris Cheatham said in an interview: 'We figured out that not a lot of people knew what is in their insurance policies... not the buyers of insurance... actually the underwriters and the brokers as well.'[81]

Furthermore, RG's tools allow insurance companies to set policy-wording benchmarks for reviewing incoming policies;[82] in other words, insurance contracts that the company did not initially draft itself. As part of this, RG deploys machine learning algorithms to parse through policies and pick out key clauses for a checklist-based review.[83] This enables insurance companies to assess incoming policies against internal standards.[84]

RG appears to be moving forward with machine learning to facilitate automation in the insurance industry. In 2018, CEO Chris Cheatham stated in an interview that the company was working on categorizing policy clauses by type (eg exclusions, war).[85] This allows algorithms to treat qualitative information like quantitative data; in this way, RG is enabling the automatic comparison of different companies' insurance contracts.[86]

**How can RG's solutions facilitate risk management
in the insurance industry?**
(Suggested answer at the end of this chapter.)

Despite regulatory pressures to give risk management greater prominence within businesses, particularly in financial services, there is still some way to go. According to one survey, a significant number of corporate risk managers report that risk is still treated as an 'afterthought' within their organization rather than as a core part of the business.[87]

So why is the role of risk management still relegated? Well, risk management is all about people; an organization can invoke best-in-class policies and deploy best-practice controls, yet still have a deficient risk management system. This is because such measures are only as good as the people behind them; their actions, in turn, are shaped by their organization's culture.

Risk management and culture in fintech

According to the FBI, the top three online frauds (by total losses) perpetrated in 2018 in the United States were email-based (US$1.3 billion), confidence/romance (US$363 million) and investment (US$253 million) scams.[88] These schemes all rely on some sort of social engineering to conduct a fraud. For example, email account compromise scams can involve bad actors pretending to be a business executive or senior decision maker to effect a transfer of funds.[89] This fraud takes advantage of the authority heuristic (see Chapter 3), much like the ethical hackers' USB attack described above.

As can be seen in the cybercrime statistics above, bad actors often rely on people making mistakes. In this regard, Shakespeare's assertion that 'the fault is not in our stars… but in ourselves',[90] is both pertinent and cogent; as people are often the weakest links in risk management systems, it makes sense to focus on shaping their actions. To this end, it is vital to get the organizational culture right.

Organizational culture is what makes the difference between what is said and what is done. While anthropological definitions may vary, 'the way we do things around here' is a useful starting point. That said, this definition may be deceptive in its simplicity, as shaping an organization's culture is anything but simple.

For starters, one must accept that there is no such thing as having no culture; whether or not it is shaped intentionally, there is something besides contractual agreements, computer code and internal policies driving outcomes within an organization. Because no business is, as yet, run entirely by robots, there is a need for human intervention. Because policies, code and rule books cannot capture all eventualities, employees are sometimes required to exercise professional judgement. It is in these situations that organizational culture is important. If no effort has been made to shape organizational culture, employees are likely to do what serves their immediate interests – often that which is expedient, easy or profitable – while taking cues from their environment to gauge the acceptability of their actions. Unfortunately, doing so does not necessarily lead to positive outcomes. Therefore, it is incumbent on financial institutions to shape their internal culture such that employees make decisions that serve organizational risk management objectives rather than their own solipsistic concerns.

Furthermore, culture is not static. It evolves in tandem with changes in organizations' internal and external environments. Therefore, it should come as no surprise that effecting cultural change within an organization is an ongoing project that must be revisited periodically.[91] This necessitates that organizations gather intelligence to help them assess how and why their culture may be changing. Such interventions could range from something as simple as an internal survey to the appointment of external consultants.

Once desired cultural changes have been identified, the question then becomes *how?* What practical measures can be implemented to effect the desired change? To this end, the organization can employ both qualitative and quantitative tools; to effect cultural change successfully, organizations must use both types of intervention.

Let's start with qualitative measures. A company's leaders are responsible for, amongst other things, providing a steer for organizational ethos;[92] however, this is more involved than writing mission statements, making speeches and providing training. Though interventions like these are certainly needed for shaping organizational culture, the most important thing is that managers do as they say, also known as 'walking the talk'. This is important because employees, like most human beings, take cues on how to behave from those in positions of power; if 'the tone at the top' is not consistent with the actions of upper and middle management, then employees will lose respect for their message. As a result, it is vitally important that both the words and actions of management align with the risk management objectives of the organization.

For example, one hedge fund manager gave his employees the minimum annual leave entitlement allowed by law. This was done on account of the hedge fund being an ambitious and hard-working organization. As the owner of the business, he was himself able to take as much leave as he wanted; but he did not. Rather, he never exceeded the minimum leave entitlement. In this way, he was living his company's ethos, thereby motivating his employees to do the same.

Employee behaviour can also be influenced by moulding organizational culture via quantitative interventions. In practice, this means putting in place incentive structures that align employee behaviour with the exigencies of organizational risk management.[93] Thus, internal appraisal procedures can be used as a risk-management tool. By assigning responsibility for risks and their sub-components to individual teams, managers and employees, organizations can make managing each risk part of someone's bottom line; such accountability incentivizes vigilance as it links risks to performance appraisal procedures. In this way, employees become risk owners.

When assigning responsibility for each risk, the level of detail must be commensurate with the desired risk management outcome at each organizational level (ie business units, teams and individuals).[94] This requires risk metrics to be relevant to each risk owner's remit; the closer to the frontline, the more granular the information needs to be and vice versa. For example, the board of a large bank is not normally concerned with the level of customer complaints of individual branches; this is the responsibility of the branch manager.

Just as responsibility is assigned top-down, information flows bottom-up. Thus, any risk management system worth its salt should aggregate low-level tactical data in a way that facilitates decision making, oversight and, crucially, timely escalation of risks up the chain of command. In this regard, it is important to ensure that desired risk management outcomes are formulated in a way that is specific, measurable, achievable, relevant and time-constrained (ie SMART);[95] otherwise a gap will emerge between what is measured (and therefore addressed) and the organization's risk management objectives.

Though the quantitative and qualitative interventions outlined above can be effective in reorientating organizational culture towards greater risk awareness, it is also possible that these cause risk owners to fall into a *silo mentality*, whereby individual business units and teams lose sight of the bigger picture. To avoid this, organizations can incentivize internal knowledge sharing, for example by seconding employees between business units.

Admittedly, many of the interventions discussed above may be better suited for larger, and more well-established financial institutions than for small fintechs. For example, many risk-management interventions require separation of duties and reporting lines in order to be effective; many small firms simply don't have the scale and staff resources to make this a reality. Nonetheless, it makes sense for fintech start-ups to consider how their culture is affecting risk management outcomes from the very beginning: when companies are in their embryonic stages, they are in a unique position to shape their organizational culture and can perhaps do so more effectively than slow-moving incumbent financial institutions.

As fintechs grow, their organizations undergo significant changes of scale: from fledgling start-ups to SMEs, and for a few, to becoming large financial institutions (eg PayPal). As a fintech grows, its organizational culture changes in tandem with its size. In this way, each stage of growth presents an opportunity to effect positive cultural change. However, there is also a risk: if the question of culture is not addressed consciously, it may develop in ways that do not serve the organization's risk-management objectives.

Because most fintechs are small organizations, it makes sense for them to start with their people and the relationships between them when seeking to effect positive cultural change. Innovative businesses tend to be led by ambitious people with high-risk appetites. As a result, many fintechs face the challenge of infusing their growth-orientated culture with a more risk-orientated outlook and, ultimately, achieve a healthy balance between the two. A good place to start is by treating revenue-preserving members of staff not as a regulatory requirement, but as valued advisers who the naturally optimistic founders come to for more sober takes on their ideas.

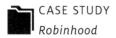

CASE STUDY
Robinhood

Robinhood is a trading app based in the United States. Since launching in 2015, the company has grown its customer base rapidly: by October 2018, it had 6 million customers;[96] in 2019, this number reached 10 million.[97] As a result, the company has received enthusiastic support from the venture capital community: in 2019, Robinhood raised US$323 million as part of a funding round that valued the company at US$7.6 billion.[98]

Robinhood allows its users to trade on a commission-free basis. The company is able to do this because it has other revenue streams: interest on cash balances, stock lending income, interchange fees on card transactions and rebates for directing trades to market makers and trading venues. In addition, Robinhood has a 'Gold' membership plan which gives users access to additional trading and investing tools.[99]

Taking payment in exchange for order flow is a common practice in the brokerage industry. Trade-executing institutions, such as market markers, are willing to pay for this because they benefit from higher trading volumes;[100] the more buyers and sellers they have, the tighter, and thus more competitive, their spreads. However, this practice has received some criticism as taking payments from third parties could give rise to conflicts of interest.[101]

However, Robinhood is adamant that it sends its customers' trades to market makers on the basis of execution quality; the company is insistent that potential rebates do not figure as part of these decisions.[102] Even so, in 2019, US regulators fined Robinhood US$1.25 million for best-execution violations.[103] Under US security industry rules, brokerage firms are required to ascertain that their best-execution arrangements give clients the best possible price given prevailing market conditions at the time of each trade.[104] This means that brokerages may sometimes have to route trades away from their preferred exchanges and/or market makers. However, during a period spanning from 2016 to 2017, it was found that Robinhood did not reasonably consider 'execution quality factors (such as price improvement) that the firm could obtain from alternative markets'.[105] According to the Financial Industry Regulatory Authority (FINRA), the body conducting the investigation into Robinhood, the company's internal documentation on best execution 'focused only on the execution quality of its pre-existing routing destinations, all of which paid Robinhood for that order flow'.[106] Though Robinhood neither admitted to nor denied these charges, it consented to FINRA's findings and settling the fine.[107]

This was not the first time that Robinhood has ended up in hot water as a result of an oversight on its part. In 2018, the company was forced to retract the announcement of a 3 per cent savings account which ostensibly would be backed by the Securities Investor Protection Corporation (SIPC), an industry body that insures cash held in investment accounts against broker failure.[108] The issue arose because Robinhood had neglected to contact the SIPC before announcing the product; had it done so, it would have learned that the SIPC only insures cash deposits intended for purchasing securities, and not savings accounts.[109]

Robinhood also has a subscription service for more sophisticated users. For US$5 a month, users get access to additional features such as more detailed (Level II) market data and access to professional research. In addition, this package comes with a margin feature which allows users to borrow against the cash in their account to purchase securities.[110]

Unfortunately, the margin feature contained a vulnerability that was exploited by users to build extremely large trading positions, seemingly for no other reason than to harass Robinhood. Worse yet, these users shared their exploits via an online message board, posting screenshots from their Robinhood accounts, thereby encouraging other users to follow in their footsteps.

To understand how rogue users were able to game Robinhood's margin features, one must first understand the idea of margin. Brokers typically allow their more sophisticated clients to borrow money against the assets (ie cash and securities) in their accounts in order to take on larger investment positions. For example, if your account is allowed 50 per cent margin, it means that if you deposit US$10,000 in your account, you can borrow another US$10,0000 to buy US$20,000 worth of securities.[111] Under normal circumstances, if you want to further increase your position size, you have to deposit more cash, which would in turn allow you to borrow more money for investing. Moreover, if the shares go down in value, you will have to put more cash into the account to preserve the 2:1 ratio of assets (cash and stocks) to liabilities (the margin); this is known as a 'margin call', which, if not met, will cause the brokerage to sell your shares to limit its own exposure.[112]

In 2019, users found a way to trick Robinhood's systems to make it seem like they had more cash in their accounts, thereby enabling them to access more margin. This process went as follows: users would purchase shares and use them to sell deep-in-the-money call options.[113] These are derivative contracts wherein the seller promises to sell shares at a certain price on or before a specified future date, known as the expiry date.[114] In exchange for making this promise, the seller receives an upfront payment, known as a premium.[115] When an option contract is said to be 'deep-in-the-money' it means that the contract price is significantly below the current market price, and often not far from expiry; as a result – and this is key – the buyer is willing to pay a premium that is very high, often not too far from the actual share price, in exchange for a small, but very likely profit.

Though the sellers of these options were obligated to sell the shares on a future date, they would hold them until expiry.[116] This, along with the cash received from the option sales, overstated the asset balance in their accounts;[117] thus, Robinhood's systems were effectively double counting large parts of users' shareholdings. This allowed some users to gain large positions by borrowing against their inflated asset balances and using this leverage to repeat the process described above several times.[118] Some users claimed to have amassed positions in the hundreds of thousands of dollars starting with account balances of just a few thousand dollars.[119] In response, Robinhood quickly restricted the offending accounts and patched the glitch in their systems.[120]

The infinite leverage hack came during a busy year for Robinhood: in 2019,[121] the company introduced fractional share trading, expanded its crypto offering, and even launched a debit card.[122] In addition, the company gained regulatory authorization to operate in the UK.[123] During that year, Robinhood also appointed new people to senior positions, including a former chief counsel at WhatsApp as Chief Legal Officer;[124] and a former SEC commissioner as the company's first independent board director.[125]

From the perspective of an independent observer, what appears to be the cultural dilemma at Robinhood?
(Suggested answer at the end of this chapter.)

Chapter summary

In this chapter we explored how bad actors can exploit systemic vulnerabilities in risk management systems and how to stop them. Unfortunately, new technologies give risk to new threats. Criminals innovate – just like the institutions they seek to attack. As a result, managing risk in fintech is a constantly evolving endeavour.

For this reason, we attempted to give the reader an overview of risk management in fintech while recognizing that the nature of the threats facing financial institutions, small and large, are bound to change as new technologies emerge. In doing so, this chapter brought together a range of topics particularly relevant to risk management in fintech: machine learning, cloud computing and organizational culture.

Though some of these areas may fall in and out of focus as new risks emerge, there is a deeper lesson to be learned from exploring such a diversity of topics: that, in order to manage risks effectively, fintechs must take a holistic view of risk management within their organizations.

That said, one must never lose sight of the glue that binds organizations together: their people. Though the risk environment will continue to change, the one constant is that human beings are, simultaneously, the greatest asset, and liability, in risk management systems. On one hand, risk management systems rely on good people to fend off bad actors; on the other, their inherent flaws are often the weakest link in such systems.

 KEY TAKEAWAYS

The most important points from this chapter are:

- Like start-ups, bad actors use technology to innovate and scale up their activities.
- When fending off attackers, organizations need both detective and predictive countermeasures while striking a balance between human intervention and automation.
- Though new technologies can create vulnerabilities for criminals to exploit, there is often a human factor underlying certain attacks.
- Incentives and the behaviour of leaders are key to effecting positive cultural change in regard to risk management.

SUGGESTED ANSWERS TO DISCUSSION POINTS

 How can RG's solutions facilitate risk management in the insurance industry?

By applying natural language processing to insurance contracts, RG digitizes the contents of individual insurance contracts, and therefore allows these to be plugged directly into insurance companies' risk management and oversight systems. In this way, RG's tools facilitate the aggregation of granular data into broader categories.

This could help insurers track their performance against individual risks, at different levels of granularity and responsibility. This could lead to better risk management and mitigation within insurance firms. For example, machine learning could be used to identify patterns in claims, which could lead insurers to insist that insureds adopt certain preventative measures as is common in the case of fire alarms and home insurance.

In addition, more granular and up-to-date data regarding underwriting performance – in essence, premiums received vs claims paid – could lead to better pricing and thus more competitive products. Finally, by facilitating reviews of insurance contracts, RG's tools may help insurers avoid contract disputes and litigation costs that may otherwise stem from human error.

 From the perspective of an independent observer, what appears to be the cultural dilemma at Robinhood?

Robinhood appears to have been suffering from a classic problem that afflicts start-ups: the problem of going too far, too fast. The company is clearly led by ambitious and growth-orientated people. This is evident in its impressive growth and its steady stream of innovations. In this context, it is not hard to see how an excessive focus on innovation and expansion (aka 'agility') may have contributed to Robinhood's various hiccups along the way, many of which suggest a lack of voices 'kicking the tyres' within the company.

To be fair, it appears that Robinhood is learning from its mistakes: the appointment of an experienced and high-profile Chief Legal Officer along with a former SEC Commissioner to its board, suggests that the company is taking legal and regulatory matters seriously.

References

1 Senior Supervisors Group (2009) Risk Management Lessons from the Global Banking Crisis of 2008, 21 October, www.sec.gov/news/press/2009/report102109.pdf (archived at https://perma.cc/AA7P-LGXS)

2 Zagaris, B and MacDonald, S B (1992) Money laundering, financial fraud, and technology: The perils of an instantaneous economy, *The George Washington Journal of International Law and Economics*, 26, 61–107

3 Financial Conduct Authority (2020) Share, bond and boiler room scams, 1 June, www.fca.org.uk/scamsmart/share-bond-boiler-room-scams (archived at https://perma.cc/JPM2-HEC3)

4 St Pauls Chambers (2020) Boiler Room Fraud, www.stpaulschambers.com/expertise/boiler-room-fraud/ (archived at https://perma.cc/BK7S-Y8WT)

5,6,7,39 Fischer, E A (2016) Cybersecurity issues and challenges: In brief, 12 August. Congressional Research Service, R43831

8,10 McAfee LLC (2018) Economic impact of cybercrime – No slowing down, www.mcafee.com/enterprise/en-us/solutions/lp/economics-cybercrime.html (archived at https://perma.cc/5696-AUNE)

9,60,73,87 Cambridge Centre for Risk Studies (2018) Risk Management Perspectives of Global Corporations, University of Cambridge Judge Business School, www.jbs.cam.ac.uk/faculty-research/centres/risk/publications/finance-economics-and-trade/risk-management-perspectives-of-global-corporations/ (archived at https://perma.cc/MB88-59S3)

11 European Commission (2018) The General Data Protection Regulation (GDPR), ec.europa.eu/info/law/law-topic/data-protection/data-protection-eu_en (archived at https://perma.cc/M3BS-TF3M)

12 The Information Commissioner's Office (2019) Intention to fine British Airways £183.39m under GDPR for data breach, 8 July, ico.org.uk/about-the-ico/news-and-events/news-and-blogs/2019/07/ico-announces-intention-to-fine-british-airways/ (archived at https://perma.cc/QY3S-RR3Z)

13 Financial Conduct Authority (2019) The Senior Managers and Certification Regime: Guide for FCA solo-regulated firms, www.fca.org.uk/publication/policy/guide-for-fca-solo-regulated-firms.pdf (archived at https://perma.cc/H3TL-4RSE)

14 Oracle & KPMG (2019) Cloud threat report, advisory.kpmg.us/content/dam/advisory/en/pdfs/2019/cloud-threat-report-2019-oracle-kpmg.pdf (archived at https://perma.cc/Z549-EBYA)

15,19,20,21,22,24 Zissis, D and Lekkas, D (2012) Addressing cloud computing security issues, *Future Generation Computer Systems*, 28, 583–92

16,17,18,23,25,26,27 McAfee LLC (2018) Cloud Adoption and Risk Report 2019, cloudsecurity.mcafee.com/cloud/en-us/forms/white-papers/wp-cloud-adoption-risk-report-2019-banner-cloud-mfe.html (archived at https://perma.cc/AG8K-3G56)

28,31,33,34,35,38 Wei, W, Li, J, Cao, L, Ou, Y and Chen, J (2013) Effective detection of sophisticated online banking fraud on extremely imbalanced data, *World Wide Web*, 16, 449–75

29,36 West, J and Bhattacharya, M (2016) Intelligent fraud detection: A comprehensive review, *Computers & Security*, 57, 47–66

30 Quah, J T S and Srinagesh, M Real time credit card fraud detection using computational intelligence, *Expert Systems with Applications*, 2008, 35 (4), 1721–32

32 Carcillo, F, Le Borgne, Y A, Caelen, O, Kessaci, Y, Oblé, F and Bontempi, G (2019) Combining unsupervised and supervised learning in credit card fraud detection, [in press] *Information Sciences* (May)

37 Ngai, E, Hu, Y, Wong, Y, Chen, Y and Sun, X (2011) The application of data mining techniques in financial fraud detection: A classification framework and an academic review of literature, *Decision Support Systems*, 50, 559–69

40,42,45,49,50,52 The Information Commissioner's Office (2012) Anonymisation: managing data protection risk – code of practice, ico.org.uk/media/1061/anonymisation-code.pdf (archived at https://perma.cc/6T3V-L68G)

41,43,44,46,51 Ohm, P (2010) Broken promises of privacy: Responding to the surprising failure of anonymization, *UCLA Law Review*, 57, 1701–31

 47 Sweeney, L (2000) Recommendations to Identify and Combat Privacy Problems in the Commonwealth: Hearing on House Resolution 351 before the Pennsylvania House Select Committee on Information Security, dataprivacylab.org/dataprivacy/talks/Flick-05-10.html#testimony (archived at https://perma.cc/RHN8-DKBX)

48 de Montjoye, Y A, Radaelli, L., Singh, V K and Pentland, A (2015) Unique in the shopping mall: On the re-identifiability of credit card metadata, *Science*, 347, 536–39 (January)

53 Townsend Security (2010) Tokenization: A cost-effective and easy path to compliance and data protection, www.townsendsecurity.com/sites/default/files/Tokenization.pdf (archived at https://perma.cc/98LQ-45YC)

54,55,56 PCI Security Standards Council (2011) Information supplement: PCI DSS Tokenization Guidelines, www.pcisecuritystandards.org/documents/Tokenization_Guidelines_Info_Supplement.pdf (archived at https://perma.cc/DD42-VJT3)

57,91–95 The Institute of Risk Management (2012) Risk culture: Resources for Practitioners, www.theirm.org/media/7236/risk-culture-resources-for-practitioners.pdf (archived at https://perma.cc/RT6M-DFUE)

58 KPMG International (2009) Never again? Risk management in banking beyond the credit crisis, London

59 Accenture (2019) Ninth Annual Cost of Cybercrime Study: Unlocking the value of improved cybersecurity protection, 6 March, www.accenture.com/us-en/insights/security/cost-cybercrime-study (archived at https://perma.cc/NB28-U23Y)

61,62,63,64,66,67 The Institute of Risk Management (2002) IRM's risk management standard, www.theirm.org/what-we-do/what-is-enterprise-risk-management/irms-risk-management-standard/ (archived at https://perma.cc/97ZS-GK6E)

65 Fintrail (2019) FinTech FinCrime Exchange (FFE), www.fintrail.co.uk/ffe/ (archived at https://perma.cc/NJL8-6HDF)

68 Thun, C (2013) Common Pitfalls in Stress Testing, Moody's Analytics, www.moodysanalytics.com/-/media/article/2012/2012-10-12-common-pitfalls-and-challenges-in-stress-testing-of-banks.pdf (archived at https://perma.cc/F8VR-WN7H)

69 Financial Conduct Authority (2019) FCA Mission: Approach to Supervision, www.fca.org.uk/publication/corporate/our-approach-supervision-final-report-feedback-statement.pdf (archived at https://perma.cc/MAK7-8U8H)

70 B3i Services AG (2019) Cat XoL Product Deployed to Customers' Production environments, 15 October, b3i.tech/news-reader/cat-xol-product-deployed-to-customers-production-environments.html (archived at https://perma.cc/8QXE-B758)

71,72 HM Government (2016) Insurance Fraud Taskforce: final report, assets.publishing. service.gov.uk/government/uploads/system/uploads/attachment_data/file/494105/ PU1817_Insurance_Fraud_Taskforce.pdf (archived at https://perma.cc/8DXB-FE9Z)

74,75 RiskGenius (2019) About RiskGenius, www.riskgenius.com/aboutus/ (archived at https://perma.cc/X5A5-25LH)

76,78,80,84 Johnston, A (2019) Quarterly InsurTech Briefing Q3, Willis Towers Watson, 23 October, www.willistowerswatson.com/en-US/Insights/2019/10/quarterly-insurtech-briefing-q3-2019 (archived at https://perma.cc/V69U-Q7K7)

77 Rodriguez, J (2019) Policy administration systems: the backbone of the policy issuance process, 23 October, in Quarterly InsurTech Briefing Q3, Willis Towers Watson, www. willistowerswatson.com/en-US/Insights/2019/10/quarterly-insurtech-briefing-q3-2019 (archived at https://perma.cc/V69U-Q7K7)

79,81 Simpson, A G (2018) Insurtech Pilots and Pivots: Learning by Doing and Undoing, *Insurance Journal*, 15 October, www.insurancejournal.com/magazines/mag-coverstory/2018/10/15/503999.htm (archived at https://perma.cc/4R29-69XL)

82,83 RiskGenius (2019) RiskGenius for carriers, www.riskgenius.com/carriers/ (archived at https://perma.cc/EL2X-NDQS)

85,86 Boyce, R (2018) Q&A with Chris Cheatham, CEO of RiskGenius, Leader's Edge, 3 October, www.leadersedge.com/brokerage-ops/itc-2018-interview-with-chris-cheatham-ceo-of-riskgenius (archived at https://perma.cc/D764-4P9H)

88,89 Federal Bureau of Investigation (2019) Internet crime report 2018, 22 April, www.fbi.gov/news/stories/ic3-releases-2018-internet-crime-report-042219 (archived at https://perma.cc/WW3W-FTB3)

90 Shakespeare, W (1599) *The Tragedie of Julius Caesar*, I (ii) 140–41, www.gutenberg.org/ cache/epub/2263/pg2263-images.html (archived at https://perma.cc/FQB8-995S)

96 Tenev, V (2018) A letter from Robinhood Co-Founder & Co-CEO Vlad Tenev, Robinhood, 12 October, blog.robinhood.com/news/2018/10/12/a-letter-from-robinhood-co-founder-amp-co-ceo-vlad-tenev (archived at https://perma.cc/8MSA-UVXG)

97 Robinhood (2019) 10 Million Thanks, 4 December, blog.robinhood.com/ news/2019/12/4/ten-million-thanks (archived at https://perma.cc/4AFE-VQC8)

98 Robinhood (2019) Robinhood Raises $323M to Democratize Finance For All, 22 July, blog.robinhood.com/news/2019/7/21/robinhood-raises-323m-to-democratize-finance-for-all (archived at https://perma.cc/S7RM-TQGS)

99,102 Robinhood (2020) How Robinhood Makes Money, robinhood.com/support/ articles/360001226106/how-robinhood-makes-money/?region=US (archived at https:// perma.cc/2K4Y-64VH)

100,101 Kenton, W (2018) Payment For Order Flow, Investopedia, 28 February, www. investopedia.com/terms/p/paymentoforderflow.asp (archived at https://perma.cc/S6TZ-KV3K)

103–107 Ong, M and Rote, M (2019) FINRA Fines Robinhood Financial, LLC $1.25 million for Best Execution Violations, Financial Industry Regulatory Authority, 19

December, www.finra.org/media-center/newsreleases/2019/finra-fines-robinhood-financial-llc-125-million-best-execution (archived at https://perma.cc/S28K-YSHF)

108,109 Rooney, K (2018) What fintech can learn from Robinhood's 'epic fail' of launching checking accounts, CNBC, 17 December, www.cnbc.com/2018/12/17/what-fintech-can-learn-from-robinhoods-epic-fail.html (archived at https://perma.cc/Q4KY-C6TE)

110 Robinhood (2020) Robinhood Gold, robinhood.com/us/en/support/my-account-and-login/robinhood-gold/ (archived at https://perma.cc/ZC85-63RQ)

113,116,118,119 Levine, M (2019) Money Stuff: Playing the Game of Infinite Leverage, Bloomberg, 5 November, www.bloomberg.com/opinion/newsletters/2019-11-05/money-stuff-playing-the-game-of-infinite-leverage (archived at https://perma.cc/F5BV-BJ8S)

111,112 Twin, A (2020) Margin, Investopedia, 21 April, www.investopedia.com/terms/m/margin.asp (archived at https://perma.cc/2YXG-3HEQ)

114,115 Farley, A (2019) The Basics of Covered Calls, Investopedia, 13 April, www.investopedia.com/articles/optioninvestor/08/covered-call.asp (archived at https://perma.cc/Y9VG-42JZ)

117,120 Fuscaldo, D (2019) Robinhood Glitch Lets Traders Borrow Unlimited Funds To Buy Stocks, *Forbes*, 6 November, www.forbes.com/sites/donnafuscaldo/2019/11/06/robinhood-glitch-lets-traders-borrow-unlimited-funds-to-buy-stocks/#425634512125 (archived at https://perma.cc/MPS6-UWKU)

121 Robinhood (2019) #RobinhoodRewind 2019, 17 December, blog.robinhood.com/news/2019/12/17/robinhoodrewind-2019 (archived at https://perma.cc/9GK2-RA57)

122 Robinhood (2019) 5 Things to Know About Cash Management, 11 December, blog.robinhood.com/news/2019/12/11/5-things-to-know-about-cash-management (archived at https://perma.cc/WJ7E-3B42)

123 Robinhood (2019) FCA Authorizes Robinhood to Operate in the UK, 7 August, blog.robinhood.com/news/2019/8/7/fca-authorizes-robinhood-to-operate-in-the-uk (archived at https://perma.cc/MHP6-HQ54)

124 Robinhood (2019) Robinhood Welcomes Anne Hoge as Chief Legal Officer, 21 November, blog.robinhood.com/news/2019/11/21/robinhood-welcomes-anne-hoge-as-chief-legal-officer (archived at https://perma.cc/YL8N-9MW6)

125 Robinhood (2019) Former SEC Commissioner, Dan Gallagher, Joins Robinhood's Board of Directors, 7 October, blog.robinhood.com/news/2019/10/7/former-sec-commissioner-dan-gallagher-joins-robinhoods-board-of-directors (archived at https://perma.cc/C3PS-XQR4)

08

Regtech and regulatory compliance

Financial regulation in a fintech context

LEARNING OBJECTIVES

This chapter will help you understand:

- How regulatory imperatives are shaping fintech.
- How regulators are responding to fintech innovation.
- Regulatory principles pertaining to Big Data and AI.
- Regulations pertaining to blockchain and cryptocurrencies.

Introduction

This chapter is about the laws and regulations that are relevant to fintech and some of the technologies discussed in this book. It is intended to set out the key regulatory issues concerning certain innovative business models and technologies. As a result, this chapter is not about financial regulation, per se. Instead, it addresses the regulatory and legal considerations pertaining to the use of innovative technologies in a fintech context.

Moreover, this chapter does not deal with the minutiae of specific rules, laws or regulations. After all, that is what lawyers are for. Instead, the aim is to examine the big-picture considerations underpinning the use of technology in finance; though individual jurisdictions may have different laws and regulations, the policymaking and regulatory objectives are often similar.

This chapter attempts to take a global view of regulation. That said, the author acknowledges that most of what is written is either UK, EU or, very occasionally, US-centric. This is because these jurisdictions have been, and continue to be, drivers of international standard setting in the domains of technology and finance. In spite of this, this chapter should be no less useful to readers outside these jurisdictions, as the underlying regulatory issues are the same.

Regulation and the global financial crisis

As discussed in Chapter 2, the global financial crisis of 2007–09 (GFC) helped foment the emergence of the fintech sector. By damaging the collective reputation of the financial industry, for example, the GFC made consumers more willing to adopt financial solutions from outside the mainstream. However, there is also the behind-the-scenes view, that the regulatory response to the GFC reimagined financial regulations and thus helped reshape the competitive arena.

Following the near implosion of the financial system in 2008, new financial regulations were introduced around the world. The aim of these was to stop future bank failures from endangering the stability of the financial system while addressing the *too big to fail* problem.[1] In this way, the post-2008 reforms were intended to prevent a repeat of the mistakes that led to the GFC.

In the United Sates, these regulatory changes came in the form of the Dodd–Frank Act.[2] This brought in a slew of new regulations, from stringent reporting requirements to restrictions on the use of banks' proprietary capital.[3] As part of this, certain large financial institutions were designated as 'systemically significant', thereby subjecting them to greater regulatory scrutiny.[4]

Meanwhile, similar reforms were enacted around the world: in the UK, for instance, this took the form of the Financial Services Act 2012, which created new regulatory authorities with enhanced supervisory powers.[5] Financial regulation, it was promised, would be more 'intrusive' and 'forward looking'.[6] Furthermore, the Banking Reform Act 2013 increased banks' capital requirements while forcing the financial separation of their retail and investment banking activities via *ring-fencing*.[7]

Although excessive regulation can be detrimental to innovation,[8] the global reform of financial services regulation since the GFC may inadvertently have facilitated fintech innovation by shifting the regulatory burden onto larger financial institutions. The financial crisis taught regulators to be more risk focussed. Given limited resources, this means that regulators have to focus on institutions that pose comparatively greater risk to their regulatory objectives. Generally speaking, this results in larger institutions receiving greater scrutiny due to their larger balance sheets and greater number of customers. As a result, small fintechs receive comparatively little scrutiny in comparison to larger institutions. In this way, more top-heavy regulation may have handed the advantage to fintechs by tempering risk appetite within large financial institutions and slowing down innovation within banks.

Such intra-jurisdictional *regulatory arbitrage* has allowed small fintechs to enjoy comparatively less scrutiny. This has left regulators in a bind: on one hand, increased competition and innovation are desirable outcomes for addressing the too big to fail problem; on the other, a greater number of firms is making regulatory oversight more difficult.[9] With their resources thinly spread, regulators are seeking new ways of overseeing the financial industry. However, as much of the current regulatory paradigm was created in response to the GFC, it may not be appropriate for regulating fintech.[10] As a result, regulators across the world are seeking new ways of supervising financial institutions: like the firms they regulate, regulators must innovate to make their internal processes faster, cheaper and easier.

Of course, such innovation is not limited to regulators: large financial institutions incur significant compliance costs in the form of professional time to ensure they comply with the minutiae of financial regulation. This is not cheap: according to an estimate by the European Commission, financial services firms spend between 0.5 per cent and 1 per cent of their annual operating costs on regulatory reporting.[11] As a result, some financial institutions are turning to technology to address the increased compliance burden.

ROBOTIC PROCESS AUTOMATION (RPA)

This term is something of a misnomer as it does not involve robots, at least not in the conventional sense.[12] In the context of RPA, a 'robot' is merely a computer that has been programmed to perform certain computer-based tasks such as opening and closing files, transferring data and filling out forms. Thus, besides freeing up staff time, RPA helps minimize errors in back-office workflows.

As back-office functions do not generate revenue, financial institutions are looking to RPA to reduce costs.[13] In some ways, this can be seen as the next logical step on from outsourcing in the journey towards back-office rationalisation.[14] What's more, RPA allows banks to incrementally digitize their operations without uprooting ageing, though mission-critical, IT systems.

On average, an RPA deployment has a payback period of *ca* 11 months.[15] Furthermore, it is estimated that a large company with 50,000 employees can increase profits by over US$30 million per annum by using RPA to automate 20 per cent of staff capacity.[16] The potential for cost savings has not escaped the eye of the insurance industry: according to one survey of insurance companies, 17 per cent of respondents expect RPA to cause a reduction in the use of outsourcing.[17]

Of course, RPA is no panacea. The robots are only as good as their underlying processes;[18] if the underlying processes change, the machines will need to be reprogrammed. Moreover, as the robots are becoming more sophisticated and, in some domains, being programmed to perform multiple tasks,[19] many jobs are at risk as a result of RPA. No surprise then, that the deployment of RPA has significant change management implications.[20]

Though jurisdictions vary, financial regulators generally have three core objectives: consumer protection, market integrity and systemic stability.[21] As the financial industry evolves with changes in technology and the emergence of innovative new business models, the risks to these objectives change. As a result, regulators must adapt to their environment and adapt their approach accordingly.

Regulatory risks in fintech business models

Though the fintech space is broader and more diverse than peer-to-peer (p2p) lenders and investment robo-advisers, this sub-section will focus on these business models. This is because both grew more prevalent in the post-crisis era. As a result, they illustrate many of the regulatory issues concerning fintech business models: as there is a significant degree of overlap in the themes discussed for both types of fintech, the prevalent issues may well apply to other fintech business models.

Both p2p lenders and investment robo-advisers promise greater financial inclusion through more accessible and cost-effective financial solutions. No doubt, this is attractive to policymakers. However, there are certain unanswered questions regarding each business model, which may affect negative consumer protection and financial stability outcomes; in other words, these business models may threaten regulatory objectives.

For starters, there may be a consumer protection issue around product understanding: as both p2p lenders and robo-advisers are new solutions, it is questionable whether consumers understand what they are signing up to. When using a smartphone or tablet to access a financial service, how many people read the terms and conditions? As many consumers mindlessly tick boxes and ignore pop-ups, there is a risk that they will miss important disclosures for the sake of preserving mental energy.

Moreover, app-based financial solutions designed to optimize the user experience may neglect important disclosures, or even mislead users. For example, a review of customer agreements from leading robo-advisers in the United States found that firms were not without potential conflicts of interest and did not hold themselves to an adequate standard in regard to serving their clients' best interests.[22] However, these details are likely to have been lost on many of their clients as any exclusions, caveats and disclaimers are often contained within lengthy client agreements.[23] As a result, many users may invest with robo-advisers and expect a higher standard of fiduciary care than the one they receive.

This misconception extends to p2p lenders. Like robo-advisers, these solutions, mobile or otherwise, often come with user agreements written in legalese. As a result, the average user has little hope of understanding these agreements. Consequently, users may not fully appreciate the risks of investing through p2p lenders.

People tend to invest in p2p schemes because they are seeking a higher yield than what mainstream banks can offer. Thus, they are anchoring their product expectations to savings accounts, which tend to enjoy some form of deposit insurance. In this way, they may succumb to the false expectation that their p2p investments, which exhibit similar characteristics to savings products (interest rates, term, etc), enjoy the same degree of protection. As a result, some may be surprised to find their investment impaired when underlying borrowers default.

The yield-seeking behaviour of some p2p investors can also have systemic effects: as investors chase yield, they take greater risks; this, in turn, depresses *yields* as there is a greater supply of credit leaving borrowers with the upper hand. The lower yield then forces yield-hungry investors to take on greater risks, thereby further depressing yields and perpetuating the cycle. A similar effect may be observed if defaults increase causing investors to become more risk averse, whereby they withdraw from the market, causing interest rates to increase; this shortage of credit means that even creditworthy borrowers will find it more difficult (and expensive) to obtain financing, thereby worsening economic conditions. Thus, p2p platforms' focus on yield may cause credit markets to become more pro-cyclical.[24] This may be particularly pronounced in markets where p2p lending is prevalent, such as the UK, where these platforms account for *ca* 15 per cent of all consumer lending.[25]

The investment robo-advice model can also be a source of pro-cyclicality. This is because robo-advisers tend to direct investors towards the same type of low-cost exchange-traded funds (ETFs). These funds passively track well-known equity indices, such as the S&P 500 by investing in all the constituent stocks of a market index. This dynamic can create bubbles as investors are, in effect, investing in a narrow range of stocks. This can give rise to a feedback loop wherein price rises attract more people to the stock market, pushing prices even higher. However, if public appetite for the stock market cools, this feedback loop could reinforce downturns in the market. With *ca* 37 per cent of invested assets in the United States held in passive investment funds like ETFs,[26] robo-driven pro-cyclicality has the potential to significantly worsen stock market crashes (for more on this, see Chapter 6).

Fintech similarities to the pre-GFC years

The more prevalent p2p and robo-advisers become, the greater their potential for systemic impact, positive and negative. If a significant number of fintechs were to fail, this may have consequences for the non-financial economy. If this sounds familiar, it is because this has happened before, most recently during the GFC.

The financial crisis of 2007–09 did not emerge in a vacuum. It came about following a period of financial innovation and historically low interest rates. This created an environment where yield-seeking institutions invested in baskets of US mortgages, the now infamous mortgage-backed securities (MBS). These investments were financially engineered to offer higher returns for comparatively less risk.[27]

The basic idea was simple as well as seductive: though individual states had experienced property market declines from time to time, US property prices had, on average, not declined for several decades. Based on historical data, it was believed that regional property markets were weakly correlated with the overall US economy, which had, from time to time, experienced recessions. In this way, banks could manufacture 'low-risk' securities by bundling together mortgages from different states and across different classes of borrowers.[28]

The apparent safety of capital and attractive yields drew investors from around the world to the US MBS market. What's more, banks found that they could make more money by following an 'originate and distribute' model,[29] which entails making home loans and then selling these on to investors and then charging a fee for servicing the mortgages. This took the risks of the mortgages off banks' balance sheets. As a result, these banks effectively became conduits between borrowers and investors. Meanwhile, investors bore the risks of financing banks' mortgages, and so became *shadow banks*.[30] This term has also been used in the context of p2p lenders as they are effectively following an 'originate and distribute' model by connecting borrowers and investors via their platforms.[31]

Of course, the parallels do not stop there: in the run-up to the financial crisis, investors were chasing yield; investors in p2p schemes are doing the same. Moreover, many pre-crisis banks were under intense shareholder pressure to maximize profits. Likewise, many fintechs face similar pressures from their financiers,[32] who favour quick growth in order to 'scale-up' their business; often, in order to make the business financially sustainable, or at least viable enough to be attractive to the next cohort of funders.

As both p2p and robo-advisers are distribution-led business models that serve to connect borrowers and investors, they retain little, if any, of the risk from the products they sell. As a result, it is not hard to see how the pressure to grow could lead some to focus on short-term customer acquisition. There is a pre-GFC precedent for this: as banks could simply pass on the credit risk of their mortgages to yield-hungry investors, there was very little incentive to screen borrowers for creditworthiness. At the same time, investors took little or no interest in the mortgages underpinning their investments; after all, these were diversified and serviced by reputable banking institutions.

With incentives thus aligned, negative consumer outcomes, such as p2p investors taking risks they do not fully understand, should not come as a surprise; indeed, this risk has been noted in relation to p2p platforms.[33] When unconstrained, the p2p business model can incentivize unsustainable lending and fraud, as was the case in China's p2p bubble, which was, at least initially, lightly regulated: as p2p lending grew in popularity, the proportion of new p2p loans to new bank loans grew to 40 per cent by mid-2016.[34] However, as defaults surged, the size of the problem spurred regulatory intervention and a nationwide overhaul of the sector ensued.[35] By mid-2018, the ratio of new p2p loans to new bank loans had fallen below 10 per cent; during the same time, the number of p2p platforms in China fell by more than a third, from around 3,000 to *ca* 1,800.[36]

Though p2p lending is growing in Europe and North America, it has yet to reach the same scale as it did in China. That said, if left unchecked, the sector could have similarly disruptive effects on consumer credit markets in the West. As p2p platforms are similar in structure to open-ended credit funds,[37] they suffer from the same potential liquidity problem: when investors want to redeem their money, the fund has to sell its underlying holdings. Unfortunately, if the underlying holdings are illiquid, a surge in redemptions could collapse the fund.[38] As p2p loans are similarly illiquid, a loss of confidence in p2p lending could cause a *run* on one or more p2p platforms.

Perhaps then, it is for this reason that many p2p lenders view the failure of a high-profile p2p platform as one of the biggest risks facing the sector;[39] such an event may trigger a rise in redemptions across the sector, which, in turn, could lead to more failures. This scenario would be a hark back to the GFC: the collapse of Lehman Brothers in September 2008 caused a run on the Reserve Primary Fund, a large *money market fund*, that had large exposures to short-term Lehman debt.[40] This collective loss of confidence caused investors to hoard cash; after all, who would fail next? As a result, the usually liquid money markets dried up, causing yet more financial turmoil.[41]

To be sure, p2p lenders have collapsed without far-reaching systemic consequences. As an example, the UK-based p2p platform Lendy collapsed in 2019.[42] Yes, investors lost money, but the failure does not appear to have had a significant effect on other platforms.

Though many of the underlying drivers (low interest rates, yield-seeking investors and distribution-led business models) in the post-crisis era are similar to those preceding the GFC, it is not clear whether a new financial crisis can emerge as a result of excessive p2p lending. There are differences between many of the fintech business models and the 'too big to fail' banks. For starters, very few, if any, fintechs have the scale of the financial institutions whose actions helped precipitate the financial crisis. Furthermore, p2p lenders are less interconnected with each other than large banks are.[43] In this way, any failures are likely to be contained, at least for now.

Ultimately, the big test for novel and fast-growing fintech business models is underway in the form of the COVID-19 outbreak and its economic aftermath.

As part of this, p2p lenders are learning whether their credit-risk models hold up in the face of economic stagnation and mounting job losses. Likewise, robo-advisers' ability to retain customers via their slick user interfaces is being tested under conditions of greater financial market volatility.

Regtech and sandboxes

Though innovative business models may pose risks to individual consumers, or indeed, the wider financial system, they also offer economic opportunity. This may come in the form of greater financial inclusion, cheaper financial products and a more competitive and consumer-friendly financial sector. As a result, regulators must try to balance these opportunities with the risks posed to their organizational objectives, just like the firms they seek to regulate.

As fintechs are innovative businesses, it makes sense for their regulators to attempt to emulate some of their innovative flair to allow for more effective and efficient regulatory supervision. Like any other business, regulators are subject to certain resource constraints. Thus, they are increasingly turning to technology to help facilitate their activities. This has given rise to the idea of 'regtech', which is a portmanteau of regulatory technology.

Just as is the case with 'fintech', the term can mean different things to different people. For our purposes it shall be taken to mean the application of technology to make regulatory supervision and compliance more effective and efficient. Thus, regtech solutions can be deployed both by regulators and the firms they seek to regulate.

To address the challenges of regulating a more dynamic financial sector, regulators use technology to facilitate data collection and enhance their oversight processes.[44] In this way, technology can help regulators gather more granular and up-to-date information; in theory, this should help regulators detect and respond to emerging risks in a more timely manner. In addition, regtech can help free up staff time that would otherwise have been spent on routine and monotonous data-gathering tasks. As regulatory authorities are constrained by their access to technological expertise,[45] saving this resource allows their tech-savvy employees to focus on value-adding activities such as thinking about emerging risks in the fintech sector or speaking directly with the firms they regulate.

CASE STUDY
Digital Regulatory Reporting

In 2018, the Bank of England and Financial Conduct Authority (FCA) launched a pilot initiative to digitize reporting processes in conjunction with six major banks. This project was branded as Digital Regulatory Reporting (DRR). Its aim was to use blockchain technology to improve the quality and consistency of the data reported to regulators. As part of the project, the participants built a prototype to facilitate regulatory reporting in two areas: mortgage lending and bank capital ratios.[46]

According to UK rules, no more than 15 per cent of mortgages sold may have credit exceeding 4.5 times the borrower's declared income.[47] In addition, Basel III Standards require banks to maintain high grade capital ratios of at least 4.5 per cent against risk weighted assets.[48] These rules were converted into computer code to allow automatic monitoring of banks' compliance with them; meanwhile, banks standardized their data to ensure consistent reporting across all participating entities.[49]

In this way, the prototype enabled the comparison of reported data against regulatory requirements. Underpinning this was a blockchain solution: each rule was programmed into a smart contract, which was then installed on nodes held at the regulators and individual banks. On each node, this contract was run against data supplied by the regulated entities. The results of these compliance checks were made available to regulators via a graphical user interface; this allowed regulators to generate compliance reports as and when required. In addition, the interface enabled regulators to request additional data directly from each firm's node via an API. To make the solution accessible to smaller firms, the prototype allowed for the option of uploading the data in Excel format.[50]

The DRR pilot can be seen as a success in the context of the UK regulatory authorities' broader approach to regtech, which the FCA views as using 'technology and innovation to deliver regulatory requirements in a more effective and efficient way'.[51] Moreover, the FCA recognizes that increases in reporting requirements since the GFC have led to a greater regulatory burden on firms.[52] According to the FCA's Director of Innovation, '*Firms face challenges in how they meet their obligations to report information to us. We think there's a real opportunity for technology and innovation to reform how they do that.*'[53]

DRR could conceivably be expanded to automatically issue fines in response to rule breaches.[54] However, this may be some way off: as part of the pilot, the regulators concluded that converting all regulation to code would be too onerous and costly.[55] As a result, they suggest approaching DRR incrementally as opposed to a wholesale overhaul of reporting systems.[56] Indeed, incremental changes in specific domains could mean significant savings for regulated firms: as an example, it is estimated that large lenders spend an average of £450,000 pa on reporting mortgage data to the regulators.[57] Thus, the regulatory authorities and industry will need to work together to identify the greatest areas of cost and inconvenience in the regulatory reporting process; in other words, their compliance 'pain points'.

How might an initiative like Digital Regulatory Reporting facilitate supervision and compliance processes in the financial industry?
(Suggested answer at the end of this chapter.)

Besides deploying technology to gather better data, regulators can seek engagement with the firms they regulate in order to enhance their own supervisory processes. This gives regulators access to business intelligence and qualitative insights from industry which can be used to inform their regulatory approach; it is also a way for regulators to disseminate best practice. What's more, engagement with regulators can benefit regulated entities: by reducing regulatory uncertainty,[58] which can be seen as a cost, such engagement helps reduce barriers to entry in the financial sector.

One way of increasing regulator–firm engagement is via a regulatory sandbox. This is a tool designed to foster in-depth regulator–firm engagement in a fintech context. As part of this, firms are allowed to experiment with novel financial solutions using real customers, albeit on a limited scale. This is done under the careful supervision of regulators on a time-constrained basis.[59]

Sandboxes allow fintechs to test innovative financial solutions in a safe environment,[60] thus minimizing the risk of inadvertently breaching any relevant laws or regulations. This allows firms to refine their solutions before rolling them out on a greater scale. Moreover, sandboxes enable regulators to instil within firms a degree of best practice in regard to risk management and compliance; as firms are keen to 'graduate' from the sandbox, they will no doubt pay close attention to the regulator's messaging.

Though sandboxes can be effective in reducing regulatory uncertainty for fintechs, they are also resource intensive as they require staff to be knowledgeable in both regulatory matters as well as technology. As a result, some financial regulators deploy fintech-specific regulatory support teams, sometimes known as *regulatory offices*. These provide basic guidance to fintechs, helping them understand regulatory requirements and how best to comply with them. Indeed, a large proportion of regulatory queries, even when they come from fintechs, do not need go through sandboxes. In this way, regulatory offices can be used as a sorting mechanism for deciding which firms go into the sandbox.[61]

Fintech-dedicated offices are a way of centralizing valuable skills and thereby leveraging them. Nonetheless, this is a tactical intervention as regulated firms still have to be dealt with on a case-by-case basis. As this approach is resource intensive, some regulators are turning to updating their rule books and guidance documents to help firms make better compliance decisions; in other words, approaching the problem strategically by attempting to minimize any confusion surrounding the rules.

Despite increasing regulatory sophistication and support for fintechs, the skills shortage at regulatory authorities is likely to persist. What's more, supervising fintechs requires a multidisciplinary approach in order to supervise the often complex fintech business models.[62] As a result, there is an opportunity for technology-savvy professionals from a diverse array of professional backgrounds to build a career in fintech regulation. Professionals with regulatory experience often command a premium in industry due to the evolving and complex nature of financial regulation.

Data protection in an AI context

In financial services, very few, if any, laws pertain directly to specific technologies. This is because financial regulators, by and large, take a *technology neutral* approach. In this way, they seek to regulate the application of technology to finance as opposed to regulating individual technologies. As a result, it makes sense to focus on the rules pertaining to areas relevant to the use of these technologies within fintech business models. In the context of machine learning and AI, this, means taking a close look at data protection rules.

Privacy and data protection are central to artificial intelligence because data, after all, is the lifeblood of the machine learning algorithms so often referred to as 'AI'. Fintechs use vast amounts of data to train these algorithms. As a result, in most customer-facing enterprises that use AI, much of this data is likely to be confidential. This opens firms up to the risk of data loss, which can significantly impact the bottom line: under UK and EU data protection laws, firms can be fined up to the higher of €20 million or 4 per cent of their annual global revenue for data protection breaches.[63]

This legislation, which applies in the UK as well as the EU, is known as the General Data Protection Regulation (GDPR). As it is perhaps the most extensive piece of legislation concerning data protection in the world, it naturally warrants further examination. Though GDPR technically only applies to firms operating within the UK or EU, many smaller jurisdictions take their cue from European regulation on account of the combined size of the UK and EU economies. As a result, it is worth considering certain aspects of the GDPR in so far as they apply to the use of AI.

The GDPR, which came into force in 2018, generally requires firms to obtain 'meaningful consent' from customers before processing their data. In general, consent must be signalled with a clear and unambiguous action, such as ticking a box. As part of this, firms must be transparent about how they intend to use customer data. Moreover, customers can withdraw their consent at any time.[64]

However, given the opacity of certain machine learning algorithms, it may be difficult to know in advance what the user's data will be used for. This makes it difficult to obtain meaningful consent in advance.[65] To address this, a graduated consent model may be called for, whereby firms obtain user consent as potential uses of their data become clearer: in practice, this could be achieved via notifications asking for consent on an incremental basis.[66]

Of course, there are certain exemptions regarding user consent. For example, it is not required when the processing of user data is necessary for the performance of a contract; in this way, using an online shopper's address and card details to fulfil an order does not require specific user consent under GDPR.[67] However, in an AI context it may be difficult to demonstrate that user data is processed specifically for the fulfilment of a contractual obligation,[68] such as the delivery of a product or service. As a result, it may be safer for fintechs deploying AI to rely on user consent rather than specific exemptions which may, at times, be difficult to prove.

When seeking user consent, firms must consider how it is obtained. For one, it cannot be inferred: just because users' data is in the public domain does not mean that they consent to its use.[69] This was a key issue in the Cambridge Analytica scandal wherein millions of Americans' social media data was used for electoral campaign purposes without their knowledge or explicit consent.[70]

What's more, passive user acquiescence to the continued use of their data does not necessarily signify consent; indeed, many people feel a mix of impotence and apathy in regard to controlling how their data is used.[71] For example, one study suggests that a majority of Americans believe that it is futile to attempt to control the collection of their personal data by private companies.[72]

Under GDPR, however, organizations cannot rely on user apathy in place of their consent. Rather, the legislation requires that processing of user data be 'fair'. In practice, this means disclosing to users how, why and by whom their data will be used. That said, this list is not exhaustive: organizations are required to disclose any additional information that ensures the fair processing of user data. In an AI context this could mean disclosing that user data is subject to automated decision making.[73]

Given the significant penalties associated with GDPR-related violations, it is not hard to see that organizations will be incentivized to over-disclose. Unfortunately, this risks defeating the purpose of the rules (ie informed user consent) as users may find themselves swamped by lengthy and complicated disclosures written in a way that most do not understand (ie legalese). In this way, users may simply skip reading the disclosures which renders them pointless.[74] As a result, there is an onus on firms to make their disclosure more accessible and user friendly. This can be achieved in novel and innovative ways: for example, the *Guardian's* website has a short video summarizing its privacy policy.[75]

GDPR confers certain informational rights upon consumers that may give rise to customer management issues in data-intensive business models. For one, where users are subject to an automated decision that materially affects them, they have the right to appeal said decision and insist on human review. There are some qualifications to this right, most notably if the user explicitly consents to automatic processing or if the processing itself is necessary for the fulfilment of a contract between an individual and the entity using their data. Nonetheless, when a firm uses large amounts of granular data to automatically profile an individual, this right is likely to apply.[76]

Furthermore, the rules give individuals the right to access their personal data in addition to information about its sources. This, along with the right to appeal some automatic decisions, places an administrative burden on firms deploying AI in any significant customer-facing capacity. As a result, these entities must design their user interfaces and underlying governance processes to uphold customer rights under the provisions of GDPR. For example, the right of data access could be upheld by providing users with a login to a dashboard containing their data and its sources.[77]

The required governance processes go beyond providing users access to their personal data. Indeed, GDPR touches on every aspect of the data lifecycle. For starters, the purpose of collecting user data must be made clear at the outset, and any subsequent changes to this must be compatible with the original purpose for which consent was sought. Failing that, the data processing entity must seek additional consent.[78]

For organizations using AI, this may restrict the degree to which algorithms can be deployed to discover and act on patterns within user data. As machine learning is, by definition, pattern recognition, it is difficult to seek consent for all potential purposes at the outset. This is because the patterns within the user data may not be known in advance. However, a distinction must be made between processing data for the purpose of identifying correlations and trends, and doing so to facilitate decisions that affect users; the latter may require further user consent, whereas this is not necessarily the case with the former.[79]

In this regard, the degree to which the ancillary purpose can be viewed as fair by the user is a key test for whether additional consent is required. This requires considering whether the new purpose falls within the reasonable expectations of the user in light of their consent to the original purpose. In addition, this means considering the impact of the new purpose on the user's privacy.[80]

When there is a change to how personal data is used that requires additional consent, the user in question must be duly notified. As part of this, the data processing entity needs to explain how their data will be used. This may be difficult in an AI context due to the complexity of the subject matter and the evolving nature of potential uses. Thus, a just-in-time consent model, whereby this is sought as and when required, may be necessary. That said, it may be possible to reduce or delay the need for consent by anonymizing user data during analytical or learning processes.[81]

The possibility of having to seek user consent more than once during the data lifecycle requires the design of customer interfaces to facilitate this. This, along with the right of access to personal data and the right to appeal certain automated decisions, necessitates that AI-deploying firms integrate data protection with their risk management and governance structures: indeed, GDPR requires 'data protection by design and by default'.[82]

Furthermore, GDPR requires firms to be parsimonious in regard to the amount of user data they collect and retain. Thus, they must not collect more data than necessary for the purpose to which the user has consented; in addition, personal data must not be kept for longer than said purpose requires. Moreover, individuals have a *right to be forgotten* whereby they can demand that their personal data be removed from an entity's systems. In this way, GDPR reduces both the likelihood of data losses as well as their potential impact on user privacy.[83]

These provisions necessitate detailed consideration by fintechs deploying AI; after all, large amounts of multivariate data are required for the ongoing calibration of machine learning algorithms. As part of this, historical user data is needed to hone the decision-making accuracy of these algorithms. Thus, in order to process user data lawfully in this way, firms may need to anonymize it; once the data has been anonymized, it is no longer personal data and therefore outside the scope of GDPR.[84] However, anonymization of data is no panacea; if the anonymization can be reversed (see Chapter 7), then the data falls within scope of the rules.

A code of conduct for artificial intelligence

As seen above, data protection rules can be highly relevant to organizations deploying AI in a consumer setting. That said, it is worth remembering that regulations like GDPR are only relevant where personal data is involved; outside the scope of such gateway regulations, there are no laws or regulations pertaining specifically to artificial intelligence – at least not in a fintech context.

Nonetheless, it is worth paying attention to what policymakers are saying about artificial intelligence, if for nothing else to inform one's view of best practice and possible future regulatory expectations. For example, whilst there is currently no AI-specific legislation planned in the UK, the House of Lords has proposed a code of conduct for the ethical use of artificial intelligence. This code contains five core principles:[85]

1 Development of artificial intelligence must be 'for the common good and benefit of humanity'.

2 Artificial intelligence should run 'on principles of intelligibility and fairness'.

3 Artificial intelligence must not be applied to the detriment of 'the data rights or privacy of individuals, families, or communities'.

4 Citizens have a right to education so that they may 'flourish mentally, emotionally, and economically alongside artificial intelligence'.

5 AI must never have the ability to autonomously 'hurt, destroy, or deceive human beings'.

Though these principles may not appear to be directly relevant to financial services, organizations deploying AI would do well to consider the spirit of each principle. For starters, Principle 1 appears to be a nod to the Hippocratic

Oath (ie 'do no harm'); Principle 5 expresses a similar sentiment in relation to autonomous AI. Thus, it is not hard to see how both can be applied to financial services, in that, taken together, these principles essentially require the AI's controller to consider the impact on its wider group of stakeholders.

Meanwhile, Principle 3 appears to be closely related to data protection, though it appears to expand on the provisions of GDPR to encompass groups of people (ie families and communities). Thus, organizations would be well advised to consider how the deployment of AI may affect the privacy of individuals as well as their family and close associates.

Furthermore, although Principle 4 appears to be targeted at policymakers, it does suggest that organizations need to be forward looking in regard to employees who will be displaced by AI-driven automation; perhaps there is another role for them within the organization which may require retraining?

Finally, there is Principle 2, which pertains to fairness and intelligibility. Algorithmic bias and fairness are addressed in a supplementary case study to this book, so shall warrant no further discussion here. On the other hand, the question of intelligibility is of particular concern in regard to deep learning algorithms, because they can be multiple layers deep:[86] this opacity makes it difficult for a humans to ascertain how these algorithms arrive at their decisions.

In certain circumstances, this can be problematic: as noted above, GDPR gives individuals the right to request an explanation as to how automated decisions that materially affect them are arrived at. If the entity has used a deep learning algorithm, it may not be able to do so in a way that is comprehensible to the average person.[87] Therefore, it may have to rely on other, more transparent algorithms when processing personal data.

Outside GDPR, the lack of transparency is not much of an issue when it comes to building algorithms that perform low-risk tasks such as spotting cats in images. After all, there is comparatively little downside to getting it wrong. The same can be said for small-ticket financial services such as mobile phone insurance: in this example, the insurer may be content that the higher accuracy provided by the algorithm may make up for the higher uncertainty (and therefore risk) caused by the lack of transparency.

However, the same approach may not be appropriate for higher-risk decision making, where getting it wrong could have serious consequences for people's personal safety or their health, for example when screening for a serious disease. The same can be said for big-ticket financial services; would average consumers be happy entrusting their financial well-being to an algorithm if they knew it could not be audited by a human?

UK policymakers appear to be aware of this problem. For instance, the House of Lords has stated that regulators should have the power to mandate the use of more transparent algorithms for high-risk decisions, even if this means using algorithms that are not as accurate.[88]

That said, there may be situations, such as flying a commercial jumbo jet, where relying on AI never becomes appropriate. Modern autopilot systems can handle most things after take-off (including landing),[89] but they are always monitored by at least one human pilot. This is because the cost of making a mistake is simply too high. Thus, in certain areas, there is a strong case for human oversight regardless of the AI's proficiency.

Though the AI code proposed by the House of Lords is not binding, it is likely to set the tone for any future AI regulation. Thus, it makes sense for financial institutions to examine these principles at length and use them as a foundation for deploying AI ethically in their businesses. In this way, they can minimize the risk of falling foul of any future regulations pertaining to AI, and thereby help futureproof current implementation of artificial intelligence.

Regulating blockchains and cryptocurrencies

Just as in the case of artificial intelligence, there are no laws specifically pertaining to blockchain technology. As a result, financial regulators have taken a gateway approach to regulating blockchain, by aiming their scrutiny on regulated domains that may be relevant to its application in a financial services context.

Moreover, a distinction has to be made between permissioned and permissionless blockchain networks: the former are, to a lesser or greater degree, private networks whereas the latter are open source and thus open to all. This is important because permissionless blockchain networks tend to be decentralized, which may hinder effective regulation.[90] Consequently, regulators may focus on the parts of the financial system that interface with these networks, the so-called gateways; in this way, regulators concerned with money laundering may turn their attention to the online exchanges where Bitcoin and other cryptocurrencies are traded against mainstream fiat currencies.[91]

Furthermore, the rapid pace of innovation and technical complexity in the blockchain space may cause regulators to favour a more principles-based approach to regulating blockchain;[92] writing a rule for every possible application of this technology would simply be too onerous. Globally, this would represent a shift towards a more European style of regulation, away from the rules-based approach favoured in the United States.

Principles-based regulation puts an onus on regulated firms to follow the *spirit of the law* and conform to best practice, even if their activities are not technically covered by the law. Thus, it may be prudent for regulated firms to treat certain blockchain-related activities as if they fall within the scope of existing regulations. For example, some cryptocurrency exchanges introduced know-your-customer (KYC) and other anti-money laundering (AML) procedures before being legally required to do so.

In addition, there is a push to update existing regulations to encompass certain blockchain-related activities. For example, the EU's fifth AML directive, which came into force in the UK and EU in early 2020, brings entities that provide cryptocurrency-related services within scope of existing money-laundering rules.[93]

Anti-money laundering and cryptocurrencies

In matters regarding money laundering, the EU takes its lead from the Financial Action Task Force (FATF), an international standard-setting body for anti-money laundering and counter-terrorist financing (AML/CFT), of which the European Commission is a member.[94] In 2019, the FATF published guidance for what it calls *Virtual Asset Service Providers* (VASPs) on how to comply with anti-money laundering rules.[95] Though individual jurisdictions may diverge from this guidance, it is nonetheless a useful starting point for fintechs involved with cryptocurrency.

The guidance defines a VASP as a person or entity that, as a business, engages in certain activities involving virtual assets on behalf of others. These activities include transacting in virtual assets, safekeeping and/or administration of virtual assets and partaking in financial services related to the issuance of virtual assets. In addition, a 'virtual asset' is defined as 'a digital representation of value that can be digitally traded or transferred and can be used for payment or investment purposes'.[96]

This definition specifically excludes fiat currencies, securities and other financial assets already captured by the FATF's existing guidance. In this way, businesses providing crypto-related services become subject to the AML/CFT regulations that similarly apply to entities providing services in fiat currencies or other financial assets (eg securities trading, exchange services, etc).

However, given the nature of cryptocurrencies, there are parts of the FATF's guidance that are unique to VASPs.[97]

As is the case with conventional financial institutions, the FATF recommends that VASPs take a risk-based approach to preventing bad actors from abusing their services to launder money or finance terror. Like conventional financial institutions, VASPs are required to consider risk factors such as geography, customer type and the nature of the service/s provided. However, there are certain risk factors which pertain specifically to cryptocurrency transactions. These include the exchange of crypto for fiat (or vice versa), the transaction obfuscation features of certain cryptocurrencies, the degree of user anonymization and the extent of decentralization within the business model of the VASP itself.[98]

The extent to which a business can be considered a VASP appears to rely on two key tests: whether it has control over its users' private keys or whether it in some way facilitates transactions on behalf of users. That said, even if an entity meets one or both of these conditions, it may not qualify as a VASP if it operates a closed-loop system such as an air miles or loyalty card programme: as the user cannot sell these in a secondary market, such 'virtual assets' fall outside the scope of the FATF's guidance.[99]

When a business has 'exclusive and independent control' over a user's private key/s, it controls their cryptocurrency. Where this is the case, the entity can be deemed to be providing safekeeping and/or administrative services and is therefore subject to AML/CFT regulations. However, where such services are ancillary to virtual asset networks in that the entity in question does not have control over the user's private key/s, its activities fall outside the scope of VASP-specific guidance: this is the case with providers of *hardware and other non-custodial wallet solutions*; as these entities do not have access to, or control over, the user's private key/s, they cannot be deemed to be providing safekeeping or administrative services in relation to the user's cryptocurrency.[100]

Outside private key control, an entity can be defined as a VASP if it has the 'ability to actively facilitate financial activity' on behalf of the user. This condition is much looser than the first, and therefore captures a wider range of entities, including Bitcoin ATMs, cryptocurrency exchanges and brokerages facilitating the issuance of virtual assets. Indeed, it even encompasses decentralized exchanges, which are software applications that allow users to transact directly via blockchain networks; though such decentralization may impede oversight for AML/CFT purposes, the entities maintaining these solutions can be deemed to be operating as VASPs on account of their facilitation of virtual asset transactions.[101]

Entities designated as VASPs are subject to the same fundamental AML/CFT requirements as conventional financial institutions providing similar services. This means conducting KYC and other customer due diligence procedures as well as complying with record-keeping requirements; in addition, VASPs are required to monitor customer accounts for suspicious transactions on an ongoing basis. Thus, VASPs must integrate AML/KYC procedures with their internal risk and oversight structures. In practice, such measures are very similar to those required of conventional financial institutions. However, the nature of cryptocurrencies imposes certain unique considerations on VASPs. For one, the opaque nature and lack of face-to-face interaction inherent to virtual asset transactions may cause VASPs to rely on digitized customer verification methods: for example, this could mean tracing the customer's IP address or cross-checking their ID numbers against national databases.[102]

Furthermore, the digital nature and opacity of virtual asset transactions means that VASPs must collect and analyse a richer array of data points for the purposes of suspicious transaction reporting; going beyond standard data points (eg geography, transaction amount, etc) and monitoring information specific to the cryptocurrency ecosystem should enable better detection of suspicious transactions. This data could include device identifying numbers, IP addresses, wallet addresses and transaction hashes.[103]

Cryptocurrencies, ICOs and securities regulation

Though the rules and regulations discussed in this chapter vary, there is a common theme throughout: the inherent complexity of the technologies deployed by fintechs pushes regulators to adopt a more principles-based stance. As a result, firms will be expected to engage with regulations based on the economic substance of their activities rather than their legal form. Fintechs cannot afford to view regulatory compliance as a box-ticking exercise.

This aspect of regulatory compliance is of particular relevance to the legal status of blockchain tokens in the investment industry: both European and US rules emphasize a substance-based approach to defining instruments as securities, and therefore the applicability of securities law.

In the United States, the so-called Howey test defines an 'investment contract' as the investment of money into a common undertaking with the 'reasonable expectation' of deriving a profit from the work of others.[104] According to the court ruling that established the Howey test, it is a 'flexible rather than static principle'.[105] Indeed, subsequent rulings have emphasized that 'form should be disregarded for substance'[106] and that 'emphasis should be on the economic realities underlying a transaction'.[107] If an instrument can be defined as an 'investment contract' involving US residents, it is subject to US securities laws: as a result, these rules capture ICO-funded start-ups in the US.[108]

Similarly, in the UK and EU, 'financial instruments' can be defined as 'transferable securities' negotiable via a capital market, under *MiFID II*; thus, though there is, strictly speaking, no legal definition for what the European Securities and Markets Authority (ESMA) calls 'crypto-assets', it is conceivable that some blockchain-related activities could still be subject to capital markets regulation.[109]

Moreover, ESMA distinguishes between different types of blockchain tokens: utility tokens – which confer access to some resource or service (eg cloud storage space) – payment tokens and investment tokens. In this way, different types of tokens may be subject to different laws on regulations depending on how they are used. For example, payment tokens may fall outside the scope of securities regulation but within that of payments regulation. What's more, hybrid tokens – those that perform multiple functions – may be subject to multiple types of regulation: in this way, a payment-investment token could be covered by payments and securities regulation.[110]

Where blockchain tokens are classified as securities, the regulated activities surrounding their use touch on several aspects of the investment lifecycle: issuance, trading and safekeeping.[111] However, investing in blockchain start-ups is a risky enterprise: according to one estimate, 30 per cent of ICO-funded projects launched in 2017 had lost substantially all of their value between January and September 2018.[112] Thus, the high probability of business failure and/or fraud, combined with low liquidity, may make investing in blockchain tokens unsuitable for a large number of retail investors. For this reason, the regulatory direction of travel in regard to blockchain investment seems to be greater investor/consumer protection: certainly, this appears to be the case in the United States, where the regulatory authorities have made it clear that crypto-exchanges and token issuers must comply with existing securities and financial market laws.[113] As US securities laws apply to transactions involving US residents regardless of where in the world these take place,[114] it may be prudent for blockchain-based fintechs to take note even though they may be located elsewhere.

Placing blockchain tokens within scope of existing securities laws imposes stringent disclosure requirements on their issuers in order to protect consumers. As a result, issuers will have to carefully consider how, and to whom, they promote their tokens. Furthermore, the move towards greater consumer protection in regard to ICOs appears to be the direction of travel in Europe as well, and is perhaps more pronounced than in the United States; indeed, regulators in some European jurisdictions, such as the UK, have proposed restricting the sale of cryptocurrency-related derivatives to retail consumers on account of their risks.[115]

Whether blockchain tokens are sold to retail or professional investors, professional intermediaries and trading platforms have a duty of care towards their clients. This requires firms to act in their clients' best interests and do so in a prudent manner. In the case of trading platforms, this means demarcating client assets from those of the firm. In this way, if the firm becomes insolvent, client assets will be protected from its creditors. Moreover, as they hold client assets, cryptocurrency trading platforms should adhere to the same record-keeping, oversight and, indeed, capital requirements to which conventional securities firms are subjected.[116]

Blockchain trading platforms commonly engage in off-chain trading. As part of this, customers deposit blockchain tokens and/or fiat currency at the exchange to trade against each other. In this way, users effectively swap certificates denoting ownership over the assets (ie fiat currency and/or blockchain tokens) while these are 'stored' at the exchange. As a result, the customers incur some degree of counterparty risk;[117] should the exchange collapse, their assets may be lost; this has happened to customers of cryptocurrency exchanges on multiple occasions, perhaps most notably in the case of the now infamous Mt. Gox in 2013.[118] As a result, there is an onus on trading to clearly differentiate between client and firm assets: in practice, this can be achieved by using different blockchain addresses for the firm and its clients.

Client asset and safekeeping rules are not unique to trading platforms or brokerages; given the nature of blockchain tokens, custodial wallet providers may also fall within scope of such regulations. This is because such firms exercise control over their clients' private keys;[119] in this way, a loss of these keys would result in a loss of client assets. In practice, some of this risk could be alleviated via multi-signature wallets, wherein transactions cannot be enacted without the authentication of each signature-holder (ie the client and the firm);[120] this would help protect clients from theft while demarcating ownership between client and firm assets.

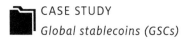

CASE STUDY
Global stablecoins (GSCs)

These are blockchain tokens backed by liquid assets with low volatility (ie short-term government securities and money market investments denominated in mainstream fiat currencies such as dollars or euros). In this way, stablecoins are an attempt to solve a core problem inherent to cryptocurrencies: their volatility. This is seen as a barrier to mainstream adoption because it prevents cryptocurrencies from fulfilling any of the core functions of money: serving as a unit of account, store of value or means of transacting.[121] In theory, backing stablecoins with a basket of low-volatility assets should reduce their volatility to that of the underlying assets and thereby pave the way to mass adoption.

In this way, creating a GSC that is useful for day-to-day transactions has the potential to make the global financial system accessible to people living in parts of the world without financial infrastructure; by facilitating capital flows to and from these areas, a GSC could alleviate poverty for more than a billion people.[122] This is no pipedream: one fintech solution has already achieved such results in parts of sub-Saharan Africa: it is estimated that M-PESA, Vodafone's mobile payments solution, has helped lift 2 per cent of Kenyan households out of poverty.[123]

With internet connectivity and mobile penetration rates growing rapidly across the developing world, there is much fanfare around blockchain-based payments solutions like GSCs. However, these solutions are not without risk: for example, concerns have been raised that they could be used for money laundering, tax avoidance and the financing of terrorism.[124]

Moreover, monetary authorities have cautioned that the mass adoption of a GSC could cause a drain on bank deposits,[125] especially in developing countries; given the perceived liquidity and inherent privacy of these tokens, people may prefer to hold GSCs in lieu of their local currencies, especially where these suffer from high inflation. After all, when current accounts pay little, if any, interest what incentive is there to keep your money in a bank?

As GSCs require the backing of low-risk liquid assets, the mass adoption of a GSC may create a shortage of such assets,[126] which banks, insurers and other large financial institutions are required to hold by law. This may create a feedback loop whereby such assets rise in value, not on account of their underlying fundamentals, but as a result of being included in the reserves of a GSC; the subsequent rise in the GSC's underlying assets may then attract speculators to the GSC, thereby increasing demand for these assets and thus perpetuating the cycle.

This problem may be particularly pronounced in open-ended schemes, whereby users can exchange fiat currency for GSC tokens and vice versa. When users want their money back, they redeem their tokens at the per-token market price of the GSC's asset pool. To satisfy user demands, the GSC operator may need to buy or sell the underlying assets. As a result, large inflows and outflows in GSCs may increase volatility in the underlying asset markets.

Some GSC operators may address this problem by making their schemes closed-ended; in this way, there is a fixed number of tokens representing a fixed amount asset. In such schemes, users get in or out by buying or selling their tokens in secondary markets. As a result, excess demand might cause coins to trade at a premium to the underlying assets. There is some historical precedent for this: during the late 19th and early 20th centuries various gold- and silver-backed currencies traded at a premium to their metal values because the functional demand for the currencies inflated their values relative to the underlying assets.[127]

Whether open- or closed-ended, GSCs may be vulnerable to losses of user confidence that could create distortions in their underlying asset markets.[128] As each GSC token represents a share in the value of the scheme's underlying assets, large redemptions in an open-ended GSC could force its operator to sell large amounts of the 'liquid' assets backing it. At the same time, a loss of confidence in a closed-ended GSC could cause it to trade at a discount to the value of its underlying assets; if the GSC is large enough, this may affect securities markets through the actions of speculators who will *short-sell* the underlying assets while *going long* in an equivalent value of GSC tokens in order to create a risk-free profit.

What are the systemic risks posed by large-scale adoption of GSCs?
(Suggested answer at the end of this chapter.)

Chapter summary

As technology will continue to evolve, policymakers and regulators will continue to play catch-up by having to update existing rules and fine-tune their oversight mechanisms. As a result, organizations may well find themselves deploying technology in contexts where there are no rules or regulatory precedents; thus, without a clear steer from regulators or rulebooks, it is best to take a principles-based approach: though technology may change, best practice and sound governance do not.

Though this approach may not protect firms from all regulatory risk, it is far better than neglecting any form of regulatory considerations on account of being 'too small for the regulators to care' or because one is using a new technology that is technically not covered by existing rules. Regulators the world over tend to look more favourably on firms that make reasonable, good faith attempts at risk management while being fair and transparent with consumers.

KEY TAKEAWAYS

The most important ideas from this chapter are:

- Like the firms they supervise, financial regulators seek to innovate by making supervisory processes more efficient and effective.

- Increasing regulatory engagement with fintechs has caused a skills shortage: they need people with the technological understanding of someone who has read this book.

- Very few, if any, financial regulations apply directly to individual technologies.

- Instead, financial regulators attempt to regulate gateway activities and the application of technologies within financial services.

SUGGESTED ANSWERS TO DISCUSSION POINTS

 How might an initiative like Digital Regulatory Reporting facilitate supervision and compliance processes in the financial industry?

As DRR-like solutions can give regulators direct access to firms' data, compliance staff at the regulated entities do not need to spend their time compiling regulatory reports. Besides saving time and expense, this also minimizes the likelihood of errors. In addition, the use of APIs and smart contracts could make regulatory reporting more secure: as firms no longer have to send data via email or post to regulators, there is a lower risk of data loss.

Furthermore, as automated reporting systems necessitate reporting rules to be coded and firms to standardize their reporting data, they help make the reported figures more comparable across firms. As a result, regulators can more accurately benchmark firms against their peers to identify outliers on which to focus their attention.

Finally, the use of graphical user interfaces to compile firm data helps regulators gain industry-level oversight, which can facilitate supervision: direct access to firms' systems and data that is nearly 'live' minimizes any time lag. This enables regulators to identify and respond to risks in a timelier manner.

 What are the systemic risks posed by large-scale adoption of GSCs?

Unfortunately, this may have further weakened public confidence in the GSC, thereby creating a feedback loop.

The relative attractiveness of GSCs may deprive localized banks of liquidity if consumers the world over prefer to use GSCs as their primary mode of transacting.

In addition, the ease and speed of transacting with a GSC may facilitate financial contagion if there is a bank run;[129] when people lose faith in one bank, they may have doubts about the system as a whole. Under such circumstances, the impact of one bank failure could be worsened by users putting their money into a GSC rather than other banks, which would otherwise have helped bolster them.

In addition, when a GSC becomes large enough, it can exacerbate asset market volatility. When there is excess demand for a GSC, its demand may create positive price spirals; meanwhile, if there is a loss of confidence in the GSC, its collapse large declines in its underlying asset markets. In both circumstances, the underlying asset values are distorted by crowd behaviour relating to the GSC rather than the assets themselves.

Finally, GSCs may help individuals evade capital controls and taxes while impeding the ability of individual countries to exercise monetary policy, particularly those whose bonds aren't included in the GSC's asset pool;[130] if such countries pursue a loose monetary policy that creates too much inflation, its residents may simply transfer their wealth into the GSC, thereby forcing said country to raise interest rates.

References

1,3,9,10,32,44 Magnuson, W (2018) Regulating Fintech, *Vanderbilt Law Review*, 71 (4), 1167–126

2,4 Coffee, J C (2011) Systemic Risk after Dodd–Frank: Contingent Capital and the Need for Regulatory Strategies beyond Oversight, *Columbia Law Review*, 795, scholarship. law.columbia.edu/faculty_scholarship/35 (archived at https://perma.cc/UB5V-6H5M)

5 Roberts, J (2013) Financial Services Act 2012: A New UK Financial Regulatory Framework, Harvard Law School Forum on Corporate Governance, 24 March, corpgov. law.harvard.edu/2013/03/24/financial-services-act-2012-a-new-uk-financial-regulatory-framework/ (archived at https://perma.cc/RU27-BFP2)

6 Wheatley, M (2013) Regulation as a spur to growth, Financial Conduct Authority [speech], www.fca.org.uk/news/speeches/regulation-spur-growth (archived at https:// perma.cc/RU3F-PWL2)

7 Allen & Overy LLP (2020) The Banking Reform Act 2013, www.allenovery.com/en-gb/ global/news-and-insights/legal-and-regulatory-risks-for-the-finance-sector/united-kingdom/the-banking-reform-act-2013 (archived at https://perma.cc/K9HT-QAV9)

8 OECD (nd) Regulatory Reform and Innovation, www.oecd.org/sti/inno/2102514.pdf (archived at https://perma.cc/F7EK-XRLQ)

11 European Commission (2019) Results of the fitness check of supervisory reporting requirements in EU financial services legislation, 7 November, ec.europa.eu/info/ publications/191107-fitness-check-supervisory-reporting_en (archived at https://perma.cc/ G45W-PAWU)

12,15,16,20 Wright, D, Witherick, D and Gordeeva, M (2018) Deloitte Global RPA Survey, Deloitte Development LLC, www2.deloitte.com/bg/en/pages/technology/articles/deloitte-global-rpa-survey-2018.html (archived at https://perma.cc/8N8F-GTK2)

13,14,18,19 Willcocks, L, Lacity, M and Craig, A (2015) Robotic Process Automation at Xchanging, The Outsourcing Unit Working Research Paper 15/03 (June, www.xchanging.com/system/files/dedicated-downloads/robotic-process-automation.pdf (archived at https://perma.cc/SS6U-FVK8)

17 PricewaterhouseCoopers LLP (2018) Actuarial robotic process automation survey report, www.pwc.com/gx/en/financial-services/pdf/insurance-rpa-survey-report.pdf (archived at https://perma.cc/XZB2-H37Y)

21 Fernandez de Lis, S (2017) Fintech: key regulatory challenges, BBVA Research, www.bbvaresearch.com/wp-content/uploads/2017/11/SFL-Panel-FinTech-LACEA.pdf (archived at https://perma.cc/E7WV-VZPY)

22,23 Fein, M L (2015) Robo-Advisors: A Closer Look, Social Science Research Network, papers.ssrn.com/sol3/ papers.cfm?abstract_id =2658701 (archived at https://perma.cc/6DFD-PNCU)

24,43 Financial Stability Board (2017) Financial Stability Implications from FinTech: Supervisory and regulatory issues that merit authorities' attention, 27 June, www.fsb.org/wp-content/uploads/R270617.pdf (archived at https://perma.cc/LRW3-3UMX)

25 Ziegler, T, Garvey, K, Ridler, S, Yerolemou, N, Hao, R and Zhang, B (2017) Entrenching Innovation: The 4th UK alternative finance industry report, Cambridge Centre for Alternative Finance, www.jbs.cam.ac.uk/faculty-research/centres/alternative-finance/publications/entrenching-innovation/ (archived at https://perma.cc/N65S-LQCA)

26 Marriage, M (2016) Passive funds take third of US market, *Financial Times*, 11 September, www.ft.com/content/4cdf2f88-7695-11e6-b60a-de4532d5ea35 (archived at https://perma.cc/7EPU-WTNH)

27,28,29,30 Brunnermeier, M K (2009) Deciphering the Liquidity and Credit Crunch 2007–2008, *Journal of Economic Perspectives*, 23 (1), 77–100

31,34,35,36,37 Claessens, S, Frost, J, Zhu, F and Turner, G (2018) Fintech credit markets around the world: size, drivers and policy issues, *BIS Quarterly Review*, 29–49 (September)

33 Financial Conduct Authority (2019) Loan-based ('peer-to-peer') and investment-based crowdfunding platforms: Feedback to CP18/20 and final rules, www.fca.org.uk/publication/policy/ps19-14.pdf (archived at https://perma.cc/53X6-ZBXE)

38 Financial Stability Board (2013) Strengthening Oversight and Regulation of Shadow Banking: Policy framework for strengthening oversight and regulation of shadow banking entities, 29 August, www.fsb.org/wp-content/uploads/r_130829c.pdf (archived at https://perma.cc/3KJ5-6H9J)

39 Ziegler, T, Shneor, R, Garvey, K, Wenzlaff, K, Yerolemou, N, Hao, R and Zhang, B (2018) Expanding horizons: The 3rd European alternative finance industry report, Cambridge Centre for Alternative Finance, www.jbs.cam.ac.uk/fileadmin/user_upload/research/centres/alternative-finance/downloads/2018-02-ccaf-exp-horizons.pdf (archived at https://perma.cc/NZ42-Q2FM)

40,41 Mishkin, F S (2011) Over the Cliff: From the Subprime to the Global Financial Crisis, *Journal of Economic Perspectives*, 25 (1), 49–70

42 Baird, R (2019) Collapse of property platform Lendy prompts FCA probe, Altfi.com, 28 May, www.altfi.com/article/5383_collapse-of-property-platform-lendy-prompts-fca-probe (archived at https://perma.cc/LC5J-LXAQ)

45,58,61,62 UNSGA Fintech Working Group, Cambridge Centre for Alternative Finance & Monetary Authority of Singapore (2019) Early Lessons on Regulatory Innovations to Enable Inclusive Fintech: Innovation offices, Regulatory Sandboxes, and RegTech, www.unsgsa.org/files/2915/5016/4448/Early_Lessons_on_Regulatory_Innovations_to_Enable_Inclusive_FinTech.pdf (archived at https://perma.cc/B78F-2FR5)

46,47–50,52 Financial Conduct Authority (2019) Digital Regulatory Reporting: Pilot Phase 1 Report, www.fca.org.uk/publication/discussion/digital-regulatory-reporting-pilot-phase-1-report.pdf (archived at https://perma.cc/2EYJ-T9ZC)

51,53 Financial Conduct Authority (2016) TechSprint: Unlocking regulatory reporting [video transcript, www.fca.org.uk/publication/documents/techsprint-unlocking-regulatory-reporting-video-transcript.pdf (archived at https://perma.cc/66G6-Z5XQ)

54 Micheler, E and Whaley, A R (2019) Regulatory Technology: Replacing Law with Computer Code, European Business Organization Law Review, 1–29

55,56,57 Financial Conduct Authority (2019) Digital Regulatory Reporting: Phase 2 Viability Assessment, www.fca.org.uk/publication/discussion/digital-regulatory-reporting-pilot-phase-2-viability-assessment.pdf (archived at https://perma.cc/BX4S-9W6G)

59,60 Zetzsche, D A, Buckley, R P, Barberis, J N and Arner, D W (2018) Regulating a Revolution: From Regulatory Sandboxes to Smart Regulation, *Fordham Journal of Corporate & Financial Law*, 23, 31–104

63 Deloitte Risk Advisory (2017) General Data Protection Regulation, www2.deloitte.com/content/dam/Deloitte/nl/Documents/risk/deloitte-nl-risk-gdpr-vision-approach.pdf (archived at https://perma.cc/W555-HLFK)

64,66,67–69,71,73,74,76–84 Information Commissioner's Office (2017) Big data, artificial intelligence, machine learning and data protection, ico.org.uk/media/for-organisations/documents/2013559/big-data-ai-ml-and-data-protection.pdf (archived at https://perma.cc/FTP3-AUGM)

65 Buttarelli, G (2016) A smart approach: Counteract the bias in artificial intelligence, *European Data Protection Supervisor*, 8 November

70 Federal Trade Commission (2019) FTC Imposes $5 Billion Penalty and Sweeping New Privacy Restrictions on Facebook, 24 July, www.ftc.gov/news-events/press-releases/2019/07/ftc-imposes-5-billion-penalty-sweeping-new-privacy-restrictions (archived at https://perma.cc/77EH-RW6X)

72 Turow, J, Hennessy, M and Draper, N (2015) The Tradeoff Fallacy: How marketers are misrepresenting American consumers and opening them up to exploitation, University of Pennsylvania, www.asc.upenn.edu/sites/default/files/TradeoffFallacy_1.pdf (archived at https://perma.cc/5SP6-ECJ6)

75 *The Guardian* (2020) Privacy, www.theguardian.com/info/privacy (archived at https://perma.cc/5ZAL-QS9A)

85,86,88 House of Lords Select Committee on Artificial Intelligence (2018) AI in the UK: Ready, willing and able? Report of session 2017–19, 16 April, publications.parliament. uk/pa/ld201719/ldselect/ldai/100/10002.htm (archived at https://perma.cc/YN92-4MCV)

87 Castelvecchi, D (2016) Can we open the black box of AI? *Nature*, 5 October 2016, www.nature.com/news/can-we-open-the-black-box-of-ai-1.20731 (archived at https:// perma.cc/PG94-H3BG)

89 Nasr, R (2015) Autopilot: What the system can and can't do, CNBC, 26 March, www. cnbc.com/2015/03/26/autopilot-what-the-system-can-and-cant-do.html (archived at https://perma.cc/ZQX8-3Q3S)

90 Bank of International Settlements (2018) V Cryptocurrencies: looking beyond the hype, BIS Annual Economic Report, www.bis.org/publ/arpdf/ar2018e5.htm (archived at https:// perma.cc/2ED7-C9RN)

91,92,108,113,114,132 Casey, M, Crane, J, Gensler, G, Johnson, S and Narula, N (2018) The Impact of Blockchain Technology on Finance: A catalyst for change, International Center for Monetary and Banking Studies, www.cimb.ch/uploads/1/1/5/4/115414161/ geneva21_1.pdf (archived at https://perma.cc/9ZTC-Q7FR)

93 Fintrail (2020) Changes to the UK's Money Laundering and Terrorist Financing Regime, 10 January, www.fintrail.co.uk/news/2020/1/10/changes-to-the-uks-money-laundering- and-terrorist-financing-regime (archived at https://perma.cc/D57M-X7HN)

94 European Commission (2019) Anti-money laundering and counter terrorist financing, ec.europa.eu/info/business-economy-euro/banking-and-finance/financial-supervision-and- risk-management/anti-money-laundering-and-counter-terrorist-financing_en (archived at https://perma.cc/M447-NUQX)

95–103 Financial Action Task Force (2019) Guidance for a risk-based approach to virtual assets and virtual asset service providers, www.fatf-gafi.org/media/fatf/documents/ recommendations/RBA-VA-VASPs.pdf (archived at https://perma.cc/6PBA-BXNV)

104–07 Securities and Exchange Commission (2017) Report of Investigation Pursuant to Section 21(a) of the Securities Exchange Act of 1934: The DAO, www.sec.gov/litigation/ investreport/34-81207.pdf (archived at https://perma.cc/LS2Q-H6AS)

109,110,111,117,119,120 European Securities and Markets Authority (2019) Advice: Initial Coin Offerings and Crypto-Assets, www.esma.europa.eu/sites/default/files/library/ esma50-157-1391_crypto_advice.pdf (archived at https://perma.cc/XAH6-D6XW)

112 Ernst & Young Global Limited (2018) Initial Coin Offerings (ICOs): The Class of 2017 – one year later, www.ey.com/Publication/vwLUAssets/ey-study-ico-research/$FILE/ ey-study-ico-research.pdf (archived at https://perma.cc/WUU9-QNCW)

115 European Banking Authority (2019) Report with advice for the European Commission on crypto-assets, 9 January, eba.europa.eu/sites/default/documents/files/ documents/10180/2545547/67493daa-85a8-4429-aa91-e9a5ed880684/EBA%20 Report%20on%20crypto%20assets.pdf (archived at https://perma.cc/U9A2-RBFQ)

116 Financial Industry Regulatory Authority (2017) Distributed Ledger Technology: Implications of blockchain for the securities industry, www.finra.org/sites/default/files/ FINRA_Blockchain_Report.pdf (archived at https://perma.cc/C3HJ-DRS9)

118 Emerging Technology from the arXiv (2014) The Troubling Holes in MtGox's Account of How It Lost $600 Million in Bitcoins, MIT Technology Review, 4 April, www. technologyreview.com/s/526161/the-troubling-holes-in-mtgoxs-account-of-how-it-lost-600-million-in-bitcoins/ (archived at https://perma.cc/JS9X-AAMT)

121 Lo, S and Wang, JC (2014) Bitcoin as Money? Current Policy Perspectives, No. 14-4, Federal Reserve Bank of Boston, www.bostonfed.org/-/media/Documents/Workingpapers/PDF/cpp1404.pdf/ (archived at https://perma.cc/P7EV-85F2)

122 Libra Association (2019) An introduction to Libra: White Paper, libra.org/en-US/wp-content/uploads/sites/23/2019/06/LibraWhitePaper_en_US.pdf (archived at https://perma.cc/8QPW-2R25)

123 Suri, T and Jack, W (2016) The long-run poverty and gender impacts of mobile money, *Science*, 354, 1288–292 (December)

124,125,126,128–30 G7 Working Group on Stablecoins (2019) Investigating the impact of global stablecoins, October, www.bis.org/cpmi/publ/d187.pdf (archived at https://perma.cc/AMZ8-UCQ2)

127 Hayek, F A (1977) Toward a Free Market Monetary System, in: Gold and Monetary Conference, New Orleans Gold, *The Journal of Libertarian Studies*, 3, 1–8

09

Looking to the future

Optimization, decentralization and personalization

LEARNING OBJECTIVES

In this final chapter we will look at:

- How the Internet of Things (IOT) will shape fintech going forward.
- The role of personalization in an increasingly automated finance sector.
- How decentralization could reimagine financial services.

Introduction

This chapter is intended to be a sober look into the future. It provides a realistic, and forward-looking, perspective on the technological trends affecting the finance sector in the short to medium term. In this way, it is hoped that readers will use its insights to inform current decision making.

This chapter makes no predictions extending beyond the next decade or so. The public record is littered with examples of bold predictions that turned out to be egregiously wrong. For instance, in 2004 the Pentagon predicted that the UK would have a 'Siberian' climate by 2020.[1] The internet does not forget.

The future is inherently uncertain, and largely unpredictable beyond the short–medium term. Therefore, rather than make outright predictions, this chapter combines the business and technological trends identified in this book to provide the reader with a glimpse into the not so distant future.

Optimization and integration

As banks respond to fintechs by making their solutions ever more convenient, accessible and cost efficient, one has to ask: what next? After all, using similar analytical techniques in combination with well-known UI/UX design principles is likely to cause financial institutions, big and small, to end up in the same place. In this way, any differences in the user experience are likely to be surface deep. So how can financial institutions differentiate themselves?

In this regard, it is useful to ask oneself, as a consumer, what kind of service proposition one would be willing to pay for. How about a visual overview of personal spending habits with estimates of near-term liquidity needs and a live net position of savings, investments and borrowings? In other words, a personal income statement and a real-time balance sheet. This would contain pie charts, complete with click-through granularity down to individual transactions and investment holdings; in addition, it would contain distribution curves comparing one's financial performance and position to historical averages, personal targets and/or similar customer profiles. What's more, these could be viewable on weekly, monthly, quarterly and annual bases and customers would be able to toggle between these at the click of a button, tap of a screen or via a short utterance.

It wouldn't stop there. This solution would mine customer data to understand their preferences, anticipate financial needs and file tax returns on their behalf; in short, it would be a personal finance department in a smartphone. Accordingly, it would deploy customers' financial resources according to their lifestyle goals, without unnecessarily infringing on their time; rather it would nudge them as and when issues or opportunities arise, and schedule monthly and quarterly review briefings. At the same time, human assistance would be readily available via a chat bot or customer-care hotline.

If the solution described above can be built for retail customers, it can also be achieved in the corporate sphere. Indeed, there are fintech apps which digitize invoice collection, payroll, management oversight and tax filings; however, none of these solutions do everything. Instead, these fintech solutions supplement finance departments by automating workflows or parts thereof. Thus, the next leap forward is likely to be driven by the integration of existing solutions to enable greater efficiencies.

The technology to facilitate such change already exists. However, in the financial sector, slow-moving back-office processes stand in the way of change: according to a 2019 survey of financial services institutions, legacy systems are seen as one of the key barriers to implementing fintech solutions.[2] Moreover, the required scale of change means that banks are forced to roll out fintech solutions incrementally; as part of this, they must focus on 'quick-wins' to improve the customer experience as part of a greater change management project.[3]

Of course, fintech solutions need not be exclusive to customer-facing domains; arguably, the biggest gains may come from deploying technology internally. In part, this will come from the digitalization and automation of back offices. However, whilst much of the focus since the GFC has been on optimizing user experiences by redesigning customer interfaces and product offerings, these same improvements have yet to be fully realized behind the scenes.

Thus, financial institutions would do well to hold themselves to a customer-facing standard when implementing internal fintech solutions: just as fintechs help their users minimize cost, inconvenience and time spent, so too should financial institutions in regard to their staff. In this context, a task-based approach to service design seems pertinent, whereby solutions are conceived to help employees perform tasks and/or overcome problems on the job.[4] In theory, this should free up staff time and energy to perform value-adding tasks such as meeting with internal or external stakeholders. This idea is not restricted to the financial sector; indeed, it may be relevant as far afield as the public sector.[5]

Real-time payments and a cashless society

In addition to reducing costs, financial institutions look to fintech as an avenue for saving time and inconvenience; in other words, they seek to reduce mental transaction costs for customers and staff alike. In this context, transacting in cash can be seen as a mental transaction cost;[6] after all, this must be manually counted and transported to the point of sale, where loose change is often imposed on the buyer. In addition, cash transactions impose additional costs behind the scenes: bookkeeping, safekeeping and trips to the bank.

To remove these costs, many institutions look to digital payments.[7] This should facilitate real-time oversight and reduce the risk of financial crime, enable faster responses to suspicious transactions and generally improve businesses' ability to redeploy their revenues in their operations; by oiling the wheels of enterprise, this increase in liquidity should help improve business profitability. For this reason, cashless initiatives are gaining traction with academics, policymakers and big business. Of course, none of this would matter without large-scale consumer buy-in, which appears to taking off: between 2012 and 2016, global non-cash transaction grew at an annual rate of *ca* 10 per cent.[8]

That said, there are hurdles to achieving truly real-time digital payments. Although card payments may seem instant from the customer's perspective, often they are not: behind the scenes, they can take several days to clear.[9] This discrepancy exists because some customer-facing institutions routinely credit customer accounts with in-transit payments before they have technically cleared. For example, a credit card provider may take payment from a customer while instantly reducing their card balance, days before the funds actually leave the customer's bank account. In this way, the card provider creates an illusion of an instantaneous transaction.

In effect, financial institutions are willing to extend short-term credit to customers for the sake of minimizing the inconvenience of having to wait for transactions to clear. As this imposes financing costs on said institutions, it begs the question: why do it? The short answer is that customers have been trained, by way of shopping online, to expect greater convenience and faster service provision. In turn, these experiences have increased customer expectations in other domains, such as financial services.[10]

The long answer is, of course, a little more complex, and quite literally so. Using short-term liquidity to create a perception of instantaneous or near-instantaneous payments can be seen as a way of making up for the deficiencies of ageing background infrastructure; indeed, a 'quick win' to improve the customer experience. At the same time, overhauling paper-laden and slow-moving back-office systems is simply too complicated, risky and costly to do in one fell swoop. Consequently, financial institutions are turning to medium-term *patches* while incrementally updating their systems.

Though financial institutions will continue to employ such workarounds for some time to come, many are adapting their systems to facilitate real-time payments (RTP). Rather than processing payments in batches at fixed time intervals – as is currently the case in many institutions – transactions are processed individually, thus enabling real-time processing.[11]

Although approaches to implementing RTP may vary across different countries, the financial industry will benefit from global adoption of ISO20022, a data standard for payment systems; the SWIFT network has committed to fully adopting this standard by the end of 2025,[12] and thereby on-board its community of more than 11,000 financial institutions.[13]

Whereas the original SWIFT system was built for speed of processing, ISO20022 modernizes payment systems to facilitate data flow. Rather than sending blocks of text, messages are marked up to facilitate the identification of information such as the recipient's name (ie <nm>) and country (ie <cntry>).

In addition, institutions can append what is called Extended Remittance Information (ERI), which is additional structured information such as references to linked documents and individual line items.[14]

The structuring of remittance data makes it machine readable, thereby enabling faster processing and more granular oversight. Moreover, the greater richness of data can facilitate better risk management, for example by training fraud detection algorithms. What's more, ERI enables payment reconciliations to be automated, or at the very least, reduces the need for phone calls, emails, and faxes.[15] Thus, implementing ISO20022 has the potential to greatly reduce transaction costs by way of shifting the burden of processing remittance data away from humans and onto machines.

With the introduction of RTP in a convenience-focussed economy, is a cashless society just around the corner? Certainly there are benefits to this: proponents of going cash-free hold that it will help prevent financial crime, such as corruption and money laundering, by establishing a digital paper-trail for all payments; in turn, this increase in transparency should facilitate poverty reduction.[16]

That said, there are also practical and ethical concerns associated with a cashless society. For starters, a cashless society is dependent on the constant availability of electricity.[17] Though power outages are a remote possibility in many developed nations, they are, nonetheless, a possibility: there is a reason hospitals have backup generators!

Moreover, a fully cashless society risks excluding those who do not have access to a bank account.[18] As these people tend to be already vulnerable members of society (eg the elderly or homeless), one has to ask whether excluding them financially is warranted for the sake of going cashless.

Besides the practical concerns highlighted above, there are also potential socio-political issues that bring into question the desirability of having a cashless society.[19] Cash gives people the option of storing their wealth outside the financial system. In itself, this is an important check on banks: if people don't trust banks, they can simply withdraw their cash and put it under the mattress. In theory, this should incentivize the banking sector to do better by their customers; without cash, this incentive disappears. Though customers can still remove their wealth from the financial system by holding physical gold or Bitcoin, they can no longer transact day to day without banks as both gold and Bitcoin are less liquid than cash. Thus, going cashless has the potential to make people beholden to the banking sector.

Such dependency would be a strong incentive not to criticize banks. In the absence of strong consumer rights, what will stop banks from shutting down a person's account for having the 'wrong' opinions? Thus, a cashless society could have devastating effects on pluralism and freedom of speech, which risks silencing investigative journalists, political activists, and dissident thinkers.[20]

Whilst we as a society must think carefully about the broader ethical issues surrounding the application of new technologies, the technologies themselves march on. Indeed, the quest to minimize transaction costs appears unstoppable. Banks migrated from the branch to our computers, then onto our phones and tablets; soon they may be part of our living room furniture.

 CASE STUDY
Banking by voice with Alexa

Although telephone banking has been around for decades, fully voice-based user interfaces had yet to become mainstream by 2020. That said, financial institutions are experimenting in this domain: in 2017, for instance, D3 Banking (D3) announced the introduction of voice-enabled banking using the Amazon Echo (aka Alexa).[21] This device records customer utterances; it then transmits these to a cloud server where they are processed using natural language processing.[22] In this way, this application of Alexa is an example of the Internet of Things (see below) in financial services.

D3 is a digital solution provider for banks and credit unions.[23] It supplies these institutions with pre-built, customizable technology solutions for consumer and business markets.[24] Speaking of its Alexa-based solution, D3's CEO, Mark Vipond, said: 'By offering voice activated banking... we are breaking down the barriers of friction and need for special knowledge from end-users.'[25]

As part of this solution, customers can check account balances, move money and review their financial goals.[26] This could make online banking more accessible to customers who lack digital skills, such as senior citizens. D3's voice banking is part of a wider platform of technology solutions.[27] This platform helps its users to gather and analyse data on their customers, something which should enable them to anticipate customer needs and personalize the customer experience: the voice assistant could, for instance, offer savings products to customer accounts that have high cash balances.[28]

Voice-based user interfaces like Amazon's Alexa have been described by some as 'virtual butlers'.[29] Of course, Amazon is not the only *big tech* player in this space: there is also Google Home and Apple's HomePod.[30] With an expanding array of features, these virtual assistants look set to play a greater role in their users' lives. Over time, and with increasing amounts of data for their underlying algorithms, these devices are likely to become increasingly conversational and more personalized (see box on affective computing below).

Although voice-enabled devices learn from recording their users' voices, and thereby become better at recognizing, and responding to, individual user input, they do make mistakes. For example, an NLP algorithm may 'mishear' a user's input and respond inappropriately or not at all.[31] To address this, users may take to simplifying their commands, providing more detail or hyper-articulating their utterances; speaking in a manner that is slower, louder and clearer than one's natural voice.[32]

How might voice-based solutions affect the customer experience when applied in a financial services context?

(Suggested answer at the end of this chapter.)

Voice-enabled user interfaces may just be a step on the way towards greater digitalization in financial services; with increasing connectivity, virtual branches, accessible via virtual reality (VR) headsets – or internet-connected spectacles – could soon be a viable alternative to physical bank branches.[33] In this way, VR technology may, somewhat ironically, recreate a user experience that is similar to attending a branch, albeit from the comfort of one's home.

However, virtual branches are unlikely to be the final destination for digitized financial services. With increasing automation, a greater number of devices will be able to act autonomously on behalf of their users. As a result, this could drastically reduce the time and input required of users. In this way, automation may diminish the role of user interfaces in the user experience.

The Internet of Things (IoT)

While the number of internet-connected user interfaces has grown rapidly since the year 2000, in the form of laptops, touchscreen phones and, more recently, smartwatches, there has also been an increase in connected autonomous devices: these are equipped with sensors that enable them to take input from their environments, such as humidity, temperature, sound and movement.[34]

This data is transmitted to applications hosted on the cloud, which, by way of analysing the data, allow 'smart' devices to respond to changes in their environment.[35] For example, an air-conditioning system could take temperature data from various parts of the home, thereby allowing it to maintain a constant temperature in each room while optimizing energy use.

Solutions like this are commonly referred to as the Internet of Things (IoT); although they have been technologically possible for some time, they were previously only accessible to the wealthy or large organizations. What makes IoT solutions different is that they are available on a retail level, and navigable via smartphone or tablet apps. This has been enabled by greater connectivity, cloud computing and, crucially, cheaper sensory technology. Thus, some of the drivers of fintech innovation are instrumental in embedding the web into the home.

Fundamentally, IoT solutions are deployed to optimize the use of resources and can be seen in both business and consumer domains. For example, digitized inventory management systems are some of the earliest known examples of IoT-like solutions.[36] However, whilst optimization – lower costs, greater convenience – is certainly an advantage, the combination of the IoT and certain other technologies holds even greater potential.

For starters, AI can be used to build more autonomous IoT-enabled solutions. However, this is a two-way street: with a greater number of connected devices, each equipped with multiple sensors, more data can be gathered to inform machine learning algorithms, and in greater detail. In turn, this allows connected devices to make data-driven decisions and thus perform their functions more autonomously. Self-driving vehicles are a good example of this. These employ a multitude of algorithms to make decisions on the road; in turn, the data gathered whilst driving – via their sensors and cameras – can then be used to further hone these algorithms.

What's more, if IoT-connected devices can be empowered with AI, they can become economic agents who can transact autonomously on behalf of their users. This can be achieved with blockchain tokens.[37] As these tokens can be used as stand-ins for fiat, they can be used for micro-transactions:[38] as blockchain tokens are digital representations of value, transacting in them, should, in theory, lower transaction costs. This is because blockchain transactions do not involve intermediaries and so can be made without the paper-laden back-office settlement processes of fiat transactions.

For example, Jaguar has experimented with compensating its users with cryptocurrency in exchange for their data. As part of this, drivers allow their cars to automatically report road data gleaned from sensors on their vehicles. In return, their digital wallets are credited with cryptocurrency which can be redeemed for coffee, parking space, and toll payments.[39]

Though the example above is relatively simple, it is not hard to see how it can be expanded upon, technologically speaking. For instance, in 2017, Toyota announced that it was exploring the use of blockchain-based car-sharing solutions in autonomous vehicles, to help car owners monetize their vehicles when not in personal use.[40] As part of this, car owners might be compensated with blockchain tokens – via a smart contract – in return for allowing other people to use their vehicles.[41] As IoT-enabled devices become more commonplace, they will start to transact on behalf of their users. In this way, things which would previously have been redundant outside personal use will become financialized.

Identity and the digital self

With evermore convenient user interfaces, instantaneous payments and IoT-enabled devices serving their users autonomously, it is not inconceivable that all this leads to the emergence of the 'digital self'. In other words, personalized digital representations of each user, designed to act on their behalf in all manner of affairs; the decisions of these AI-enabled tools will be informed by vast swathes of user data captured from a variety of user interfaces.[42]

To a degree, such solutions already exist. For instance, robo-advisers make investment recommendations on behalf of their user's expressed preferences (aka user data). What's more, the exchange-traded funds that many robo-advisers recommend make algorithmic investment decisions themselves: for instance, investing in the 100 largest companies on the London Stock Exchange in proportion to their market capitalization is an algorithmic investment strategy, however passive.

In the future, however, it is likely that the application serving us will take input from a variety of sources.[43] This could include our online search history, financial transactions, shopping carts, driving habits and even our private conversations. As the technology already exists for recording, and capitalizing, on these data sets, the obvious next step is to integrate these.

In both business and consumer spheres, the core strategy of many disruptors appears to be convenience optimization. Thus, the current spate of fintech innovations will, at some point, require integration as a way of reducing users' oversight and time costs. Perhaps then, it is unsurprising that novel platform-based financial institutions, which combine various fintech innovations, are flourishing at the expense of more established financial institutions (see Chapter 1).

In order to integrate technology-enabled solutions, user identities must first be digitized. To some degree, this has already happened organically:

many websites allow people to log in using their Facebook credentials, for example. Similarly, online retailers require a user's email address to set up an account; the same address can then be used to authenticate transactions via an online payment processor such as PayPal.

However, these functionalities do not constitute a fully-fledged digital identity system; hitherto, the focus has been on transaction authentication, not user verification.[44] As a result, these systems rely on third-party financial institutions to confirm user transactions. In turn, these institutions rely on government-issued documentation, such as passports or driving licences, to verify user identities. In this way, the online identity systems of Silicon Valley are but digital veneers of existing paper-based systems.

Moreover, these digital veneers are not centralized, whereas the underlying systems are: most governments, for instance, keep a database of all driving licences in issue. This separation – of our digital and physical identities – allows people to adopt multiple online identities. Whilst this may be attractive from a privacy perspective, it also enables financial crime; indeed, certain online frauds would be harder to pull off if all e-mail accounts were linked to their users' government-issued IDs.

Of course, the potential benefits (fraud reduction, AML, etc) of centralized digital identity systems may not outweigh the potential risks that such systems pose to civil liberties. Regardless, such concerns have not stopped some countries from digitizing their citizens' identities. India's *Aadhaar* (Hindi for 'foundation') initiative is perhaps the most extensive example of this: in 2008, the Government of India launched this programme to give each of the country's 1.2 billion people a digital identity.[45] One of the programme's core aims was to increase financial inclusion and access to public services; with an estimated 52 per cent of Indian adults not using financial services as of 2008,[46] this intervention can be seen as an effort to alleviate poverty in the world's largest democracy.

This appears to have worked: between 2011 and 2017, the proportion of people over the age of 15 with a financial institution account grew from 35 per cent to 80 per cent.[47] What's more, high denomination (500 and 1,000 rupee) bank notes were banned in 2016 in an effort to combat money laundering and tax evasion in what was a highly cash-centric economy:[48] according to a 2014 estimate, around 90 per cent of consumer payments were conducted in cash.[49] These reforms are facilitating the digitization of India's economy: for example, digital payments grew by *ca* 18 per cent from 2016 to 2017, from US$17 billion to US$20 billion.[50] Moreover, India's GDP grew at an annualized rate of around 7.5 per cent between 2014 and 2019.[51]

However, pro-digitization reforms are not unique to India: in 2019, countries in the Eurozone stopped issuing €500 banknotes, though existing notes continue to be legal tender.[52] Given that most people in more mature economies already have bank accounts, it seems likely that financial institutions, and not governments, will be play the leading role in managing digital identity systems.

As financial institutions have the user interfaces and requisite infrastructure for managing millions of customer accounts, they could play a key role in digital identity systems.[53] When banks sign up new customers, they are essentially verifying their identities from scratch; whereas the Indian Government started with a central authority that would collect basic information about its citizens,[54] banks merely need ask their customers for more verifiable data. Indeed, they already have the scale and sophistication to collect and store this information securely.[55]

In this way, banks could digitize their customers' identities on behalf of governments. To facilitate this, governments could formalize implementation standards, as has been done in the case of Open Banking in the UK, and thereby provide institutions with a common framework for managing their customers' digital identities. Alternatively, this could be achieved via a consortium of financial institutions, which would verify and manage customers' digital identities centrally.[56]

That said, more decentralized approaches to identity management do exist: in a distributed identity solution, for example, user verification relies on multiple third-party institutions,[57] such as utility companies or tax authorities. In practice, APIs (see Chapter 1) would be used to access to third-party systems in order to provide and/or verify user information.

 CASE STUDY
ConsenSys's uPort: Distributed identity

'We have arrived at a breakthrough in how we can build trust into all of our systems. We are at the beginning of the next revolution, the Trust Revolution.' These are the words of Joseph Lubin, the founder of ConsenSys, a Switzerland-based blockchain company, and developer of uPort.[58] The company, which was founded in 2014, is notable because it develops applications for Ethereum, an open-source blockchain system which Lubin co-founded.[59]

Like Bitcoin, Ethereum is a blockchain network; however, its features differ significantly. Whereas Bitcoin is backed by the energy costs incurred by its miners, Ethereum derives its value from a different commodity: computing resources. To understand why this is important, one must first appreciate that Bitcoin derives its scarcity from the fact that it can only be created via the process known as mining; like gold mining, this entails energy and hardware costs.[60] By expending computing resources, miners earn the right to issue Bitcoin, hence the term 'proof of work'.[61] This system is necessary for deciding who gets to add the next block to the blockchain, and thus for reconciling the ledger (see Chapter 5).

On the other hand, the Ethereum network reconciles its ledger via a proof-of-stake model, whereby network nodes get to mine blocks in proportion to their holdings of the Ethereum token,[62] which is known as Ether.[63] As part of this, Ethereum miners host decentralized applications,[64] because proof of work is much less energy intensive than proof-of-stake. In this way, the Ethereum network is effectively a decentralized cloud system; to access applications on the network, users pay miners in Ether,[65] which creates a natural demand for the token. As a result, the Ethereum blockchain is effectively a currency system backed by processing power.

Although the Ethereum network consumes the same resources as Bitcoin (ie energy, hardware and labour), it transforms these into something more useful: if the Bitcoin token can be described as 'digital gold', then Ether can aptly be described as digital gold jewellery. This metaphor is fitting because jewellery making, which enhances the value of the gold, requires skill and creativity – just like software development.

The decentralized applications running on Ethereum are known as 'DApps'.[66] Though it may seem perplexing that computer programs can be hosted on a blockchain, you might recall from Chapter 5 that blockchain transactions are no more than transfers of information and that computer programs are no more than lines of code. As Ethereum is an open-source system, anyone can use it to launch a DApp.[67] Moreover, these applications are managed independently of the Ethereum Foundation, the non-profit that supports the Ethereum network.[68]

The uPort solution is an example of a DApp. It is an identity-management solution that allows users to store and manage their data via the Ethereum blockchain. The application itself functions like a cryptocurrency wallet wherein private keys are used to authenticate transactions. Of course, no tokens are sent; instead, users sign transactions to grant counterparty access to their data in order to verify their identities.[69]

In 2019, ConsenSys announced a partnership involving uPort, PwC and Onfido, a global identity management provider. As part of this, the uPort solution would be experimented with for user verification purposes in financial services. Commenting on this, uPort's strategy and operations lead, Alice Nawfal, said: 'We see an increased demand for secure and privacy-preserving solutions that facilitate personal data sharing between financial institutions. Our view is that consumers will eventually be able to build dynamic, robust financial identities based on data from all financial institutions they have accounts at, and be able to port their identities across service providers.'[70]

What are the opportunities and risks of using uPort in financial services?
(Suggested answer at the end of this chapter.)

If a person's identity can be digitized and its verification decentralized, can the same be done for a financial institution? Corporations, after all, have, in many jurisdictions, rights and responsibilities that are similar to those of individuals. What's more, the required digitization and decentralization has already begun:[71] individuals work from home, office-based work flows are being automated and IT infrastructure is moving onto the cloud.

Decentralized financial institutions?

Decentralization has been underway for some time in finance. By disintermediating and unbundling financial services, fintechs have undermined the role of centralized financial institutions (see Chapters 1 and 2). Of course, these fintechs then congregate on financial platforms. However, given that the requisite technologies already exist – in the form of APIs, blockchain and AI – for the further decentralization of financial services, it may only be a matter of time before these platforms themselves are decentralized.

Arguably, decentralized organizations already exist, in the form of open-source communities. However, as these communities rely on their members to donate their time and effort to support the project at hand, they are not private enterprises. Indeed, very few corporations can rely on their shareholders for unremunerated work like open-source communities do.

What's more, decentralized private organizations are not a wholly untested idea: for instance, in 2016, the decentralized autonomous organization (DAO) was launched. This was an Ethereum-based enterprise whose projects would be decided by polls of its members. As each member's votes were weighed in proportion to their holding of DAO tokens, this process was comparable to shareholder resolutions at an AGM. In addition, DAO tokens were exchangeable for Ether tokens.[72]

Management of the DAO was decentralized as projects would be proposed and voted on by its members. Once a project had been accepted, it would be delegated to a contractor via a smart contract, who, on successful completion, would be payable in Ether.[73] In this way, the DAO was at the same time a shareholder corporation, crowdfunding platform and a cryptocurrency.

The DAO's launch in May 2016 garnered much excitement, attracting US$130 million worth of funding from *ca* 18,000 investors.[74] However, the DAO did not last long: just over a month into its life, a hacker exploited a loophole in the DAO's contracting mechanism to steal US$70 million worth of ETH from its treasury.[75] Subsequently, the DAO collapsed; this was followed up by an SEC investigation which found that the DAO may have breached US securities laws by issuing unregistered securities in the form of its blockchain tokens, though no enforcement action was subsequently taken.[76] The world, it seemed, was turned off decentralized organizations, for the time being.

The human touch: the edge in an automated economy

Throughout this book we have examined how technology is being applied to make financial services faster, cheaper and easier; in this chapter, we explored how the continuation of this trend will facilitate greater automation and decentralization in financial services. Thus, in a future of increasingly sophisticated robo-advisers, automated voice-assistants and even decentralized organizations, it is pertinent to ask: how can individual financial institutions differentiate themselves?

In Chapter 3, we examined how behavioural economics and careful interface design can be used to optimize the user experience. However, if all financial institutions pursue similar optimization strategies, differentiation will be limited; though branding may vary, different solutions will feel similar, thus limiting the depth of the user experience. Moreover, self-service solutions have been shown to struggle with customer retention.[77]

Therefore, financial institutions must consider the role of humans when deploying new technologies within their businesses. How, will depend on the target users and their so-called 'pain points'; in this context, one can interpret the idea of a 'customer' more widely, to include internal stakeholders. After all, if a lack of human contact adversely affects customer retention, perhaps it also affects staff morale and employee performance?

Regardless of whether they are internal or external, customers share certain inherent preferences. These are human agency, transparency of effort and authenticity.[78] Those seeking to create unique user experiences should be mindful of these when deploying human resources as part their technology-enabled service offerings. Consequently, each preference warrants further elaboration.

For starters, the desire for human agency is straightforward: users want experiences that are the work of human agency rather than that of machines.[79] For this reason, consumers are willing to pay a premium for handmade products, such as jewellery or gift cards.[80] This dynamic may explain the fact that people are willing to pay for financial advice delivered by humans, despite the lower cost and increasing sophistication of robo-advisers.

Furthermore, users desire an observable human effort in service of their needs; that is to say, they want to see that someone is doing something to help them.[81] This may explain the reluctance in some people with regard to using chat bots; some customers just prefer to speak with another human being. Indeed, Britain's first bank without branches, First Direct – which prides itself on having been 'open 24/7/365 since 1989' – has a UK-based call centre, despite the fact that its customers are 19 times as likely to engage with the bank digitally than over the phone.[82] In this way, some customers, regardless of the efficacy of the user interface, may continue to prefer a human interaction.

AFFECTIVE COMPUTING

As many people still desire a 'human touch' as part of their user experience, work is underway to make user interfaces that are emotionally intelligent, or at least appear so in the eyes of the user. This involves building systems that can recognize and respond to human emotions, which is known as affective computing.[83] Due to the complexity of this, affective computing is a multidisciplinary field, which draws on computing, psychology and cognitive science.[84]

While humans gauge each other's emotions by picking up on verbal and non-verbal cues – both consciously and subconsciously – computers attempt to detect patterns in user input. For example, an emotionally agitated person may exhibit certain sound wave frequencies in their speech. As a result, the range and depth of emotional signals exhibited by humans can be an obstacle to their interpretability by computers; indeed, human beings often misread each other's emotions.[85] Moreover, in order to interpret human emotions, computers must gather and integrate different pieces of information in real time. This is complicated by the fact that people express emotions in diverse ways, and often do so idiosyncratically.[86]

Finally, customers desire authentic experiences.[87] Of their key preferences, this is perhaps the most difficult to manufacture; as there is a risk of being perceived as disingenuous if one tries too hard, any efforts to appear authentic must be subtle. For example, restaurants that prematurely display their year of founding as part of their branding may appear déclassé to more discerning customers, because they recognize the trick that the restaurateur is trying to play on them.

In this regard, established financial institutions have a potential advantage over fintechs: in a globalized and digitized world that feels increasingly uncertain to many, people are drawn towards the tangible, that which has history and a connection to the local community. Established banks can play to these desires by highlighting their historical roots, serving local businesses and engaging the local community via their branches; this is a potential edge that digital-only fintechs simply do not have.

The customer preferences highlighted above give us an idea of how financial services organizations can redeploy employees who will be displaced by automation over the coming decade. Thus, the onus is on financial institutions to identify workflows that are likely to be automated. As advances in AI will enable the automation of jobs that rely on accessing and storing data, many administrative roles will become increasingly computerized.[88] Moreover, as the algorithms grow more sophisticated, workflows that rely on pattern recognition are likely to go the same way.[89] This transformation is well underway in some areas of finance: for instance, in the year 2000 Goldman Sachs employed *ca* 600 equity traders at its New York City office; by 2017, it employed just two traders there, plus around 200 software engineers.[90]

On the other hand, workflows that involve high degrees of creativity and/or emotional intelligence are forecast to be less susceptible to automation.[91] That said, such predictions are based on other predictions about the future of technology. As a result, they are inherently uncertain as the speed and nature of technological developments can and will surprise even the keenest observers. While it is difficult to foresee how new technologies will shape the world, it is at least as difficult to say exactly when.

Chapter summary

This chapter looked at several technological trends that will shape financial services over the next decade: digitization, automation and decentralization. However, financial institutions that deploy new technologies in their businesses must not forget to integrate their services and to personalize these. Thus, the financial industry's answer to fintech disruption may, in some respects, be surprisingly low tech: more convenient solutions with a human touch.

KEY TAKEAWAYS

The key takeaways from this chapter are:

- As financial services become progressively cheaper, faster and more convenient, the next source of value may be found in integrating disparate technology solutions.

- Banks can play a key role in furthering digital identity management due to their existing scale and sophistication.

- With increasing automation and digitization, consumers may find value in services that include a human touch.

SUGGESTED ANSWERS TO DISCUSSION POINTS

 How might voice-based solutions affect the customer experience when applied in a financial services context?

Personalizing financial services by addressing users by their first name, for example, and by anticipating their needs may improve customer retention. Also, being able to review one's financial situation and goals without having to endure extra screen time is likely to be attractive to convenience-hungry customers. Indeed, this may help customers stay within their budgets and meet their savings targets as they may feel 'in control' of their financial situation as a result of the greater oversight afforded to them (and thereby feel motivated to take greater responsibility for meeting their goals).

In addition, anticipating customer needs and, on this basis, recommending additional products to them can give customers the feeling that they are receiving a personalized service. That said, these recommendations need to be genuinely helpful and relevant to each customer's needs; otherwise, they will feel too much like an up-sell and therefore inconvenience the customer. After all, having to consider whether a recommendation is helpful can be seen as a mental transaction cost.

Finally, users may become frustrated if they have to repeat themselves, hyper-articulate or provide additional details in order to get the voice assistant to do their bidding. In addition, as users are accustomed to doing things on screen, they may have difficulty retaining any information they receive in an auditory format.

What are the opportunities and risks of using uPort in financial services?

Opportunities

- Faster access to financial services as identity can be verified via the uPort app.
- Reduction in behind-the-scenes paperwork/back-office costs.
- Reduced risk of data loss on the part of financial institutions as they have to hold less customer data.
- Digitization of customer data may enable data mining to detect opportunities and threats.

Risks

- Customers could lose their private keys due to negligence or cyberattack.
- Concentration of data means that one breach could lead to the loss of the customer's most sensitive data.
- Speed of service provision also enables faster cyberattacks (eg by using digital ID to take out loan).
- Therefore, financial institutions need a user interface and procedures that will allow customers to reset their passwords/report attacks.
- Such contingencies/countermeasures could mimic those of email providers.
- Two-factor authentication may not suffice for mobile-based apps.

References

1 Townsend, M and Harris, P (2004) Now the Pentagon tells Bush: climate change will destroy us, *The Guardian*, 22 February, www.theguardian.com/environment/2004/feb/22/usnews.theobserver (archived at https://perma.cc/RK7Q-4LDN)

2 PricewaterhouseCoopers (2019) Crossing the lines: How fintech is propelling FS and TMT firms out of their lanes, Global Fintech Report, https://www.pwc.com/gx/en/industries/financial-services/assets/pwc-global-fintech-report-2019.pdf (archived at https://perma.cc/MC4Z-YCZE)

3,10,50 Badi, M, Dab, S, Drummond, A, Malhotra, S, Muxi, F, Peeters, M, Roongta, P, Strauß, M and Sénant, Y (2018) Global Payments 2018: Reimagining the Customer Experience, The Boston Consulting Group, 18 October, www.bcg.com/publications/2018/global-payments-reimagining-customer-experience.aspx (archived at https://perma.cc/UKQ2-AMSJ)

4 Bettencourt, L and Ulwick, A W (2008) The Customer-Centred Innovation Map, *Harvard Business Review*, 86 (5), 109–14 (May)

5 Martinho-Truswell, E (2018) How AI Could Help the Public Sector, *Harvard Business Review*, 53–55 (January–February)

6 Szabo, N (1999) Micropayments and Mental Transaction Costs, www.fon.hum.uva.nl/rob/Courses/InformationInSpeech/CDROM/Literature/LOTwinterschool2006/szabo.best.vwh.net/berlinmentalmicro.pdf (archived at https://perma.cc/8X8L-BKA3)

7,11 Deloitte Consulting LLP (2015) Real-time payments are changing the reality of payments, https://www2.deloitte.com/content/dam/Deloitte/us/Documents/strategy/us-cons-real-time-payments.pdf (archived at https://perma.cc/V4N6-BLEQ)

8 Gapgemini and BNP Paribas (2018) World Payments Report 2018, worldpaymentsreport.com/wp-content/uploads/sites/5/2018/10/World-Payments-Report-2018.pdf (archived at https://perma.cc/VK4T-JZLX)

9 Large, J (2005) Clearing and settlement in payment card schemes, The Global Treasurer, February 14, www.theglobaltreasurer.com/2005/02/14/clearing-and-settlement-in-payment-card-schemes/ (archived at https://perma.cc/JB5L-LZLB)

12 Swift (2020) ISO 20022 Programme, www.swift.com/standards/iso-20022-programme (archived at https://perma.cc/LK6Z-EJAR)

13 Swift (2020) About Us, www.swift.com/about-us (archived at https://perma.cc/5E3L-BYVY)

14,15 Swift (2019) ISO 20022: Better data means better payments - Why correspondent banking needs ISO 20022 now, www.swift.com/swift-resource/229416/download (archived at https://perma.cc/G88Y-D7E4)

16 Desai, M (2020) The benefits of a cashless society, World Economic Forum Annual Meeting, 7 January, www.weforum.org/agenda/2020/01/benefits-cashless-society-mobile-payments/ (archived at https://perma.cc/C4WL-KBHL)

17 Hardekopf, B (2020) Is a Cashless Society Good For America?, *Forbes*, 24 February, www.forbes.com/sites/billhardekopf/2020/02/24/is-a-cashless-society-good-for-america/ (archived at https://perma.cc/T625-LUNR)

18 Federal Reserve Bank of San Francisco (2019) Impacts of Cashless Business on Financial Inclusion, 19 August, www.frbsf.org/our-district/about/sf-fed-blog/impacts-cashless-business-financial-inclusion/ (archived at https://perma.cc/FXK8-YDBH)

19,20 Sajter, D (2013) Privacy, Identity, and the Perils of the Cashless Cociety, in *Culture, Society, Identity - European Realities*, papers.ssrn.com/sol3/papers.cfm?abstract_id=2285438 (archived at https://perma.cc/3P9D-WQ9P)

21, 25–28 Businesswire (2017) D3 Banking Introduces Intelligent Voice Banking with Amazon's Alexa: Natural language interactions provide a simple and intuitive way of banking, 22 February, www.businesswire.com/news/home/20170222005349/en/D3-Banking-Introduces-Intelligent-Voice-Banking-Amazon%E2%80%99s (archived at https://perma.cc/U5R3-EMFL)

22 Amazon.com, Inc. (2020) Alexa and Alexa device FAQs, www.amazon.com/gp/help/customer/display.html?nodeId=201602230#GUID-1CDA0A16-3D5A-47C1-9DD8-FDEDB10381A3__GUID-A596C73E-1A6B-4385-B1AC-F8A09EF2EBC6 (archived at https://perma.cc/5BP2-MCHE)

23,24 D3 Banking Technology (2019) Platform, www.d3banking.com/platform/ (archived at https://perma.cc/57JS-MT3K)

29,30 Porcheron, M, Fischer, J E, Reeves, S and Sharples, S (2018) Voice interfaces in everyday life, in The ACM CHI Conference on Human Factors in Computing Systems, Montréal, Canada

31,32 Myers, C, Furqan, A, Nebolsky, J, Caro, K and Zhu, J (2018) Patterns for how users overcome obstacles in voice user interfaces, in The ACM CHI Conference on Human Factors in Computing Systems, Montréal, Canada

33 BNP Paribas (2017) Virtual reality: step into the future of banking, 9 August, group. bnpparibas/en/news/virtual-reality-step-future-banking (archived at https://perma.cc/ C2XF-NBHS)

34 Bandyopadhyay, D and Sen, J (2011) Internet of Things: Applications and Challenges in Technology and Standardization, *Wireless Personal Communications*, 58, 49–69

35 Lee, I and Lee, K (2015) The Internet of Things (IoT): applications, investments, and challenges for enterprises, *Business Horizons*, 58, 431–40

36 Palattella, M R, Dohler, M, Grieco, A, Rizzo, G, Torsner, J, Engel, T and Ladid, L (2016) Internet of Things in the 5G Era: Enablers, Architecture and Business Models, *IEEE Journal on selected areas in communications*, 34 (3), 510–27

37,38 Huckle, S, Bhattacharya, R, White, M and Beloff, N (2016) Internet of Things, Blockchain and Shared Economy Applications, *Procedia Computer Science*, 98, 461–66

39 Khatri, Y (2019) Jaguar Land Rover Plans to Give Drivers Crypto in Return for Their Data, Coindesk, 29 April, www.coindesk.com/jaguar-land-rover-plans-to-give-drivers-crypto-in-return-for-their-data (archived at https://perma.cc/6NUX-T9QG)

40,41 Toyota Research Institute (2017) TRI Explores Blockchain Technology for Development of New Mobility Ecosystem, www.tri.global/news/toyota-research-institute-explores-blockchain-technology-for-development-of-new-mobility-ecosystem-2017-5-22 (archived at https://perma.cc/3KRN-H8BZ)

42,43 Domingos, P (2015) *The Master Algorithm: How the quest for the ultimate learning algorithm will remake our world*, Penguin Books, London

44,53,55,56,57 McWaters, J, Bruno, G, Galaski, R, Drexler, M and Robson, C (2016) A Blueprint for Digital Identity: The role of financial institutions in building digital identity, World Economic Forum, www3.weforum.org/docs/WEF_A_Blueprint_for_Digital_ Identity.pdf (archived at https://perma.cc/DS5U-JUHE)

45,54 Banerjee, S (2016) Aadhaar: Digital inclusion and public services in India, in World Development Report, World Bank Group, pubdocs.worldbank.org/en/655801461250682317/ WDR16-BP-Aadhaar-Paper-Banerjee.pdf (archived at https://perma.cc/49QD-FBPD)

46 Honohan, P (2008) Cross-country variation in household access to financial services, *Journal of Banking and Finance*, 32, 2493–500 (May)

47 World Bank (2018) The Little Data Book on Financial Inclusion 2018, openknowledge. worldbank.org/handle/10986/29654 (archived at https://perma.cc/UY3C-7598)

48 Agarwal, S (2018) India's Demonetization Drive: A necessary jolt towards a more digital economy?, 1 September, www.forbes.com/sites/nusbusinessschool/2018/09/01/indias-demonetization-drive-a-necessary-jolt-towards-a-more-digital-economy/#39e486423dc3 (archived at https://perma.cc/3DUE-3C4Z)

49 Euromonitor, Passport (2015) in: Govil, S, Whitelaw, D and Spaeth, P (2016) Perspectives on accelerating global payment acceptance, Visa Inc, usa.visa.com/visa-everywhere/global-impact/accelerating-electronic-payments-worldwide.html (archived at https://perma.cc/G3JD-7T5A)

51 Boone, L, Joumard, I and de la Maisonneuve, C (2020) Structural reforms are key for a more prosperous and inclusive India, OECD, 3 December, oecdecoscope.blog/2019/12/05/structural-reforms-are-key-for-a-more-prosperous-and-inclusive-india/ (archived at https://perma.cc/5XWT-7U5X)

52 European Central Bank (2020) Banknotes, www.ecb.europa.eu/euro/banknotes/html/index.en.html#500 (archived at https://perma.cc/Q3H5-GXZH)

58,69 ConsenSys (2015) UPort: The wallet is the new browser, 1 October, media.consensys.net/uport-the-wallet-is-the-new-browser-b133a83fe73 (archived at https://perma.cc/C4TK-TKX6)

59 ConsenSys (2020) About us: ConsenSys is a market-leading blockchain technology company, consensys.net/about/ (archived at https://perma.cc/HE57-5LVZ)

60,61 Nakamoto, S (2008) Bitcoin: A peer-to-peer electronic cash system, bitcoin.org/bitcoin.pdf (archived at https://perma.cc/6N5N-2NPQ)

62,64 Buterin, V (2020) Ethereum Whitepaper, 27 May, ethereum.org/whitepaper/ (archived at https://perma.cc/QWQ6-BN6M)

63,65 Ethereum Foundation (2020) What is Ether (ETH)? 11 April, ethereum.org/eth/ (archived at https://perma.cc/Y9VS-MF5A)

66,67 Ethereum Foundation (2020) What is Ethereum? 13 May, ethereum.org/what-is-ethereum/ (archived at https://perma.cc/3GA8-JBA6)

68 Ethereum Foundation (2020) About the Ethereum Foundation, 8 May, ethereum.org/foundation/ (archived at https://perma.cc/GKJ4-77DK)

70 ConsenSys (2019) PwC and Onfido to Join uPort's Portable Identity Effort in the UK Finserv, 23 September, consensys.net/blog/press-release/uport-with-onfido-pwc-_-sibos-2019/ (archived at https://perma.cc/GM5J-DM6H)

71 Kypriotaki, K N, Zamani, E D and Giaglis, G M (2015) From Bitcoin to decentralized autonomous corporations, in Proceedings of the 17th International Conference on Enterprise Information Systems, 284–90

72,73 Jentzsch, C (2016) Decentralised autonomous organization to automate governance – final draft – under review, archive.org/stream/DecentralizedAutonomousOrganizations/WhitePaper_djvu.txt (archived at https://perma.cc/RVW2-BFFL)

74 Simonite, T (2016) The 'Autonomous Corporation' Called the DAO is Not a Good Way to Spend $130 Million, MIT Technology Review, 17 May, www.technologyreview.com/s/601480/the-autonomous-corporation-called-the-dao-is-not-a-good-way-to-spend-130-million/ (archived at https://perma.cc/A9UV-DJJR)

75 Falkon, S (2017) The story of the DAO – its history and consequences, Medium, 24 December, https://medium.com/swlh/the-story-of-the-dao-its-history-and-consequences-71e6a8a551ee (archived at https://perma.cc/R75X-ZKW8)

76 Securities and Exchange Commission (2017) Report of Investigation Pursuant to Section 21(a) of the Securities Exchange Act of 1934: The DAO, www.sec.gov/litigation/investre port/34-81207.pdf (archived at https://perma.cc/LS2Q-H6AS)

77 Scherer, A, Wangenheim, F and Wünderlich, N (2015) The value of self-service: Long-term effects of technology-based self-service usage on customer retention, *MIS Quarterly*, 39 (1), 17–200 (March)

78,79,81,87 Waytz, A (2019) When customers want to see the human behind the product, *Harvard Business Review*, 5 June, hbr.org/2019/06/when-customers-want-to-see-the-human-behind-the-product (archived at https://perma.cc/YSH9-4ZLB)

80 Fuchs, C, Schreier, M and van Osselaer, S M J (2015) The handmade effect: What's love got to do with it? *Journal of Marketing*, 79 (2), 98–110

82 HSBC Bank plc (2020) About First Direct, www2.firstdirect.com/press-releases/about-first-direct/ (archived at https://perma.cc/H952-DEJD)

83,84 Banafa, A (2020) What is Affective Computing? BBVA Group, 6 June, www.bbvaopenmind.com/en/technology/digital-world/what-is-affective-computing/ (archived at https://perma.cc/Y887-EH2U)

85,86 Picard, R W (2003) Affective computing: Challenges, *International Journal of Human-Computer Studies*, 59, 55–64

88,89,91 Frey, C B and Osborne, M A (2017) The future of employment: How susceptible are jobs to computerisation?, *Technological Forecasting & Social Change*, 114, 254–80

90 Byrnes, N (2017) As Goldman Embraces Automation, Even the Masters of the Universe Are Threatened, MIT Technology Review, 7 February, www.technologyreview.com/s/603431/as-goldman-embraces-automation-even-the-masters-of-the-universe-are-threatened/ (archived at https://perma.cc/Z472-6QP2)

GLOSSARY

Aadhaar : The Hindi name for India's digital identity system. This translates to 'foundation' or 'base'.

Algorithm : A set of instructions that can be executed by a computer. For example, an investment algorithm may buy gold when it trades below its average price for the preceding 52 weeks.

AML/CFT : Anti-money laundering/combatting the financing of terrorism; rules and procedures designed to impede the flow of money to and from criminal enterprises and terrorist activities.

Anchoring : When an individual's decision making is disproportionately influenced by the first pieces of information they are exposed to, as these frame the evaluation of additional information.

Artificial intelligence (AI) : The deployment of computer programs acting with some degree of autonomy so that they meet the Turing Test.

Bid–ask (aka bid offer) : The price you can achieve if you want to transact in a financial market now. Under these circumstances, the buyer will pay the higher price and the seller will receive the lower price; the difference (ie the spread) goes to the market maker.

Big Data : Quantitative decision-making methodologies that involve large-scale data sets and extensive data management systems.

Big tech : A handful of large, well-known technology companies based in the United States. These include Microsoft, Google, Facebook and Amazon.

Captive : A subsidiary company set up within a group of companies with the intention of providing insurance services exclusively within the group.

Cashless : Transacting electronically without the use of cash or other tangible assets.

Choice overload : The result of being exposed to too many choices and/or information, which impedes rational decision making.

Cost-leadership : Seeking to compete by offering a product/service for the lowest price; one of Porter's generic strategies.

Cryptocurrency : A blockchain token used as a currency system (eg Bitcoin).

Cryptography : The branch of mathematics concerned with concealing information, thereby securing it from prying eyes.

Decision fatigue : A cognitive phenomenon that arises when a person is exposed to a succession, or multitude, of choices that renders them progressively less capable of making rational decisions.

Derivative : A security that derives its value from another asset. For example, if you buy gold futures, you benefit if the price of gold goes up; meanwhile, your counterparty, the person that sold you the gold futures, suffers a loss, and vice versa.

Differentiation : The opposite of cost-leadership in that one tries to compete by offering a product/service that is, or at least perceived is to be, unique; according to Porter, this is done to justify charging a higher price.

Differentiation focus : Similar to above, but where one deploys a differentiation strategy in a particular market segment.

Digital native : A person who grew up as the internet became a mainstay in most households or someone who does not remember life before the internet.

Digitally : Pertaining to activity that has a networked, and usually web-enabled, technological underpinning. For example, transacting digitally could be taken to mean transacting via an application that relies on being connected to the internet.

Dis-economies of scale : The opposite of economies of scale; when an entity gets too big, it incurs additional costs as a result of its size, such as increased monitoring and audit costs. In addition, the objectives of management are frustrated by individual actors pursuing their own goals, sometimes to the detriment of the organization as a whole.

Disruptive innovation : A theory of competition developed primarily by the Harvard scholar Clayton Christensen. Herein, innovators disrupt established players by pursuing overlooked customer segments within their markets in order to build a foothold before moving on to more lucrative segments.

Distributed-ledger technology (DLT) : Same as blockchain technology.

Economies of scale : Where the increasing size on an entity gives rise to a competitive advantage. Bulk purchase discounts from suppliers are an example of this; as is brand recognition.

Efficient market hypothesis (EMH) : The theory that it is impossible, other than by chance, to outperform financial markets because all available information is already reflected in market prices.

Encryption : The concealment of information by turning it into something else (such as a hash). The opposite of decryption.

Ethical hackers : Consultants that are paid to break into systems in order to expose vulnerabilities.

Fear Index : A 2011 thriller by author Robert Harris about a hedge fund with a mind of its own.

Financial technology (fintech) : The application of technology to finance to make it faster, cheaper, more convenient and more accessible.

GFC : The global financial crisis of 2007–09, sometimes referred to as the credit crunch.

Going long : The act of buying a security in order to profit from a gain in its price.

Hardware and other non-custodial wallet solutions : A cryptocurrency wallet that does not rely on a third party for safekeeping of the user's private keys. This is commonly a USB-based device.

Hash : The output of a hashing algorithm

ISO20022 : An international standards framework for transaction communications between financial institutions.

Keylogging : Software that keeps a record of everything that is typed on the user's keyboard.

KYC : Know your client/customer; anti-money laundering procedures wherein a firm seeks to ascertain the identity of new customers and gain an understanding of the customer's rationale for seeking its services.

Letter of no action : A document issued by the US Securities and Exchange Commission to an entity or individual conducting a financial activity of uncertain legality; the letter effectively guarantees no further enforcement action by the SEC provided that its conditions, as set out in the letter, are met.

Liquidity : The idea that securities become cheaper and easier to trade the greater the size of the market as a result of intragroup competition between buyers and sellers.

Maturity transformation : The result of banks having multiple borrowers and depositors. In this way, depositors do not need access to their money at the same time, which enables the bank to lend out their deposits over longer time horizons, thereby securing higher returns.

Mid-price : The average of the bid and offer prices in a market; in other words, the halfway house between the prices preferred by buyers and by sellers.

MiFID II : A piece of EU legislation (Markets in Financial Instruments Directive), that regulates trading venues and service providers in connection with shares, bonds, investment funds and derivatives.

Money-market fund : A fund that invests in short-term bank deposits/debt securities.

Mortgage-backed securities (MBS) : An investment that is backed by a bundle of mortgages, such that the investor receives a diversified stream of mortgage payments in return for incurring default risk.

Negative network externalities : Where the increasing size of a network leads to negative outcomes for its participants. See Network effect below.

Network effect : The idea that a network becomes more useful and/or valuable to its participants as it increases in size (ie 'connections').

Network externality : Similar to network effect, though can be positive and negative.

Nudges : A subtle change in a person's environment intended to guide their decision making towards a preferred outcome.

One-stop shop : The notion that you can get all your financial needs met by one provider, thereby eliminating the inconvenience of having to deal with multiple institutions. Some supermarkets operate a more holistic version of this model by offering, in addition to food, petrol, electronics, financial services and clothing.

Online banking : The conduct of banking affairs via an internet browser or smartphone application. In many cases, this removes the need to attend bank branches.

Passive investment : An investment strategy that does not seek to outperform the stock market by picking individual stocks; rather, one invests in the whole market index, thereby securing the average return for the market.

Patch/Patches : A workaround or fix for software bugs or other operational problems.

Peer-to-peer (p2p) lender : A platform that connects savers with borrowers; by disintermediating banks, this should, in theory, secure both higher savings rates and lower borrowing rates.

Private key : A unique password that confers access to a single public address on a blockchain.

Proof of work : A hashed output starting with a certain number of zeros that a Bitcoin miner must find to add the next block of the Bitcoin blockchain. The requisite number of zeros varies according to the amount of computing power on the network so that a new block is added roughly every 10 minutes.

Public address : The location on a blockchain that pertains to a specific private key; in other words, a location that is only accessible to the holder of the private key.

Regulatory arbitrage : The act of relocating to a jurisdiction with laxer laws and/or regulations in order to minimize regulatory scrutiny and compliance costs.

Regulatory office : In the context of fintech, this is a team within a regulatory authority that specializes in the regulation of fintechs, and is thereby able to provide more sector-specific support to fintech start-ups.

Right to be forgotten : An individual's right to ask a search engine or other data repository to remove their personal data. Under GDPR, this is called the right to erasure.

Ring-fencing : A post-GFC regulatory intervention (primarily in the UK and EU) that requires banks to separate their retail and investment banking activities by funding sources and into separate legal entities. This is intended to avoid a repeat of the financial crisis wherein the risky activities of firms' investment banking arms endangered their otherwise healthy retail businesses.

Risk : The possibility that something good or bad may happen.

Run : When a large number of depositors decide to withdraw their funds from a bank, thereby causing its collapse. This can also happen in the context of other financial institutions, such as when investors decide to withdraw their capital from an open-ended investment fund.

Scientific management : An efficiency-driven management theory that emphasizes worker specialization, workflow planning and extensive performance measurement.

Securitization : When a promise of future cash flows such as mortgage payments, rental income or life insurance premiums is sold as an investment to a third party, thereby turning the initial contract into a security.

Security/Securities : A financial instrument/s that can be bought and sold; a financial instrument is a promise of future cash flows such as a stock or bond.

Shadow bank : A non-bank entity that invests in securitized bank loans or other forms of debt, and in doing so, takes on credit risk like a bank.

Short-selling : The act of borrowing a security and then selling it in order to profit from a fall in its price. To make the lender of the security good, the short-seller has to buy the security back on the market and return it to them; if this has fallen in value, the short-seller makes a gain.

Silo mentality : The problem that arises when teams and departments take a too narrow view of their goals/risks and lose sight of the bigger picture facing their organization.

Spirit of the law : The idea that, in order to comply with the law, one must comply with it in principle, rather than on a mere technical basis. This is intended to prevent people from gaming the rules.

Spread : The financial gain a financial intermediary makes from connecting two transacting parties (ie buying low, selling high). For example, a bank will pay a lower interest rate on deposits than the one it charges borrowers.

Stack : An arrangement of technological modularities and/or solutions into multiple layers such that each layer relies on the layers below it.

Stored at rest : When data or information is stored digitally and not being used.

SWIFT : The Society for Worldwide Interbank Financial Telecommunications is a member-owned cooperative and network for financial messaging services.

Symbolic interactionism : The idea that people attribute symbolic significance to objects that are prevalent in social interactions.

Technology acceptance model (TAM) : An analytical framework for technology adoption. It holds that perceived ease of use and perceived usefulness are core drivers of technology adoption.

Technology neutral : A policy stance wherein policymakers and regulators seek to regulate the application of technologies in the context of, say, financial services, rather than favouring or disfavouring individual technologies.

The cloud : A catch-all to describe any computing that takes place on a remote, third-party computer. For example, storing images online can be described as being on the cloud.

Token : In the context of tokenization, a stand-in number that is used in lieu of a user's card number or other sensitive details when authenticating transactions.

Too big to fail : The idea that some financial institutions are so large that their collapse would bring down the financial system; thus, these institutions are believed to have an implicit bailout guarantee as it is believed governments would be forced to intervene to save the financial system. This dynamic can be problematic as it incentivizes reckless risk-taking in financial institutions.

Turing Test : A standard for assessing whether a machine can be held up as 'artificial intelligence'; if the machine can perform a task with a degree of proficiency that is equivalent to, or better than, what a human being would be capable of, then it can be considered to be artificial intelligence.

Two-sided markets : A market centred around an entity – or platform – with at least two stakeholder groups, wherein the entity's actions with regard to one group influences outcomes for the other/s.

Un-bundling : The idea that traditional banking models that offer their customers a complete suite of products are coming undone by smaller fintechs that pry away their customers by offering them better/cheaper individual products.

Virtual asset service provider (VASP) : An entity that provides services concerning virtual assets such as blockchain tokens. According to international anti-money laundering guidance, this includes activities pertaining to the exchange, administration, safekeeping, and issuance of virtual assets.

Voice assistant : A web-enabled console and/or smartphone application that reacts to users' voice input.

White-labelling : Selling a product under one's own brand that is produced/serviced by someone else. For example, many own-brand supermarket products are white-labelled.

Wisdom of the crowds : The notion that mean estimates from a large group are proficient at estimating/predicting uncertain facts and outcomes because extreme estimates/predictions cancel each other out.

XaaS : Everything as a service; the idea that technology can transform products into services that are to be rented rather than purchased. Software-as-as-service is a prime example of this.

Yield : The annualized rate of return which can be achieved by buying a security at prevailing prices; the lower the price, the higher the potential return.

INDEX

Page numbers in **bold** indicate glossary items